HANS CHRISTIAN ANDERSEN AND THE ROMANTIC THEATRE

Hans Christian Andersen and the Romantic Theatre

A study of stage practices in the prenaturalistic Scandinavian theatre

FREDERICK J. MARKER

UNIVERSITY OF TORONTO PRESS

© University of Toronto Press 1971
All rights reserved
Printed in the United States of America for
University of Toronto Press
Toronto and Buffalo
ISBN 0–8020–5242–8
ISBN 0–8020–0022–3 (microfiche)
LC 74–151377

For Gudrun and Henry

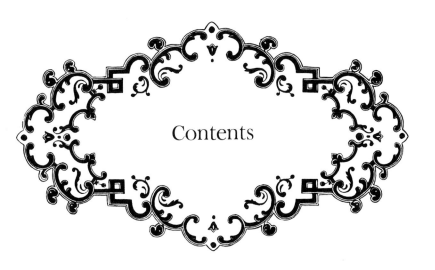

Contents

Illustrations

Acknowledgments

DURING THE COURSE of its development this study has enjoyed the benefit of advice and encouragement from a wide variety of sources. I would be sorely remiss, however, if I did not specify certain particular debts of gratitude which I feel deeply.

It is a pleasure to acknowledge my indebtedness to the staffs of the Danish State Archives, the Royal Library, the University of Copenhagen Library, the Danish Theatre Museum, and the H.C. Andersen Museum in Odense. In particular, the Royal Theatre in Copenhagen has shown me great hospitality and co-operation over a period of many years.

A Fulbright fellowship to Denmark supported my research in its earliest stages. Two Humanities Research grants from the University of Toronto have enabled me to pursue later investigations abroad. The book has been published with the help of a grant from the Humanities Research Council of Canada, using funds provided by the Canada Council.

Among those from whose critical advice and friendly scrutiny this study has profited immeasurably, A.M. Nagler and the late John Gassner of Yale and Clifford Leech of the University of Toronto stand uppermost in my mind. In preparing the manuscript for publication the editorial guidance of Miss Jean C. Jamieson and Mrs Rosemary Shipton has rescued me from numerous pitfalls.

Without the assistance so generously proffered by such individuals and institutions as these, the work of writing this book would have been far more arduous; without the incalculably great and incredibly optimistic contributions of my wife Lise-Lone, it would have been impossible.

F J M

Foreword

FOR THOSE WHO PREFER to view drama solely from a literary vantage point and for others who persist in regarding theatrical values as subordinate or even negative qualities in a play, this book, and the theatre of the nineteenth century which is its subject, may well prove a disappointment. The romantic theatre, for all its imaginative vigour and eagerness for experimentation, holds an appeal chiefly for those who basically *like* theatre – unabashed, total theatre, unashamedly spectacular, unforgettably pathetic. Yet even in terms of literary influence it is a serious distortion to ignore the debt – in the areas of form, subject matter, and philosophical bias – which the exponents of naturalism owed to the theatre and drama of the prenaturalistic period.

Particularly in Scandinavia this period was a transitional one of interaction and flux which, while retaining certain characteristics of the eighteenth-century theatre, developed new tendencies, directions, and techniques that led gradually and with little fanfare to the emergence of a new style in the 1880s: naturalism. However, despite universal critical agreement about the significance of Ibsen and Strindberg as creators of modernism, no sustained attempt has previously been made to describe and delineate the nineteenth-century theatrical context out of which these major Scandinavian playwrights evolved. Strindberg's celebrated Preface to *Miss Julie* is endlessly reprinted and admired, but little or no consideration is usually given to the theatrical conventions and practices to which he refers. It is this gap in our knowledge of the prenaturalistic theatre in Scandinavia which the present study has sought to make smaller.

Hans Christian Andersen (1805–1875), or H.C. Andersen as he is more correctly referred to in Denmark, stands squarely astride the romantic period in Scandinavia. As a playwright his career extended from his debut in 1829 to the production of his last play in 1865. Although he is recognized as a great artist in the medium with which his name has become synonymous, his extensive output as a dramatist has been neglected. Yet he himself placed serious emphasis on his work in the theatre, and a glance at the chronology at the back of this book – listing twenty-five original Andersen plays produced for a total of more than 1000 performances – dispels any notion that he was a closet dramatist similar to Shelley, Coleridge, or Dickens. Andersen possessed, above all else, an astute sense of practical theatre. His dramatic works – embracing vaudevilles, opera libretti, romantic dramas, and romantic comedies – represent an almost perfect cross-section of the nineteenth-century repertory; their production history affords a panorama of the popular components of the colourful, picturesque romantic stage picture.

Andersen was not the period's 'best' dramatist: Adam Oehlenschläger (1779–1856) was a finer poet, J. L. Heiberg (1791–1860) a keener wit, Henrik Hertz (1798–1870) a more obvious forerunner of Ibsen. Yet none of these playwrights embraces as much of the rich variety and scope of the romantic theatre as Andersen. The production history of his plays at the Danish Royal Theatre has been made the organizational focus of this study because it affords a veritable microcosm of important mid-nineteenth-century dramatic forms and theatrical styles. Equally worthy of our attention are the frequently incisive comments and observations about the theatre and drama made by Andersen as he travelled restlessly through Europe and attended other leading playhouses of his day. Relegated to the realm of myth, however, has been the stereotyped notion of Andersen as a frustrated and totally unsuccessful closet dramatist – a notion often perpetuated, it seems to me, by critics who have not inconvenienced themselves by reading his plays. Nor, of course, is Andersen the only nineteenth-century playwright to have fallen victim to the labelling malaise.

The non-reader of the Scandinavian languages is at a serious disadvantage in attempting to unravel the strands of development in the drama before Ibsen. The bulk of English translations of Andersen, in terms of his work as a whole, is astonishing: Elias Bredsdorff's *Danish Literature in English Translation* lists a bibliography of translations of his prose writings, particularly his tales, that fills sixty pages! In his own lifetime eighteen of his tales, two of his novels (*The Two Baronesses* and *To Be, or Not to Be?*), one of his travel books (*Pictures of Sweden*), and the definitive edition of his autobiography (*The Story of My Life*) appeared in England even before they were published in Denmark; in the United States ten of his tales were published for the first time anywhere in the *Riverside Magazine for Young People*. Nevertheless, despite his position in the English-speaking world and although his works for the stage were known both in Germany and in the other Scandinavian countries, not one of his twenty-five original plays has ever been made available in English. Lest this be taken as a reflection on their quality, it is well to add that, while the same few standard Scandinavian plays continue to appear in versions which more or less resemble the original, not a line of dialogue from the plays of such major influences on Ibsen as Oehlenschläger, Heiberg, or Hertz is easily accessible to the English reader today. (The only exceptions are the bombastic and forgotten nineteenth-century translations of Oehlenschläger's *Hakon Jarl* and Hertz's *King René's Daughter*, but even these are not often encountered.) The present book has attempted to cope with this situation by being as explicit as possible about plot when introducing the reader, perhaps for the first time, to a wide range of nineteenth-century Scandinavian plays, and by referring to all Danish titles in English translation, giving the original alongside at the first mention.

Equally unfamiliar to most scholars will be the unique theatrical research material preserved in the library of the Royal Theatre in Copenhagen – records which form the core of this study's investigation of prenaturalistic stage practices. Because the Royal Theatre held a major place among the European playhouses of this period, moreover, many of these conventions and techniques have direct parallels in the rest of Europe as well. Aspects of staging can be reconstructed from a collection of handwritten folio volumes in the Royal Theatre archives which contain detailed descriptions and the actual ground plans for hundreds of settings. The sources on staging are supplemented by a series of inventories which specify the scenery in the Royal Theatre stock room at a given time. A third group of handwritten volumes, maintained by the stage manager and known as *Regieprotokoller*, are protocols listing sets, costumes, props, dates, and casts for each production. Costuming practices are illuminated by a collection of complete costume lists and, in the case of Andersen's plays, twelve surviving costume drawings. Among the documents pertaining to acting, the *Regiejournal*, a daily, chronological record of rehearsals and performances, sheds new light on nineteenth-century rehearsal practice. Various printed 'Actors' Regulations' also provide important facts about performance style. These theatrical sources are further enriched by an assortment of miscellaneous manuscripts, letters, and the collected decisions of the Royal Theatre dramaturge, as well as by a gallery of original unpublished scene designs, some of the best of which have been included in this study in order to introduce three of the foremost prenaturalistic stage designers, Aron Wallich, Troels Lund, and C.F. Christensen.

In evolving an over-all picture of theatre practice in the last century, additional details have been culled from the financial records and accounts of the Royal Theatre preserved in the Danish State Archives (Rigsarkivet), the collection of prompt copies, musical scores, and Andersen Papers in the Danish Royal Library, the newspaper and periodical files housed in the University of Copenhagen Library, and the rich storehouse of prints and memorabilia in the Danish Theatre Museum.

The prologue and the complimentary epilogue to this book are intended to provide a logical framework for its principal concern. They sketch in brief strokes the eighteenth-century background from which the romantic theatre developed, and the movement toward the modern concept of the director that occurred at the close of Andersen's career.

An opening chapter explores the early artistic and cultural impressions of Andersen's youth, impressions which shaped his interest in the practical theatre and were of immense initial importance in his development. At the age of fourteen, unsuspecting, proud, ambitious, and hopelessly inept, he blundered into the cultural environment of the Danish capital, eager for guidance and needing it as urgently as ever any young author did. A little more than three decades later, in 1852, another young man, named Henrik Ibsen, journeyed to Copenhagen in search of similar experience and contact with the influential men of Danish theatre. One of those whom he visited was H.C. Andersen, who recommended the plays of the Austrian dramatist Ferdinand Raimund to the young director's attention. The suggestion was a characteristic one. The subtle harmony of theatrical fantasy and realism in the Viennese fairy-tale genre was the hallmark of much of Andersen's dramaturgy as well, and it was this same blend, combined with an ideology borrowed from Kierkegaard and a structure borrowed from Heiberg's untranslated masterpiece *A Soul After Death*, that Ibsen would soon turn to his own use in a play like *Peer Gynt*.

In November 1872, less than three years before Andersen's death, his play *More than Pearls and Gold* was given its hundredth performance at Casino Theatre, the popular independent playhouse which he had helped to establish. The aging author, accompanied by his protegé William Bloch, who would himself before long become the foremost naturalistic director in Scandinavia, was welcomed with an anonymous prologue written for the occasion. In its description of the characters with which Andersen had peopled the 'wondrous, living, and illustrated/Album' of his play, it touched on those elements of theatricality and fantasy so central to the theatre of romance:

> *King of the fairies, who sleeps on a cloud!*
> *Salamanders, the Seasons, trolls, and sprites*
> *And all that merry, motley crowd*
> *From the kingdom of fancy and truth.*

HANS CHRISTIAN ANDERSEN AND THE ROMANTIC THEATRE

Eighteenth-Century
Danish Theatre

THE DANISH ROYAL THEATRE was built on its present site on Kongens Nytorv in Copenhagen by the court architect, Niels Eigtved, in 1748. It is therefore one of the oldest functioning theatres in Europe. During the eighteenth century Eigtved's noble building and its machinery underwent a number of alterations, the most thorough being a major rebuilding in 1772 under the direction of the architect C.F. Harsdorff, in the course of which the stage was greatly expanded and the scenic machinery improved. Harsdorff's plan for the rebuilt playhouse is seen in Fig. 1. The original stage had been fitted with four rows of flat wings on each side, and Harsdorff added two additional rows which are projected in his drawing. The proscenium opening measured slightly more than twenty-nine feet in width; the lower half of the plan depicts the horseshoe-shaped auditorium with its side boxes.

Although the stage underwent subsequent changes and improvements from time to time, the original building continued to function throughout most of the nineteenth century. It was not until 1874, a year before Andersen's death, that the theatre for which he had written his plays was finally demolished and replaced by the present Royal Theatre building. The razing of the old theatre was a symbolic act as well, marking the end of the prenaturalistic system and the advent of a new style.

Before turning to Andersen's plays as they relate to the theatrical practices of the nineteenth century, valuable perspective may be gained by recalling, as a general point of comparison and departure, some of the more important features of the eighteenth-century theatre in Denmark.[1]

1 I am indebted for my conclusions about this earlier period to the informative studies of Torben Krogh.

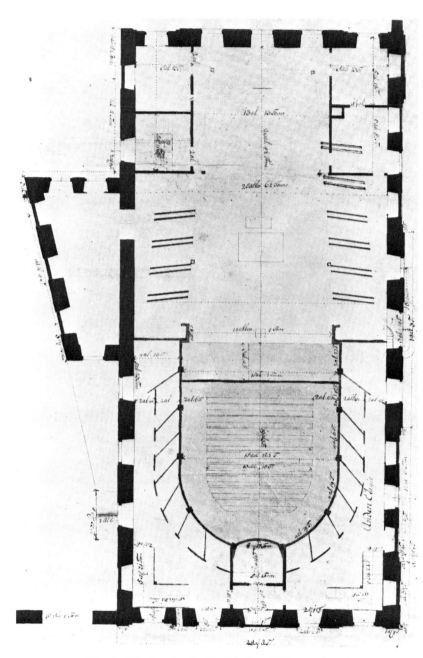

1 Harsdorff's plan for the Danish Royal Theatre (1772)

It is commonly realized that the standard stage setting throughout the eighteenth and early nineteenth centuries consisted of loose flat wings, backdrops or shutters, and overhead borders. The box set or closed room of the modern theatre, with its real walls and ceiling, first appeared in Denmark in 1829, when the celebrated choreographer August Bournonville used it for the ballet *La sonnambula*. Its use did not become general, however, until several decades later; for the first productions of nearly all of Andersen's plays at the Royal Theatre wing-and-border sets were used. In contrast it may be borne in mind that the box set had already been introduced in France and Germany at the close of the eighteenth century.[2]

The older type of setting derived from the chariot-counterweight system evolved in the Renaissance by the 'Great Sorcerer' of stage mechanics, Giacomo Torelli. Side wings were fastened to carriages or 'chariots' running in slots in the stage floor; the chariots were capable of being moved simultaneously beneath the stage by means of ropes attached to a windlass, allowing a new group of wings to be rolled forward before an open curtain. Scene changes were facilitated by the use of double chariots in each wing position (marked by double lines in Fig. 1); in addition to the set of wings visible to the audience, a second set was mounted and ready to replace them. A further improvement occurred in 1826 with the installation of triple chariots, thereby making it possible to hang three separate settings simultaneously.[3] Similarly the backdrop and borders in such a setting were designed for convenient raising and lowering with the aid of ropes and winches. Thus an *a vista* scene shift could be accomplished in the shortest possible time, and was further implemented by the practice of alternating the use of deep and shallow, or 'carpenter,' scenes.

As Richard Southern has ably argued, visible transformations were an integral part of the theatrical spectacle.[4] In fact, the practice of lowering the curtain, even between acts, for the purpose of concealing a change of scene met with sharp criticism. Hence, in a review of Goethe's *Claudine von Villa Bella*, the Danish author and critic K.L. Rahbek spoke out strongly against this procedure as unbefitting a royal theatre.[5] Similarly a production by Freibach's German troupe in Odense in 1791 was criti-

2 Cf Bergman, *Regi och Spelstil*, p. 26
3 'Fortegnelse paa Ombygninger, Forandringer og Forbedringer ved Det Kongelige Comediehus' 1824–50 (Royal Theatre library)
4 See his *Changeable Scenery*, p. 17
5 *Minerva* (March 1787), p. 261

cized because between acts 'the curtain fell each time, apparently so that the shortcomings of the machinery would pass unnoticed,' despite the fact, as the reviewer continued, that such scene changes frequently constituted the most interesting element for the audience.[6] Throughout the eighteenth century, a theatre's store of basic types of settings fell as a rule into certain fixed categories, representing a room, a forest, a street, a seascape, a gothic hall, and so on. The same sets were re-used continually in changing combinations with illusory set-pieces added to create variety – a practice which survived far into the following century. 'The setting we will ignore,' remarked the gifted Danish critic Rosenstand-Goiske in 1771, 'since it is, so far as we know, used for other plays and consequently not appropriate.'[7] An example, no doubt an extreme one, of such a collection of standard settings is found, incidentally, in Andersen's own recollection of the small store of stock décors possessed by the provincial dramatic company in Slagelse during his school years there. The inventory consisted of a front curtain on which a fountain was painted, its spout emanating directly from the prompter's hole; a street décor painted to represent Slagelse Square; and a forest décor painted on the back wall itself, so that the company was obliged to place a new moon which it acquired in *front* of the tree tops![8]

Allowing for the imaginative nature of Andersen's anecdote, it was nonetheless not uncommon, especially in the provincial theatres, to utilize stock settings under the most inappropriate circumstances. Concerning the stock forest décor at Odense Theatre, one critic remarked in 1796: 'The setting should, it is true, have been a laurel grove; but as none was to be found in the old décor inventory ... the spectators had to be content with a common oak or beech forest.'[9] That one may expect to encounter similar stylistic incongruities at the Royal Theatre far into the nineteenth century is suggested by Andersen's dismay at seeing palm trees and cactus in an 1840 production of Donizetti's *La fille du régiment*, in which the scene is laid in the Tyrol.[10] The truth of Andersen's observation can, more-

6 *Hefteskriftet Almeennyttige Samlinger til Hiertets Forbedring, Kundskabernes Ubdredelse og Stundom til Moerskab* (Odense 1791), XXIII, 309

7 Rosenstand-Goiske, *Den dramatiske Journal*, I, 4

8 *H.C. Andersens Levnedsbog 1805–1831*, ed. H. Topsøe-Jensen, p. 100

9 *Mennesket, En Journal af blandet Indhold*, ed. Søren Hempel (Odense 1797), I, 1 (the only issue), 154–5. *De kgl. allene autoriserede Fyens Avertissements Tidender*, XCVI (1796) criticized the use of this décor for a street.

10 See his *Mit Livs Eventyr*, II, 140

over, be tested by examining the Royal Theatre archives. Although the setting used for *La fille du régiment* was predominantly Tyrolean, borrowed chiefly from *Wilhelm Tell*, the front wing, on which a Madonna picture was painted, was taken over from Bournonville's celebrated ballet of the Italian Campagna, *Festival in Albano/Festen i Albano*. In this ballet's setting the wing in question is described as follows: 'No. 1 and No. 2 wings stage left are likewise painted as a wood *in tropical character* and on No. 1 wing is painted a board with a Madonna picture.'[11] There can be no doubt that Andersen's recollection of tropical vegetation in the Tyrol was fully accurate.

Closely related to the incongruous combination of settings is the fact that in many cases scene changes in the eighteenth-century theatre were not complete but only partial. This meant that only the backdrop was shifted, while the side wings remained unaltered. 'In the tragedy two rooms were depicted which alternated with each other,' wrote one reviewer of an Odense production, 'but this change took place as usual by each time allowing the backdrop to fall or be raised. The side wings were still the same.'[12] Although 'partial changes' are not unknown even in the modern theatre, in the eighteenth century they frequently served to shatter illusion and were therefore a common critical target. 'When the scene changes here,' complained Rosenstand-Goiske in a review, 'it happens by raising the drop, but the wings which were in the palace, together with the red ceiling, remain. We would like to know whether this is a fault of the machinist or a defect in the theatre?'[13] The installation in the Royal Theatre of triple wing chariots in 1826 presumably helped to eliminate the necessity of partial scene shifts. Nevertheless, it was still possible at mid-century for Andersen to point out with chagrin that 'they offer us day-wings with sunlight streaming through, while in the background we have an open balcony looking out on a dark blue, starry sky!'[14]

Furniture and other objects standing on the eighteenth-century stage presented a substantial problem. The setting was, as we have seen, usually shifted with the curtain open and all furniture had therefore to be cleared before the *changement* began. Allowing the same furniture to remain on

11 *Fortegnelse over Decorationer til Balletter, Divertissementer og Entréer*, 43, and *Decorationer til Syngespil*, 199–200 (Royal Theatre library)
12 *Almeennyttige Samlinger*, XXIII, 315

13 *Den dramatiske Journal*, I, 47. See also *Almeennyttige Samlinger*, XXIII, 298, 350, et al.
14 *Mit Livs Eventyr*, II, 140

the stage throughout could hardly be expected to strengthen scenic illusion. 'The patience of the spectators,' asserted an account of Odense Theatre in 1796, 'cannot continue to tolerate seeing a Count's sofa remain standing in a painter's chamber, only to be carried out later by the servants of two different gentlemen as though it were goods pawned for delinquent taxes.'[15] The usual solution to this dilemma was to make the servants or supernumeraries in a scene responsible for carrying all furniture off the stage with them. The survival of this practice in the nineteenth century is exemplified in the stage manager's notes for Andersen's singspiel, *The Bride of Lammermoor/Bruden fra Lammermoor*, staged in 1832: '(2nd act) The table and the benches are removed from the stage by the supernumeraries.'[16] It is easy to appreciate the elation of the Danish theatre man J.D. Preisler when, during a study trip through France and Germany in 1788, he encountered at the theatre in Mannheim chairs and tables painted in such a manner that they 'could serve for all rooms without being removed.'[17]

One of the most important factors influencing eighteenth-century theatre practice and acting style was stage lighting. The principal sources of illumination in this period were footlights, candles or lamps filled with tallow placed behind the loose wing pieces, and chandeliers. In order to brighten the forestage, the auditorium at the Royal Theatre had been illuminated from the earliest period with five small chandeliers during the performance, a practice unchanged by Harsdorff's alterations. This custom was naturally imitated in a more primitive fashion by the provincial companies, and it supplied Andersen with a series of colourful theatrical reminiscences. 'A little iron chandelier with candles hung down under the ceiling,' he wrote of the theatre in Slagelse. 'They dripped so badly that beneath them there was always an open space, no matter how full the house otherwise was.'[18] At the Royal Theatre, footlight and side illumination were provided chiefly by 'lamps' – specially designed containers filled with liquid tallow and placed in conjunction with polished metal reflectors. It was not until 1819 that candle lighting at the Royal

15 *Bidrag til ... Fyens Avertissements Tidender*, XCVI (1796)

16 *Decorationer til Syngespil*, p. 114

17 See his *Journal over en Reise*, II, 117

18 *H.C. Andersens Levenedsbog*, p. 100. Similar recollections are found in

Andersen's prose works *Skyggebilleder af en Rejse til Harzen* (1831) and *Billedbog uden Billeder* (1840): see his collected works, *Samlede Skrifter*, VII, 115 ff; VIII, 34

Theatre was replaced by the more flexible and reliable oil-burning Argand lamps, invented by Aimé Argand in 1783.[19]

While the foreground of the eighteenth-century stage was thus bathed in light from the footlights, wing lamps, and chandeliers, it was difficult or impossible to light the background, and the stage proper was relatively dark by modern standards. This fact was not as disadvantageous as it might first appear, however, because the subdued illumination undoubtedly lent a special romantic atmosphere of its own to the scenery and the figures of the actors. Nevertheless, a favourite method of dispelling some of the gloom on the stage was the arbitrary inclusion of all types of light sources, including lamps, candles, transparencies, and so on, within the setting itself. Since this practice was followed regardless of whether the scene represented daytime or not, inconsistencies frequently arose. 'Why it is necessary to have lamps hanging in the prison we do not know, since this wretched setting requires daylight,' commented Rosenstand-Goiske in connection with the production in 1770 of an adaptation of Moore's *The Gamester*.[20] 'It was common practice this evening for the robbers to light their pipes with the wing candles,' complained a reviewer of an Odense production, 'despite the fact that the scene represented daytime.'[21]

These lighting conditions had a marked influence on the placement of actors on the stage because they demanded unmitigated foreground playing. The practice, stemming from the time of the Renaissance, of always coming forward on the stage to face the audience squarely – actors 'should never act in profile nor turn their backs to the spectators,' stated Goethe's *Rules for Actors*[22] – was followed for very practical reasons: so that the actor might be seen and heard. This simple, basic condition was one of the principal factors determining earlier theatrical practice, and the majority of rules governing placement of persons on the stage may be considered in this context.

In the absence of a stage director or a blocking plan in the modern sense, certain additional placement rules were adhered to for the sake of order whenever several persons appeared onstage together. By far the most important rule of placement concerned the traditional semicircle on the forestage, an arrangement into which the actors automatically assembled when there was a group onstage. The obligatory semicircle was

19 Overskou, *Den danske Skueplads*, IV, 600
20 *Den dramatiske Journal*, II, 23
21 *Alm. Samlinger*, XXIII, 350–1
22 Quoted in Nagler, *A Source Book in Theatrical History*, p. 429

very seldom violated, and the positions of the principal actors were shifted only if absolutely necessary. 'While an actor is speaking he ought never to walk about unless he is forced thereto by great necessity,' the experienced theatre man Leone di Somi had noted in the Renaissance.[23] In the theatre of the eighteenth and nineteenth centuries, animation was achieved mainly in the often decorative and processional entrances and exits and in the movement of the supernumeraries in the middle plane. Grouping in the semicircle on the forestage was according to rank, so that persons of higher rank and ladies were always placed on the right side of the stage and, in a group of three or more, always occupied the centre position. Brissard's frontispiece to Molière's *Impromptu de Versailles* (produced 1663) is in reality an excellent illustration of this kind of placement. This same convention continued to survive in the nineteenth century, moreover, long after its original motivation, dim candle lighting and poor acoustics, had disappeared. Two leading German innovators at the turn of the century, Iffland and F.L. Schröder, tacitly accepted the semicircle tradition without objection as a natural and unalterable fact. 'Sind mehrere Personen auf der Bühne, so müssen sie in halben Zirkel stehen,' asserted Schröder; 'der dadurch sehr leicht gebildet wird, wenn der in der Mitte stehende *nur eben* Alle sieht, und von Allen *nur eben* gesehen wird.' [When several persons are onstage, they must stand in a semicircle which can very easily be formed when the middle man is *just able* to see everyone, and can *just* be seen by everyone.][24] The predominance of the semicircle in France at the time of the English guest performances in Paris in 1827 can be divined from a comment in *Le Courier français* (13 September 1827) which, in expressing admiration for the original English scenic arrangements, added: 'Chez nous, quand cinq ou six personnages se trouvent à la fois sur le théâtre, ces personnages forment un demi-cercle devant la rampe, et trop souvent celui qui ne parle pas, regarde dans les loges, ce qui détruit espèce d'illusion.'

The latter part of this French critic's complaint brings to mind another important convention for scenic behaviour, contained in the maxim: 'No one must be free on the stage.' This principle came into operation whenever an actor remained before the audience without having lines to deliver.

23 Nicoll, *The Development of the Theatre*, p. 256

24 Meyer, *Fr. L. Schröder*, II, 209. See also A.W. Iffland, 'Fragmente über

einige wesentliche Erfordernisse für den darstellenden Künstler auf der Bühne,' *Almanach für Theater- und Theaterfreunde auf das Jahr 1807*, 179

Many rules were offered for filling in such empty spaces in the dialogue, depending, according to the critic K.L. Rahbek, on whether (a) one is simply listening or has something else to do, (b) one is affected by what is being said or not, and (c) if affected, whether this reaction can be seen by the other characters or only by the audience.[25] Precepts were then laid down by Rahbek for each of these conditions, but in all cases the admonition against being 'free on the stage' was reiterated. Indeed, the art of pantomime and reaction was regarded very seriously in the older acting style. Francesco Riccoboni, in his classic *L'art du théâtre*, devoted an entire chapter to *Le jeu muet*, characterizing this aspect of acting as of the utmost importance but complaining that few actors commanded it properly.[26] Two related factors made the question of pantomime of primary critical significance in the eighteenth century: the absence of a stage director to guide the actors in this respect, and the fact that an average of between two and five rehearsals was the norm for any production at the Royal Theatre. The exaggerated critical preoccupation with reaction and dumbshow which persisted through the nineteenth century may even seem somewhat difficult to understand today, when this side of an actor's characterization develops naturally in the course of the numerous and extensive rehearsals, under constant supervision of a director, which form the basis for any modern production. Under a system of few rehearsals with very little direction, however, there was real danger that a less experienced actor having no lines to speak would simply stand and gaze idly out at the spectators.[27]

Another result of few rehearsals was the problem of role memorizing, which constituted a favourite target for critical reprimands throughout the eighteenth century.[28] The prompter maintained a position of magnified importance: the actors kept their eyes on him, their best ear towards him, and even talked to him if need be, neglecting the audience out front for the sake of 'the oracle in the hole,' as he was ironically called by Rahbek.[29] When the prompter could not help, the actors stammered, twisted their lines, or worse. 'Mad. Meyer displayed a charming figure

25 *Breve fra en gammel Skuespiller*, pp. 246–7, 335

26 *L'art du théâtre*, pp. 75 ff

27 Cf *Den dramatiske Journal*, I, 12, 46, and *Alm. Samlinger*, XXIII, 293

28 For numerous instances, see Krogh's edition of the Royal Theatre's oldest daily journal, *Det Kgl. Teaters ældeste Regiejournal 1781–1787*, pp. 15, 18, 42, et al.

29 Rahbek, *Om Skuespilkunsten*, p. 91

for the stage,' remarked *Odense Theaterblad* in a review in 1804. 'Pity she had not studied her part, and her memory, if it was in use at all on this occasion, so betrayed her that she was distracted enough to exit through the wall' – ie, through the open side wings.[30] Despite a ceaseless barrage of criticism and imposed fines, however, failing memories continued to rely on the prompter. When the entire cast was in fact letter-perfect in their parts, this was considered something quite extraordinary. Preisler, whose journey took him to Strasbourg, remarked of the French troupe there: 'The prompter was not heard, and admire I must the excellence of all in memorizing.'[31]

In the absence of a stage director the actor devised independently, without particular regard for the total ensemble, a jeu de théâtre or a coup de théâtre with which to enliven a scene. He was aided in his work both by the distinct types of roles that existed and especially by the theatrical handbooks, based on the works on oratory by Cicero and Quintilian, by writers like Riccoboni and Sainte Albine, who set down working rules for significant aspects of the actor's craft. Particularly important were the precepts for gestures, movements, and positions which characterized this style. Actors were expected to perform with ultimate grace and beauty, and all clumsiness or gracelessness was banished from the stage. The Danish critic J.C. Tode's comment in 1789 is illustrative of this ideal: 'Nothing is more displeasing to the eye than to see a theatre person standing in a forced, affected, slouched manner ... naturally, unforcedly, and firmly you must stand.'[32]

At first glance the recurring demand that gesture and movement should be 'unforced' and 'natural' might appear deceptively modern. The cry for 'naturalness' in any era, however, must be seen in the light of that period's conception of the meaning of the term, a conception having no particular relationship to what is considered 'natural' today. The eighteenth-century ideal in this respect was governed by a seeking for the classic and statuesque form. The prescribed method for achieving this ideal was, characteristically, through intensive ballet instruction for all young, aspiring actors. As a whole the five ballet positions played a crucial role regarding the stage movement of eighteenth-century players. Riccoboni, for example, whose work comprised an indispensable acting

30 *Odense Theaterblad*, 1 (1804), 6
31 *Journal over en Reise*, 1, 162
32 See *Dramatiske Tillæg til Museum*,

Kritik og Antikritik (Copenhagen 1789), p. 62

handbook, emphasized regarding stance that the second position was 'the most natural and the most simple.'[33] Goethe noted that the fourth dance position provided 'a beautiful contemplative pose (for a young man, for instance).'[34]

The end goal of this striving towards the statuesque was *Schöne Wahrheit*, the beautiful form. The importance of idealizing a role in conformity with this concept was an omnipresent influence in the older acting style. The actor played in large, sustained *affects*, or over-all expressional phrases (Hazlitt liked to refer to one 'predominant feeling' or 'ruling passion'), at the same time expressing this affect with so vital a grace – so 'fair an attitude' – that it was also perceived as beauty. This theatrical ideal was formulated most succinctly by Goethe in his *Rules for Actors* (section 35): 'First of all, the player must consider that he should not only imitate nature but also portray it ideally, thereby, in his presentation, uniting the true with the beautiful.'[35] These words might well stand as a motto over the art of acting in the eighteenth century, particularly in the period after neoclassicism, with its worship of the idealized and the statuesque, had begun its conquest of the theatre.

This brief 'prologue' summarizing the chief theatrical conventions governing eighteenth-century Danish theatre has its place here for two reasons. Andersen's initial acquaintance with theatre in Odense and Copenhagen was with these traditions; furthermore, because a wholly different set of practices and conventions did not emerge in reality until the breakthrough of naturalism certain of these older conventions continued to manifest themselves during the nineteenth century in the productions of Andersen's plays. The radical changes brought about by naturalism in the eighties, however, were prepared for during the period of transition which was romanticism, and the older eighteenth-century traditions were gradually altered or revised by a multitude of new impulses and stylistic developments during the important thirty-five years in which H.C. Andersen was writing for the Royal Theatre in Copenhagen.

33 *L'art du théâtre*, p. 6   35 *Ibid.*, p. 429
34 Nagler, *Source Book*, p. 430

ONE

Early Impressions

NO ASPECT OF HANS CHRISTIAN ANDERSEN'S ART can successfully be separated from his personal experience. Each of his major novels was autobiographical. He himself remarked that his fairy-tales had been with him all his life 'like seeds in the mind, needing only a current, a ray of sunlight, a drop of distilled wormwood, to burst into flower.'[1] Similarly, his work as a playwright grew out of specific exposures to stylistic trends and impulses in the romantic theatre of his time. A whole series of autobiographies makes Andersen's life an open book. *Das Märchen meines Lebens ohne Dichtung* appeared in connection with the first edition of his collected works in German, published in Leipzig in 1847. This formed the basis for the authoritative two-volume work, *The Story of My Life | Mit Livs Eventyr*, issued in Denmark in 1855; its continuation was published for the first time in New York in 1871, appearing in Copenhagen five years later. Finally, a youthful manuscript written in 1832–3, entitled *The Book of Life | Levnedsbogen*, was the object of a sensational literary 'find' in 1926. Each of these delightful autobiographies is filled with detail describing his childhood in Odense, from his birth there on 2 April 1805 until he set out in 1819 as a stowaway on the stagecoach to Copenhagen, and his subsequent formative years in the Danish capital. The early theatrical impressions which he records introduced him to a wide range of the genres and personalities forming the general background of Danish theatrical life in the first half of the nineteenth century.

Andersen's first recorded encounter with the living theatre was with a

1 Topsøe-Jensen, *H.C. Andersen og andre Studier*, p. 37

German version of a great Danish classic, Ludvig Holberg's *The Political Tinker | Den politiske Kandestøber*, which he saw at Odense Theatre in 1812.[2] This three-act musical adaptation of Holberg's comedy represented a highly popular nineteenth-century genre, the 'musical' derived from a classic play or novel – a genre to which Andersen would return in his own operatic adaptions of Walter Scott and Carlo Gozzi. Similarly, the next play which he recalls at Odense Theatre, *Das Donauweibchen* by K.F. Hensler and Ferdinand Kauer, exemplifies another genre to become important in his playwriting, the Viennese *Zauberposse*. The combination of the comic, the fantastical, and the supernatural in Hensler and Kauer's 'romantisch-komische Zauberoper in 3 Akten' scored an instant success in Odense. The impression it made on Andersen was so lasting that twenty years later Caroline Walter, the actress whom he had seen in the leading role, joined in his imagination with the celebrated opera singer Maria Malibran to form the model for the character of Annunziata in his first novel, *The Improvisator | Improvisatoren*.[3]

Yet a third theatrical event singled out in Andersen's childhood recollections is the guest appearance of Giuseppe Casorti's international pantomime and tightrope troupe in Odense from December 1814 to March 1815. Casorti's performances at Prices' Theatre in Vesterbro provided one of the highlights in the cultural life of Copenhagen during this period, and his work formed a link between the older traditions of the commedia dell'arte and their preservation in a Danish tradition of masked comedy that has survived until the present day. Casorti's *Harlequin Foreman of the Threshers* captured Andersen's imagination, and later the figures of the Italian masked comedy continued to hold a fascination for him, appearing in such dissimilar works as his opera *The Raven | Ravnen* and the prose collection *Picture Book without Pictures | Billedbog uden Billeder*.

From the financial collapse of Görbing Franck's troupe in 1815 until 1820, Odense was without a professional theatre. 'People,' relates Odense Theatre's official historian ruefully, 'would rather see a trained horse that came here, or Goldkette's stilt-dancers, Geisselbrecht's puppets, and the

2 On the date of this performance see Topsøe-Jensen, *Omkring Levenedsbogen*, p. 108. General influences of Holberg on Andersen's writing are discussed in Topsøe-Jensen, *H.C. Andersen og Holberg*, and Brix, *H.C. Andersen og hans Eventyr*.

3 Andersen, *Mit Livs Eventyr*, 1, 192–3. Hansen, *Die Entwicklung das National-Theaters in Odense*, provides a lucid general discussion of the theatre in Odense; see especially pp. 192–8.

strong Madam Paulsen who could lift several persons in her hair, and could endure having an anvil laid upon her breast and a piece of cold iron hammered on it till the metal became hot'.[4] To make up for the lack of 'legitimate' theatrical entertainment an amateur dramatic society was organized in 1816, in which Andersen took an intense interest and which subsequently provided him with material for a number of entertaining episodes in his novels.[5] However, by far the most significant theatrical event in Odense during these years was the annual summer visit of the Royal Theatre company, which performed plays with complete cast and equipment and which was invariably greeted with enthusiasm by the local populace. Andersen's admiration for these actors knew no bounds; 'I looked up to them as to earthly gods,' he later wrote with disarming frankness.[6] Their repertoire in the summer of 1818 included romantic tragedies of Adam Oehlenschläger and popular operettas of Grétry, D'Alayrac, and Isouard. This encounter proved decisive for the course of Andersen's future career, firmly establishing his lifelong obsession with the theatre.

He obtained permission to watch the performances from the wings and made several appearances as a supernumerary. In this capacity he spoke his first line on stage as the page in Nicolo Isouard and C.G. Etienne's highly popular *Cendrillon*.[7] This adaptation of the Cinderella story was flavoured with humourous and sentimental elements characteristic of this type of opéra comique; hence the evil stepmother was made a comic stepfather, and an Italian Renaissance setting, a wizard named Alidor, and an exciting disguise intrigue were added. The highpoint of this operetta occurs, meanwhile, shortly after Andersen's line as the page; Anine (Cinderella) sings a charming French song in gavotte rhythm about a peasant girl named Colinette who cannot thrive in the atmosphere of the court:

> *Car on ne peut ici s'expliquer sans détour,*
> *Il n'est point de plaisir, de bonheur, sans l'amour.*

In the pauses Anine dances accompanied by a tambourine, the rhythm of

4 Schmidt, *Meddelelser om Skuespil*, p. 64
5 See *Kun en Spillemand*, pp. 289–90, and *Lykke-Peer*, p. 26
6 *Mit Livs Eventyr*, I, 51

7 Cf Torben Krogh, 'H.C. Andersen og Æskepot,' *Dagens Nyheders kronik* (20 Jan 1955)

2 Anine's dance scene in the second act of
Isouard and Etienne's opéra comique, *Cendrilion*;
Mlle Alexandrine St Aubin of the Paris Opéra Comique

which is indicated in Isouard's score. The graceful charm of this moment, an impression of which is conveyed in Fig. 2, so fired Andersen's imagination that a year later in Copenhagen he called on solo ballerina Anna Schall and, removing his boots and using his broad hat as a tambourine, proceeded to perform Anine's number from memory in the hope that the unusual audition might secure him an engagement at the Royal Theatre![8]

The production of *Cendrillon* by the Royal Theatre company also influenced Andersen in a less spectacular manner. Music from the score reappears in two of his later vaudevilles, and, in a wider sense, the tone of many of his plays and fairy-tales bears subtle echoes of the sentimental moral precepts of the wise magician Alidor concerning the importance of 'blessed peace of mind.' Moreover, the Royal Theatre performances at Odense Theatre in 1818 prompted and influenced his earliest, highly primitive attempts at playwriting. In his father's military account book he transcribed snatches of songs and arias as well as a list of titles for twenty-five projected dramas – the majority of which died mercifully in the planning stage.[9]

Given these experiences, inspired by his less than peripheral association with the Royal Theatre performances, and armed with the ingenuous conviction of a fourteen-year-old, H.C. Andersen set forth alone in September 1819 on his singular journey to the capital to become a royal actor. Once in Copenhagen, the romantic fascination which the provincial playhouse in Odense had held for him quickly faded in the glow of the more professional atmosphere of the Royal Theatre itself.[10] His arrival coincided with the emergence of a new theatrical style throughout Europe, particularly in France and England. The new stylistic ideals, differing in many respects from the more formalized and abstracted theatrical system of the eighteenth century, led gradually to the dissolution of that system. In 1827 Victor Hugo's preface to *Cromwell* proclaimed a charter of freedom from

8 An illustration of Andersen himself in this dance scene appeared during his lifetime in the Dutch edition of *Mit Livs Eventyr*, *Zija Leven vertelt*. See R. Neiiendam, *To Kvinder i H.C. Andersens liv*, p. 10 and Topsøe-Jensen, *H.C. Andersens Brevveksling med Edvard og Henriette Collin*, III, 251

9 See *Mit Livs Eventyr*, I, 42–3; Brix, *Det første Skridt*, pp. 10–11; Collin,

H.C. Andersen, p. v. The account book is preserved in the Collin Manuscript Collection of the Royal Library.

10 Thus, some ten years after his departure, Andersen rejected without hesitation an offer to appear on the stage at Odense; see Collin, *H.C. Andersen*, p. 150, and Bille and Bøgh, *Breve til H.C. Andersen*, p. 82

the remaining neoclassical restrictions on drama. The English guest performances in Paris in 1827–8 and the productions in 1829 and 1830 of
Dumas' *Henri III et sa cour*, Vigny's *Othello*, and Hugo's *Hernani* marked the
real breakthrough of the new romanticism on the Continent.[11] The new
scenic goals of 'Walter Scott romanticism' – more piquant and illusory
settings, greater emphasis on local colour, and the concept of the theatre
as *eine lebende Bildergallerie* (the favourite phrase of the brilliant German
designer K.F. Schinkel) – were to be felt strongly in many of the productions which Andersen saw at the Royal Theatre during the twenties.

The first production he attended on Kongens Nytorv was Kreutzer and
Favières' three-act operetta *Paul et Virginie*.[12] This experience, joined with
his vivid recollection of Galeotti's spectacular romantic ballet *Raoul Barbe-
Bleue / Rolf Blaaskæg*, which he presumably saw sometime in 1821, formed
the stimulus for an episode in his novel *Only a Fiddler / Kun en Spillemand*,
in which the young hero Christian is taken to the theatre for the first time.
Andersen's fictionalized reaction to the sensational ballet is noteworthy:
'The music resounded like human voices, indeed like the whole world of
nature ... The curtain rolled up, Bluebeard's murdered wives hovered in
white linen about their murderer's bed. The music was the mighty
language of the dead, and [Christian's] imagination followed the entire
romantic poem on powerful wings ... The life of the theatre seemed to
him to be a magical picture of joy and beauty.'[13] This enthusiastic description represents Andersen's initial encounter with a significant phase
of the cultural life of the Danish capital. Vincenzo Galeotti (1733–1816),
the internationally famous Italian choreographer who had staged half a
hundred ballets at the Royal Theatre during his career, is the man generally considered to be the creator of the Danish ballet's illustrious traditions
– traditions which his gifted successor August Bournonville (1805–1879)
built upon and renewed in the romantic spirit, preparing in the process
for the introduction around mid-century of more complex and integrated
mises-en-scène for opera and drama. Hence *Raoul Barbe-Bleue* introduced
Andersen to the typical elements of early romanticism, including an
effectively exotic setting by the Italian designer Cocchi, picturesque

11 Bergman, *Regi och Spelstil*, pp. 17–89,
provides a fine discussion of the implications of the new romantic elements
in France and Germany. For England,

see, *eg*, Nicoll, *History of English Drama*,
IV, 1–57
12 *Mit Livs Eventyr*, I, 56; *H.C. Andersens
Levnedsbog 1805–1831*, pp. 56–8
13 *Kun en Spillemand*, chap. XVI, p. 122

tableaux, intense portrayal of strong emotions, and a liberal seasoning of the mysterious, the mediaeval, and the supernatural. The 'magical picture' with which he was so fascinated formed, in reality, the highpoint of Galeotti's ballet. On the night before his wedding Bluebeard is asleep on his couch, which is lit by a single lamp; in a dream the ghosts of his first four slain wives appear behind a transparency and act out terrible death threats. In an enchanting dance the beautiful Isaure, Bluebeard's next wife-to-be, then enacts love and happiness, after which a flaming prophecy of death appears on the wall. Bluebeard awakes in terror and the dreadful vision vanishes. This scene sent a shudder of horror through the audience, and Bournonville reported dramatically that the suspense provoked several nerve cases among the spectators.[14]

Andersen, as the foregoing has implied, ranks as one of the finest observers and recorders of theatrical productions in the nineteenth century. A similar recollection of Meyerbeer's spectacular opera *Robert le Diable*, which he saw in Paris in 1833 and also described in *Only a Fiddler*, demonstrates both the quality of his perception and the fact that Danish theatre was fully in the mainstream of European romanticism. For, like *Raoul Barbe-Bleue*, *Robert le Diable*, in which its talented designer Ciceri employed every trick of perspective and stage lighting, featured the supernatural and sensational aspects of romantic theatre. 'The moon shines into the gloomy hall where crumbling grave monuments stand,' relates Andersen. 'At the hour of midnight the candles in the ancient brass chandeliers suddenly begin to glow, the tombs open, and the dead nuns rise up. By the hundreds they raise themselves from the graveyard and hover; they seem not to touch the ground ... Suddenly the shrouds fall, they all stand in full-bodied nakedness, and a bacchanal begins.' 'It could drive one mad!' he added in a letter on the production to a friend.[15]

Music and ballet continued to exert a significant influence on Andersen during his earliest years in Copenhagen. Under the patronage of the Italian opera singer and pedagogue, Giuseppe Siboni, and the Danish romantic composer, C.E.F. Weyse, he received a thorough introduction to contemporary romantic music. Through the friendship of the Swedish ballet dancer and instructor, Carl Dahlén, he gained admission to the

14 Bournonville, *Mit Theaterliv*, III, 216. On this ballet in general, see Krogh and Kragh-Jacobsen, *Den kongelige danske Ballet*, pp. 172–3

15 This letter, of 27 July 1827, was addressed to Ludvig Müller. *Kun en Spillemand*, pp. 311–12, and Bille and Bøgh, *Breve fra H.C. Andersen*, I, 127

Royal Theatre as a ballet pupil in the summer of 1820.[16] In this capacity he was permitted to watch all performances from the wings or from the ballet box in the third balcony. There is no reason to doubt his own very modest opinion of his dancing ability. However, although his youthful efforts to conquer the Royal Theatre stage as a performer are in one sense mere footnotes to the history of his later achievements, they continue to arouse interest because for the fifteen-year-old Andersen they constituted a formative experience of immense importance.

In such pearls of storytelling as *Moster* and *Lykke-Peer*, he has recaptured the atmosphere of the ballet school and the milling backstage life he observed there. To gain an accurate idea of the productions in which he actually did appear at the Royal Theatre, however, one may best turn to the 150-year-old historical documents themselves, several of which have lain unnoticed in the theatre's archives. Also aiding in the search is a small 'theatrical diary' in Andersen's handwriting, begun on 4 September 1820 and preserved in the Collin Manuscript Collection of the Royal Library. In this diary he catalogued the repertoire presented at the playhouse on Kongens Nytorv during 1820 and 1821, marking each title that impressed him with an asterisk and noting those momentous occasions on which he himself trod the boards as an extra.

Following an abortive crowd-scene appearance in D'Alayrac and Marsollier's operetta *Les deux petits savoyards* in 1820 – he was frightened offstage again by an actor who tried to make his remarkably ungraceful appearance the butt of a public joke – Andersen enacted 'a musical servant' in Galeotti's colourful pantomime ballet *Nina* in January 1821. In this ballet about a young, passionate girl who is mad from love, his particular task was to impersonate one of the two musicians who play for Nina and soothe the distraught girl with a melody that recalls her lover. The two musicians were placed farthest forward on the stage, and Andersen was deeply flattered that the bewitching Anna Margrethe Schall, who played Nina, paid him particular attention – 'probably I presented a very comical figure,' he later admitted.[17]

In April of the same year, Andersen appeared as one of the trolls in Carl Dahlén's four-act heroic ballet, *Armida* – on which occasion his name

16 On this period in Andersen's career, see R. Neiiendam, 'Da H.C. Andersens navn første gang blev trykt,' pp. 207–15, Jan Neiiendam, 'H.C. Andersen og Hofteatret,' pp. 3–11, and F.J. Marker, 'H.C. Andersen as a Royal Theatre Actor,' pp. 278–84

17 *Levnedsbogen*, p. 78

was entered for the first time in the archives of the Royal Theatre, together with that of Johanne Pätges, who as Johanne Luise Heiberg (1812–1890) was to become Scandinavia's foremost actress and the central figure in an ensemble of scenic artists unrivalled in Europe.[18] The action of *Armida*, based on Gluck's opera and derived from Tasso's *Jerusalem Delivered*, takes place during the First Crusade; the seductive Saracen sorceress Armida ensnares the crusader Rinaldo, without whose help Jerusalem cannot be freed. Rinaldo lives intoxicated with love on Armida's enchanted island until he is freed from the spell by a colleague, the crusader Ubaldo, who leads his wayward friend back to battle. Wearing a 'hideous mask' as one of Armida's eight trolls, Andersen's first stage business was to seize Rinaldo's sword and shield, while a frightful storm and a bolt of lightning destroying Armida's altar brought down the curtain. By no means less spectacular was the appearance of Andersen in the finale. Here the trolls are conjured out of the ground and gather on a cliff together with Armida, who hurls a bolt of lightning at Rinaldo's departing ship. The cliff collapses with the trolls 'falling in various violent positions' – Bournonville later recalled that Andersen fell headlong out of a crevice![19] The curtain fell as Armida ascended in a fiery car drawn by dragons and the trolls sank back into the ground.

Despite Claus Schall's music and the ballet's many spectacular effects, *Armida* proved unsuccessful. Nonetheless, it did provide Andersen with both a delightful 'nimbus of immortality' – the sight of his name in print for the first time on the programme – and a vivid introduction to the kind of spectacular theatricality so typical of the romantic theatre at this time. In his first major prose work, *A Walking Trip | Fodreise fra Holmens Canal*, a collection of fantastic sketches in the manner of the German romantics, Andersen recalled, in an impressionistic, Hoffmann-like vision capturing the essence of nineteenth-century theatre, the very effects he had seen at close range on stage in *Armida* a few years before: 'The curtain rolled up, and one saw an enormous kaleidoscope which was very slowly turned. Cliffs with waterfalls, burning cities, clouds raining fire, and wrecked ships tumbled haphazard among one another.'[20]

After transferring to the Royal Theatre's Opera Academy in the 1821–2 season – the final phase in his fruitless struggle to become an actor –

18 Cf Torben Krogh, 'På jagt efter et navn,' *Det Kgl. Teaters Program*, VII (1958–9)

19 Bournonville, *Mit Theaterliv*, III, 2, 48
20 *Fodreise fra Holmens Canal*, p. 43

Andersen figured as a supernumerary in a number of other productions. The fragment of his theatrical diary that survives from this season mentions roles in Oehlenschläger's *Axel and Valborg*, Simon Mayr's exotic singspiel *Lanassa*, and *Zoraïme et Zulnar*, an operetta set in Granada with a score by the successful French composer Boieldieu, whose better-known *La dame blanche* had a decisive influence on Danish theatre. To test the accuracy of his diary and other recollections, one may turn to the records of the Royal Theatre, particularly those costume lists which have survived for the productions in question, in search of Andersen's name among the supporting players. Although it was previously assumed that the appearance of his name in the Royal Theatre archives as a minor actor was limited to a single page from the ballet protocol for *Armida*, a more patient search has shown otherwise.

In a list of 'dance personnel' for Holberg's *Maskarade*, for instance, we encounter his name and learn that he danced 'an English dance and waltz' with a certain Miss Bolstrup on this occasion. Similarly, in a costume list dated 1821 for Thaarup and Schultz's Danish pastoral idyl *The Harvest Festival / Høstgildet*, we meet him as one of the peasants dressed in bright rustic attire, coloured scarf, blue and white woollen stockings, and peasant boots. Finally, as one of seven 'Brahmins' in *Lanassa*, set in East India during the time of Henri IV, he made his personal contribution to the piquant exoticism of the operetta in a costume consisting of 'red pantaloons, jumper and tights, yellow tunic, yellow drapery, unstained leather shoes, yellow turban, and yellow waistband.'[21] This seems, incidentally, considerably less bare and less drastic than the embarrassing Brahmin outfit so vividly described by Andersen in his earliest autobiography: ' ... tight, flesh-coloured clothing over the whole body, only a small belt, otherwise the whole back and chest completely bare. With hair shaved to a tiny wisp, we looked dreadful.'[22]

Several other dates starred with an asterisk in the theatrical diary from these early years are noteworthy because they represent additional points of contact between Andersen and the wider artistic context in which he would develop. The first of these dates, 8 October 1820, marks the initial Copenhagen performance of the overture to Carl Maria von Weber's opera *Der Freischütz*, which after its formal Danish premiere in 1822 became

---

21 'Dragter og Requisiter til Lanassa,' ten-page manuscript in the Royal Theatre library.

22 *Levnedsbogen*, p. 84

an outstanding popular favourite. The influence of this pearl of early German romanticism on Andersen may be judged simply from the number of
times he returns to it in his writings and private papers. The sensational
romantic effects and woodland mystique of *Der Freischütz*, particularly in
the celebrated second act scene in the Wolf's Glen where Casper conjures
Zamiel, the Evil One, exerted an irresistible appeal to Andersen's imagination. The very stage directions for the Wolf's Glen scene capture in a para-
graph the quintessence of this kind of scenic romanticism: 'A weird,
craggy glen, surrounded by high mountains, down the side of one of which
falls a cascade. A thunderstorm is coming on. In the foreground a tree
shattered by lightning and rotten inside, so that it seems to glow. On the
knotty branch of another tree a huge owl with fiery eyes. Caspar, in shirt-
sleeves, is making a circle of black stones; a skull is in the centre. The moon
throws a lurid light over all.'[23] On 12 October 1827 Andersen again
noted this opera in his theatrical diary, and little more than a year later
he included the Wolf's Glen scene in his kaleidoscope of nineteenth-century
scenic effects in *A Walking Trip*. In 1831 Weber's opera figured in a letter
from Andersen in Hamburg: 'The theatre has four tiers besides the
parterre, and what settings there were! In *Der Freischütz*, where the Wolf's
Glen is presented, will-o'-the wisps appeared and the Wild Huntsman was
in brilliant transparencies, while similar clouds rushed across the stage in
the strangest shapes.'[24] As late as 1846 he attended another production of
this opera in Lyon by a German company from Zürich, but found to his
dismay that the dialogue was omitted and only the music was presented.[25]

Dyveke, O.J. Samsøe's Danish national-historical tragedy from 1796,
was among the most admired national plays of this period and is starred
several times in the first year of Andersen's theatrical diary. Thomas
Bruun's original stage settings for this drama were among those most frequently borrowed and re-used in the nineteenth century to convey the
appropriately gothic atmosphere of romantic theatre; as such they reappeared in a number of Andersen productions. Moreover, the historical
subject-matter of Samsøe's play, dealing with the mediaeval King Christjern II and his mistress Dyveke, was later taken up and reworked by
Andersen in his romantic drama *Dreams of the King / Kongen Drømmer*.

The works of Adam Oehlenschläger, including *Axel and Valborg*, *The*

23 English text by Natalia MacFarren
and Th. Baker. Copyright, 1904, by
G. Schirmer, Inc.

24 Bille and Bøgh, *Breve fra H.C. Andersen*, I, 79

25 *Mit Livs Eventyr*, II, 7–8

Robber Fortress / *Røverborgen*, and *The Sleeping Potion* / *Sovedrikken*, occupied a prominent place in Andersen's early theatrical experience, just as they eventually did in Ibsen's at mid-century. Andersen's romanticism is intrinsically Oehlenschlägerean; as the Danish critic Hans Brix once remarked, it was Andersen's destiny that he lived in the Golden Age of Danish romanticism and that Oehlenschläger was its greatest exponent.[26] Young Andersen read the master diligently; an inept but oddly fascinating doggerel poem, dated 17 October 1821 and dedicated to 'my benefactor Herr Professor Oehlenschläger' from 'Hans Christian Andersen, pupil at the Royal Theatre,' is our first piece of evidence testifying to the lasting relationship between the older and the younger poet.[27]

In the Scandinavian drama of the first quarter of the century Oehlenschläger is unquestionably the major figure. In 1802 his *Poems* introduced the conscious establishment of a new movement in Danish literature, aimed at breaking with older traditions and championing the spirit of German romanticism. In the years that followed, he created a series of romantic verse dramas which adhered to his concept that 'the noblest object which a poet can bring to the stage is beyond a doubt a historical deed.' Strongly influenced by the later classicism of Schiller in *Wallenstein, Maria Stuart*, and *Die Jungfrau von Orleans*, he forged the Nordic heroic genre synonymous with his name in plays like *Hakon Jarl* (1807) and *Palnatoke* (1809). Side by side with this development, the versatile dramatist derived inspiration from French classical tragedy for such poetic dramas of love and duty as *Axel and Valborg* (1810) and *Hagbarth and Signe* (1815), in the latter of which he consciously set out to 'sail even some degrees closer to French classicism.' The popular artist-hero of German romanticism is also represented in Oehlenschläger's *Correggio* (1809), originally written in German and widely read in Germany during the first half of the nineteenth century. Yet a fourth vein in this playwright's rich production is suggested by the imaginative dramatic poem *Aladdin* (1805), drawn from a story in the *Arabian Nights* and so successful that Goethe's inscription in Oehlenschläger's autograph book was simply 'dem Dichter des Aladdin.'

Although Oehlenschläger's writing continued to undergo a series of further developments and he remained the nominal laureate of Danish letters until his death in 1850, his influence waned in the second quarter

26 *H.C. Anderson og hans Eventyr*, pp. 221, 111

27 See Topsøe-Jensen, *H.C. Andersen og andre Studier*, pp. 327–8

of the century as the critical and artistic views of J.L. Heiberg and his adherents gained ascendancy. Andersen regarded Oehlenschläger in the twenties as 'the one person above all that I mentally bowed down to, and looked up to in every respect.' Yet he would soon outdistance his idol's reputation, writing not without satisfaction in a letter from 1844 that 'although Oehlenschläger is far greater than I, the fact remains that in Germany I am the best known author, the author one prefers to read.'[28]

While still on the threshold of his career, however, Andersen was dismissed from the Royal Theatre school in June 1822 and placed, on the recommendation of State Councillor Jonas Collin and at the expense of the Crown, as a student in Slagelse Latin School, thereby putting an abrupt end to his ambitions of becoming an actor. It was obvious to those having eyes to see that his unique talent lay in another direction. 'His lanky frame and clumsy gestures seemed less well suited to ballet,' wrote August Bournonville of his first encounter with the poetically inclined ballet pupil, 'and my father [the French ballet-master Antoine Bournonville] therefore asked him whether he might not prefer the spoken drama, upon which the young man requested permission to recite one of his own poems. Its content I have forgotten, but this much is certain: I had the immediate impression of genius and, far from finding him ridiculous, it seemed to me that he was determined to get the best of us rather than the other way around.'[29]

The provincial dramatic societies of Slagelse and Elsinore, where he moved in 1825, held little inspiration for Andersen. All the more enthusiastic then was his reaction during a school vacation in Copenhagen in December 1825 to a new genre which had already set the capital in a furore, and which provided the direct impetus for the start of his own career as a dramatist – the vaudeville as developed in France by the prolific Eugène Scribe and introduced in Denmark by Johan Ludvig Heiberg. Dr Heiberg, after a brilliant doctoral dissertation in Latin on Calderón in 1817, quickly came to dominate Danish intellectual life in this period in a variety of capacities. As a playwright (Heiberg has remained second only to Holberg as Denmark's most performed dramatist), publicist, philosopher, theatre manager, and unofficial cultural arbiter, he represented the concept of romanticism as an elegantly refined parlour game.[30]

28 *Mit Livs Eventyr*, I, 95, and Topsøe-
  Jensen, *H.C. Andersen*, p. 363
29 Bournonville, *Mit Theater liv*, III, 3, 250

30 See Fenger, *The Heibergs*, for a study
  in English of this important figure

Although Heiberg's later achievements in the realm of romantic drama and literate comedy – particularly the masterful doomsday satire of mindless society entitled *A Soul after Death | En Sjæl efter Døden* (1841) – are considerable, perhaps his most popular contribution as a playwright was his systematic introduction of the Scribean vaudeville comedy to Scandinavia. Andersen's diary describes in glowing terms Heiberg's *King Solomon and George the Hatter | Kong Salomon og Jørgen Hattemager*, the play which marked the birth of the Danish vaudeville and which Andersen saw a month after it opened at the Royal Theatre in November 1825.[31] He found its witty parody of the Huntsmen Chorus from *Der Freischütz*, 'Was gleicht wohl auf Erden dem Jägervergnügen,' particularly entertaining, which no doubt inspired the use of the same pompous fanfare melody in his own vaudeville *Parting and Meeting | Skilles og Mødes*. His general reaction to the vaudeville genre was one of boundless enthusiasm and admiration for Heiberg's light, revue-like mixture of lyricism, jest, and satire. 'It was a Danish vaudeville,' Andersen later recalled, 'blood of our blood, one felt, and therefore it was received with jubilation and replaced all else. Thalia held a carnival on the Danish stage, and Heiberg was her chosen favourite.'[32]

The production in April 1826 of *The April Fools | Aprilsnarrene*, written by Heiberg especially for his future wife Johanne Luise, firmly established the thirteen-year-old actress as a star and the thirty-five-year-old dramatist as a major force in Danish theatre. His skill as a translator and importer of French vaudevilles is reflected in Andersen's delight less than two years later with the Heiberg adaptation of Scribe and Delavigne's *La somnambule | Kjærlighedsdrømme*. This popular piece, about a love affair which is resolved by the charming romantic sleepwalker Ernestine, is singularized by the fact that Scribe tried for the first time to give the vaudeville a sentimental, serious turn – a characteristic adopted by Andersen in his later sentimental vaudevilles. Heiberg's brilliantly polemical Hegelian 'demonstration' of the superiority of the vaudeville to other genres, entitled *On the Vaudeville as a Dramatic Form* (1826), was not only a momentary critical sensation but was still being referred to by Ibsen thirty years later.[33] Following Heiberg's early successes a landslide of vaudeville-comedies with and without music engulfed the Danish stage, drawing with it Andersen's own debut as a dramatist in 1829.

31 See Collin, *H.C. Andersen*, p. 99   33 See *Ibsen Letters and Speeches*, p. 16
32 *Mit Livs Eventyr*, I, 99

Two other Danish dramatists of note emerged as initial products of the vaudeville rage. Fascinated by the topicality of Heiberg's first vaudevilles, Henrik Hertz made his debut as a playwright in 1827 with a five-act satire of amateur dramatics entitled *Burchardt and his Family | Hr. Burchardt og hans Familie*, and *Moving Day | Flyttedagen*, a satire of contemporary apartment-hunting, appeared the following year. His most successful play in this vein remains, however, the delightful character comedy about a family which mistakenly believes they have hit the jackpot in the lottery, *The Savings Bank | Sparekassen* (1836). Hertz's extensive production as a dramatist also included such lyrical romantic dramas in mediaeval settings as *Svend Dyring's House | Svend Dyrings Hus* (1837) and *King René's Daughter | Kong Renés Datter* (1845). The latter, one of Hertz's best plays, expresses the theme of the erotic awakening of a young woman in terms of the delicate image of a blind girl who gains her sight. Hertz's central character, Jolanthe, seems closely akin to Andersen's figure of Lara in *The Improvisator*, based in turn on Andersen's encounter with a blind girl in Naples during his tour of Italy in 1833–4.

At mid-century Jens Christian Hostrup (1818–1892) also achieved lasting success with two plays which sprang directly from the tradition of the topical vaudeville-comedy. *The Neighbours | Genboerne* (1844) and *Adventures on Foot | Eventyr paa Fodrejsen* (1848) are festive comedies of Danish student life which combine occasional touches from Andersen's fairy-tales and the Viennese fairy-tale comedy with the revue-like satire and idyllic lyricism of the vaudeville genre.

No purpose would be served in the present study by comparing the untranslated plays of these dramatists with those of Andersen in terms of literary 'merit.' The point has already been made that none of his contemporaries represents as fully as he that rich variety and range of theatrical styles and dramatic forms which make up the romantic theatre in Scandinavia. His unique position in the intellectual and literary environment of his age is further suggested by the curious way in which he stands in relation to the other significant writers of the period. Henrik Hertz first attracted attention on the literary scene with his contrived poetic satire *Letters from a Ghost | Gjengangerbreve* (1830), written anonymously in the style and in the persona of the eighteenth-century poet Jens Baggesen. In Hertz's polemical espousal of Heiberg at the expense of Oehlenschläger and his followers, Andersen found himself publicly ridiculed for the first – but not the last – time in Danish literature. Søren Kierkegaard

(1813–1855) took the trouble to write his first book, *From the Papers of Someone still Alive | Af en endnu Levendes Papirer* (1838), as an attack on Andersen's novel *Only a Fiddler*. J.L. Heiberg's cutting satire in *A Soul after Death* addressed itself specifically to two of Andersen's romantic dramas. In his later life this most unusual of all Danish authors would seek consolation for this insular pettiness in his world renown, adding with barely concealed bitterness: 'It matters not to have been born in a duck-yard if one has been hatched from a swan's egg.' At twenty-five, however, Hertz's ambush found him unprepared: 'I met even well-dressed people who in passing would, with grinning faces, make a mocking remark to me. We Danes have a great penchant for ridicule, or to phrase it in nicer terms: We have a sense for the amusing and that is why we have so many comic dramatists.'[34]

The kaleidoscope of genres and influences to which Andersen was exposed in his youth – the comedies of Ludvig Holberg, the Viennese *Zauberoper*, the pantomimes of Giuseppe Casorti, the French opéra comique, the spectacular pantomimic ballets of Vincenzo Galeotti, the gothic sensationalism of *Raoul Barbe-Bleue* and *Robert le Diable*, the ghosts and goblins of the *Freischütz* genre, the stately Nordic romanticism of Adam Oehlenschläger, the sparkling urbanity of Johan Ludvig Heiberg – represents the state of the Copenhagen theatre at the time when he began to write. This theatre comprises the context within which his artistic intentions as a dramatist should be evaluated. Obviously his early impressions were gradually supplemented or supplanted by a multitude of other stimuli from a lifetime of intensive theatre-going. As one of the pioneers of rail travel Andersen visited every corner of Europe. In the course of twenty-nine extended trips outside Denmark, he became a seasoned playgoer in the great theatre capitals – Paris, London, Munich, Vienna, and elsewhere – and witnessed at first hand the art of the greatest names in all phases of nineteenth-century theatre – Rachel, Ristori, Ciceri, Dingelstedt, Charles Kean, and many more. However, the 'living picture-gallery' of his early theatrical impressions stands as a sufficiently representative crosscut exposing the principal outlines of the cultural and theatrical environment which gave rise to his plays.

34 *Mit Livs Eventyr*, I, 119

TWO
The Plays of H.C. Andersen

'IN DENMARK there is but one city and one theatre,' wrote Kierkegaard in 1848,[1] and his characteristic comment suggests the central place occupied by the Royal Theatre in nineteenth-century Danish culture and society. Architecturally as well as intellectually, it dominated the daily life of Copenhagen; it was 'the most important daily and nightly topic of conversation,' Andersen declared, and it 'ranked among the finest in Europe.'[2] It is no surprise, then, that Andersen's very existence revolved around the imposing playhouse on Kongens Nytorv. His lodgings were always within easy walking distance of it. On most evenings he could be found in the stalls together with the foremost figures of the Danish Golden Age – Oehlenschläger, Thorvaldsen, Heiberg, Kierkegaard – first as a young, promising author, eventually as the renowned mid-point of Scandinavian romanticism. As a dramatist, Andersen turned eagerly and early to the theatre as the best source of the personal admiration and financial support he so desperately sought. He regarded his plays very seriously in comparison with his other work; the stage to him was a 'mighty platform' from which it was possible to 'proclaim for hundreds what would hardly be read by ten.'[3] As one of the most widely read novelists in Europe and as a world-renowned writer of fairy-tales, he continued to wage the struggle for acceptance and recognition in the theatre that he had begun long before as 'a musical servant' in *Nina*.

In Andersen's own pessimistic, persecuted view – although not in terms of production statistics or of theatrical history – his struggle ended in

1 Søren Kierkegaard, *Samlede Værker*, XIV (Copenhagen 1963), 118

2 *Mit Livs Eventyr*, I, 215
3 *Ibid.*, 218

defeat. The Brandes myth of Andersen as 'the hunted animal in Danish literature' has persisted, and posterity has had little to add to this evaluation.[4] However, as a playwright Andersen forms an important transition between two periods. He belongs among the younger exponents of romanticism, but at the same time points ahead toward the realism which eventually triumphed in the 1870s. The production history of his plays provides a microcosm of the exotic, historical, idyllic, and topical elements that were the popular components of the colourful, romantic stage picture. And it was to the Copenhagen theatre which Andersen's plays reflect that a young apprentice was sent from Bergen on a travelling scholarship in 1852 to learn his craft – an apprentice whose name was Henrik Ibsen.

Andersen's early puerile efforts in the 'tragic' genre were clearly bewildered products of his youthful encounters with the more sensational aspects of romantic theatre. His first complete play, a 'tragedy in five acts' entitled *The Forest Chapel | Skovcapellet*, was written at the age of sixteen in the hope that it would provide money with which he might continue his schooling.[5] It is an example of hardboiled terror romanticism adapted from a German short story published in C.N. Rosenkilde's periodical *Brevduen* (nos 19 and 20, 1819); he was fortunately dissuaded from submitting it to the Royal Theatre. With his next effort, however, a 'patriotic tragedy' called *The Robbers of Vissenberg | Røverne i Vissenberg*, Andersen became bolder. It was written in two weeks and submitted anonymously to the Royal Theatre in 1822, which reacted by replying in a letter dated 16 June 1822 that it did not in future wish to receive 'plays which to such a degree as this display a lack of all elementary education.'[6] Although only a single scene of this play, published in A.P. Liunge's magazine *Harpen* (XXXII, 1822), survives, the melodramatic dialogue in the robbers' den gives ample evidence of the drama's exaggerated *sturm und drang* tendencies. Yet a third 'tragedy' was finished by Andersen in 1822, a play entitled *Alfsol* which acquired its subject matter from the historian P.F. Suhm's *Nordiske Noveller* (1783) and its style from Oehlenschläger and the Danish novelist B.S. Ingemann. Although rejected for production, *Alfsol* marked the turning point in its author's life since it provided the

4 See Topsøe-Jensen, *H.C. Andersen og andre Studier*, p. 35
5 The play is unpublished; the manuscript is in the Royal Library,

Collinske Samling 18, 7, with corrections by Andersen's tutor.
6 Collin, *H.C. Andersen*, p. xv

impetus for the Royal Theatre's decision to support his further education. He expressed his gratitude by dedicating his first book, published at his own expense under the pseudonym William Christian Walter (his own middle name plus his two favourite authors, Shakespeare and Scott!) and containing *Alfsol*, to the 'exalted Royal Theatre management.' The few copies of the book still in existence belong among the costliest rarities of Scandinavian literature.[7]

Although any of these early, youthful gothic tragedies can be criticized on virtually every count, they nevertheless bear unmistakable evidence – as the Royal Theatre management also realized – of raw poetic talent. It is noteworthy that when Andersen, having completed his formal education, made his debut as a practising dramatist in 1829, it was in a genre which directly parodied the stiff, solemn, and sentimental style of these first tragedies.

For the most part, however, Andersen's uncompleted or unproduced plays have little bearing on his relation to the practical theatre of the nineteenth century. Similarly, four of his translations produced at the Royal Theatre, including Scribe's *La quarantaine* (as *Skibet*), Bayard's *La reine de seize ans* (as *Dronningen paa 16 Aar*), Dorvigny's *La fête de campagne, ou L'intendant comédien malgré lui* (as *En Comedie i det Grønne*), and Meyerbeer's *Le pardon de Ploërmel* (as *Dinorah*), are only indirectly relevant to his personal artistic intentions as a playwright and assume only an incidental place in this discussion. Nevertheless, despite these exclusions, original plays and opera libretti by Andersen produced at the Royal Theatre between 1829 and 1865 account for a total of twenty-one works, embracing such widely diverse forms as vaudeville, opera or singspiel, romantic drama and fantasy, and romantic comedy. (For convenience a chronological list of these plays, with translated titles, has been included in the Appendix.) Several of them were later performed at the private Casino Theatre, for which Andersen also wrote four additional dramatic fantasies, but no reliable production records of the Casino performances have survived.

VAUDEVILLE

Andersen wrote for a theatre where musical genres played an extremely important role in the repertory. A large number of its performers were

---

7 See Cai M. Woel's facsimile edition of *Gjenfærdet ved Palnatokes Grav* (Copenhagen 1940)

talented both as singers and as actors, and it possessed an excellent orchestra with distinguished traditions. Therefore it is not surprising to discover that vaudeville, opera, and singspiel are dominant forms in his dramaturgy.

Vaudeville, unlike opera or operetta, is characterized mainly by the fact that the melodies which are interspersed among the dialogue are borrowed from recognizable popular songs, operatic arias, and the like. The traditions of this genre reach back to the harlequinades of the Italian commedia dell'arte players in the service of Louis XIV.[8] A new ditty sung to a borrowed melody was called at this time a 'Pont neuf' after the busy Parisian thoroughfare where the events of the hour were set to verse and sung to recognizable tunes, also known as vaudevilles. The word 'vaude-ville' is thought to derive from *chanson du Vau* (or *Val*) *de Vire*, a district in Normandy; it was applied in the sixteenth century to a type of popular ditty.[9] At the beginning of the nineteenth century, the privileged patent theatres in Paris retained the right to perform legitimate plays, whereas the remaining houses were obliged to confine themselves to 'lyrical-musical' drama. This law was easily circumvented, however, by giving the pieces performed at the minor theatres a musical appearance and by interrupting the dialogue occasionally with short, topical song numbers. These plays were known as *pièces en vaudeville*.[10]

The objective of Scribe and his co-workers in this genre was not to write for the sake of the songs, but on the contrary to shape these small plays in the form of a comedy, topical, light, piquant, and without particular poetic pretensions. In the French vaudeville the songs contained topical points and jokes formed in rapid couplets, whereas J.L. Heiberg, master of the Danish vaudeville, regarded the songs as more elaborate 'decorations on the dialogue.'[11] The French couplets were therefore much shorter, more abrupt, and more numerous than the extensive musical numbers in the vaudevilles of Heiberg and Andersen.

The successful production at the Royal Theatre in 1825 of Karl von Holtei's vaudeville-influenced 'musical farce' *Die Wiener in Berlin* led directly to the introduction of the Danish vaudeville with the performance

8 Krogh, *Heibergs Vaudeviller*, p. 5; see also Klinger, *Die Comedie-Italienne in Paris*, p. 188

9 Cf *Oxford Companion to the Theatre*, p. 822

10 On the burletta-vaudeville tradition in England, see Nicoll, *History of English Drama*, IV, 137–47

11 See his *Prosaiske Skrifter*, VII, 59

in the same year of Heiberg's *King Solomon*. Andersen's enthusiastic discovery of the new genre has already been described, and he was not long in following Heiberg's example. In 1829 he made the first of several efforts in this genre with his vaudeville-parody, *Love on St Nicholas Tower, or What Says the Pit | Kjærlighed paa Nicolai Taarn, eller Hvad siger Parterret*. This short, delightful farce treats the star-crossed love affair of Ellen, daughter of the 'knight' (ie, watchman) of St Nicholas Tower, and the brave little tailor Søren Pind, about whom we learn:

> *A tailor is a rosebud here below,*
> *A butterfly that flutters to and fro,*
> *Too fragile, thin, and pale*
> *To withstand the wild and stormy gale.*[12]

Together this engaging pair battle the stormy gales of destiny, embodied in the person of Peer Hansen, a watchman from a neighbouring tower who also seeks Ellen's hand in marriage. The play is a characteristic student parody of the romantic tragedy of destiny, in which watchmen and tailors assume heroic poses and speak stilted verse. The farcical element in the action was further heightened by means of numerous topical points of reference in the setting, the music, and the dialogue. Satirical jibes at actual persons, especially Adam Oehlenschläger, proved particularly upsetting to the more conservative elements; reviews in *Maanedsskrift for Litteratur* (1, 1829, 543) and *Kjøbenhavnsposten* (22 May 1829) both reproached the young playwright for having parodied 'our finest tragedies.' Three years later, Andersen was ready to express appropriate contrition for having 'really believed at that time that parody of something excellent, or use of something truly moving, might be permitted in jest without thereby having a bad heart.'[13] *Mea culpa.*

The Royal Theatre readers' report of *Love on St Nicholas Tower*, which has not previously been printed, is so characteristic of contemporary opinion regarding vaudeville and parody that it deserves to be cited at some length:[14]

That the vaudeville *Love on St. Nicholas* by no means corresponds to my ideas about the purpose and dignity of drama is hardly necessary to point out. Should it, how-

---

12 Andersen, *Samlede Skrifter*, XII, 6

13 *H.C. Andersens Levnedsbog*, p. 190

14 Loose sheet in the collection 'Det Kgl. Teater: Censurer 1821–29' (Rigsarkivet)

ever, despite my dissent, secure majority support, I must at least request that a
fellow citizen is not mentioned on the stage in order to evoke a shameful laughter,
as is the case on p. 35 and elsewhere.[15] It is high time to stop the boyish foolishness
that more and more dominates our stage, and which naturally finds all-too-ready
support from the crowd of boys in the house ... Furthermore, I feel that the
Theatre would act ignobly and unwisely to parody, by favouring such examples
as this, some of the most beautiful situations and scenes which adorn our theatre.

31 Dec. 1828   RAHBEK

If the author, as I do not doubt, observes with dutiful care the foregoing hints by
my colleague, I do not believe that the present vaudeville should be rejected; the
original turn at the end of the play, the fine, flowing verse, and the vigorous action
throughout speak in its favour; at any rate I regard it as one of our best vaudevilles, and vote unconditionally for its acceptance.

5 Jan. 1829   G.H. OLSEN

Olsen, theatre manager, and Rahbek, author and critic, represented
established, eighteenth-century conservatism; both were sixty-nine at this
point, Olsen died the same year and Rahbek a year later. The conservative
establishment triumphed, however. Despite the success of the play's
unusual ending in which the audience is allowed to decide whether or not
the tailor wins Ellen, its appearance at the close of the season, coupled
with a heated controversy concerning the leading actress, resulted in a
short run of only three performances.

Andersen's subsequent vaudevilles helped to shape the genre which
Thomas Overskou later defined as 'a small, delicately drawn comedy stemming from local affairs, daily events, or piquant situations.'[16] The theme of
the love affair threatened by circumstances remained the predominant
one. In his later vaudevilles, however, Andersen abandoned almost entirely the satirical, burlesque tone for which *Love* had been criticized. Thus in
writing *Parting and Meeting*, which takes for its background the visit of
Spanish troops to Odense in 1808, his aim, as he hastened to assure an
acquaintance in a letter dated 11 April 1831, was now a sentimental, rather
than a satirical, vaudeville. 'Do not imagine,' he declared, 'that my
new vaudeville will ridicule the dear town of my birth; no, the play is sen-

---

15 The reference is to *Samlede Skrifter*,
xii, 14: 'She sits often in a corner,
Humming me a song by Bay,' ie,
composer Rudolph Bay (1791–1856).

16 Overskou, 'Johan Ludvig Heiberg og
den danske Vaudeville,' *Danmarks ill.
Almanak for 1861*, 90

timental, very serious, written from the heart. I read some scenes for Heiberg recently, and they pleased him greatly because of the melancholy tone.'[17] Andersen benefited greatly in this vaudeville from the detailed, skilful dramaturgical hints on construction provided by Heiberg.[18] Following a sharp initial rejection by the Royal Theatre in 1833, a revised version of *Parting and Meeting* consisting of two short, separate but related plays was accepted for production in November 1835.[19] In the first playlet, *Spaniards in Odense / Spanierne i Odense*, Augusta falls in love with a dashing Spaniard, Francesco, who is stationed in Odense. However, her sense of duty persuades her to marry Ludvig, childhood sweetheart, as the Spanish troops march away in the distance. The sequel, *25 Years After / Fem og Tyve Aar derefter*, presents the same characters 'twenty-five years later' in Elsinore – a novelty to which the actors, in the opinion of the critic for *Dagen* (19 April 1836), proved unequal in their depiction of the age changes. The sentimental conclusion to this romance unites the daughter of the now-widowed Augusta, Louise, to Diego, the son of a Spanish ambassador who proves to be none other than Augusta's sometime soldier, Francesco.

Lovers' intrigues also provided the main themes in two other Andersen vaudevilles. *Mikkel's Parisian Love Stories / Mikkels Kjærlighheds Historier i Paris* is a brief vaudeville monologue composed for a benefit for the celebrated Danish comedian, Ludvig Phister, and performed twice in 1840. Mikkel, a character revived from an earlier Heiberg vaudeville, relates his amorous adventures in the French capital. In *The Bird in the Pear-Tree / Fuglen i Pæretræet* the quarrel of two neighbours provides the comic background for the amorous intrigue of Herman and Henriette; here, too, love surmounts all obstacles, including a fence erected between the feuding neighbours' gardens and figuring prominently in the action. A high point in this atmospheric genre sketch is Andersen's rich characterization of Counsellor Arents, who in spite of his basically friendly nature becomes entangled in the neighbour dispute over the pear-tree. His outburst when he is finally compelled to recognize the fact that his daughter's heart has been captured by the son of the enemy suggests his nature:

17 Bille and Bøgh, *Breve fra H.C. Andersen*
     I, 89; cf *Mit Livs Eventyr*, I, 109
18 See Heiberg's letter to Jonas Collin
     dated 22 Nov. 1833 in Collin, *H.C.
     Andersen*, pp. 215–21; cf Bille and
     Bøgh, *Breve til H.C. Andersen*, pp. 109–

     10, and Topsøe-Jensen, *Brevveksling
     med Jonas Collin d. Ældre*, I, 99–100
19 The reader's report is reproduced in
     Hetsch, *H.C. Andersen og Musikken*, pp.
     33–7

THE PLAYS OF H.C. ANDERSEN 37

Where is my daughter! Don't look at me like that!
I know very well where she is! But it's a lie![20]

Following two successful summer performances in 1842, *The Bird in the Pear-Tree* was entered in the regular repertoire with Scandinavia's leading actress, Johanne Luise Heiberg, in the role of Henriette. Notwithstanding her services and the play's initial popularity, however, it was soon attacked by Andersen's opponents and, in the wake of polemical articles and hissing in the theatre, it was taken off the programme after four performances. 'For the past two weeks not a single sin has been committed in Denmark,' wrote *Corsaren* (11 Nov. 1842), one of the most vitriolic of the many polemically minded periodicals at this time; '*The Bird in the Pear-Tree* is no longer applauded, on the contrary it was hissed.' Heiberg, the authoritative voice of Danish culture and intellectual endeavour, succeeded in elegantly damning the play with faint praise: 'It belongs to that species of small creatures,' he commented in his influential *Intelligensblade* (XIX, 1842), 'whose inclusion in our theatre-menagerie it would be pedantic to oppose, since it can be said of them that if they do no good, neither do they do any harm; they are too small for that, too insignificant, and too innocuous.'[21] The bitterness caused by this hostility to his play pervades Andersen's diary entries for this period: one such entry notes that his depressed mood inspired him with the idea for his best-known fairy-tale, *The Ugly Duckling*.[22]

One of Andersen's most successful works for the stage, however, was the vaudeville farce *The Invisible Man on Sprogø | Den Usynlige paa Sprogø*, 'a dramatic jest in one act with chorus and songs' which he admittedly tailored to suit a particular landscape setting originally designed for Henrik Hertz's unsuccessful vaudeville, *Flight to Sprogø | Flugten til Sprogø*.[23] Following a summer performance in 1839 which became a personal triumph for the actor C.M. Foersom in the title role of Blomme, the gullible merchant who is made 'invisible,' the play went on to become a popular favourite at the Royal Theatre, where it ran for twenty-two per-

20 *Samlede Skrifter*, XI, 192. Jensen, 'H.C. Andersens dramatiske Digtning og det moderne Teater,' has presented a good evaluation of this vaudeville, to which Rostand's *Les Romanesques* (bet-

ter known as *The Fantasticks*) bears some resemblances.

21 See Heiberg, *Prosaiske Skrifter*, VII, 287–90

22 4 July 1842, Collinske Samling 7, 1

23 *Mit Livs Eventyr*, I, 219

formances, and at Casino and Odense Theatre. 'Gulling' was another common subject in vaudeville. In *The Bird in the Pear-Tree*, Arents is gulled at the end in order that the lovers can be united. In *The Invisible Man* the entire dramatic situation is based on the 'gulling' of the central character, the enthusiastically credulous Agent Blomme ('I am a Sunday-child, am I! / O, I see more than meets the eye!') who is stranded with his family on the island of Sprogø, and is made to believe that three drops of liquid in a glass of wine together with a magic incantation have the power to render him invisible.

The play was singled out by the critics for its '*musical* element, which Andersen used here with great taste and effect.'[24] One of the most basic and significant characteristics of the vaudeville genre, as we have already noted, was its borrowing of appropriate melodies from well-known and popular tunes.[25] The function of music as an intrinsic dramatic element in this genre, intended as part of the total effect, represents a key to its performance style. Hence the strength of Andersen's vaudevilles is to a great degree to be found in his talented and entertaining melody selection.

The lively Danish interest at this time in Spanish songs and dances can be traced to the garrisoning of Spanish troops at Odense in 1808, an event which had a profound influence in Denmark and was the direct background for *Parting and Meeting*, in which such songs were introduced. Similarly, in *The Invisible Man* a 'Jaleo di Xeres,' a popular Andalusian dance in 3/4 time, played a vital part in the action. It was danced by the importunate suitor Theodor to entertain Agent Blomme and his party, and the play itself was first titled *Jaleo di Xeres*. The motive behind Andersen's choice of this particular dance may meanwhile be sought in the popularity it had achieved when it appeared in Auber's *Le domino noir* in January 1839 and in Heiberg's vaudeville monologue *Yes / Ja* one month later.

A comparable interest in popular Tyrolese songs is reflected in their frequent use in the vaudevilles of both Heiberg and Andersen. Thus in Andersen's adaptation of Dorvigny's *La fête de campagne*, produced in 1840, Dalby's humorous verse on nature was set to a highly popular and melodious *Tyrolienne* composed by the opera singer Maria Malibran and already familiar to the Danish audience from Heiberg's 1833 vaudeville *Danes in Paris / De Danske i Paris*.[26]

24 *Portefeuillen for 1839*, IV, 42. See also *Dagen*, 17 June 1839, and *Berlingske Tidende*, 17 June and 5 Oct. 1839

25 Heiberg, *Prosaiske Skrifter*, VI, 44
26 *Samlede Skrifter*, XXXI, 14; cf Heiberg, *Vaudeviller*, III, 140

It was, however, not alone such dance tunes and popular 'hits' which were adopted for use in the vaudeville. Familiar opera and singspiel arias also provided favourite material for vaudeville melodies. Andersen, in emulation of J.L. Heiberg's example, derived music for his vaudeville texts from such composers as D'Alayrac (*Azemia*), Isouard (*Cendrillon*), Auber (*Fra Diavolo, Le domino noir, Le maçon*), Boieldieu (*La dame blanche, Jean de Paris, Le petit chaperon rouge*), Weber (*Der Freischütz, Preciosa*), Weyse (*Ludlams Hule*), Kuhlau (*Lulu*), and, in particular, Mozart (*Die Zauberflöte, Die Entführung aus dem Serail, Don Giovanni*). This list alone indicates the impressively wide acquaintance with the nineteenth-century opera repertoire which Andersen (and his audience) possessed.

Vaudeville and parody went traditionally hand in hand, and in most cases Andersen employed the music of these operas and singspiel in a satirical manner, setting intentionally incongruous words to the serious music. Thus in *Love on St Nicholas Tower* the lovely, sentimental Romance from E.H. Méhul's opera *Joseph*, 'A peine au sortir de l'enfance, quatorze ans au plus je comptais,' served as the melody for a highly colloquial and satirical re-telling by Peer Hansen of the story of his youthful arrival in Copenhagen: 'I had fourteen years on my backside, but still I was tending the geese.'[27] In addition, two highlights of this performance were a tailors' chorus which cavorted to the strains of a delicate elfin dance from F. Kuhlau's romantic Danish opera *Lulu*, and a burlesque of Mozart's 'Vivat Bacchus' from *Die Entführung aus dem Serail* which provided the tower watchman Ole with a spirited and farcical entrance song, 'Vivat Destiny!' Andersen again returned to Mozart's music in *Parting and Meeting* and *The Invisible Man*. In the former, the festive, sweeping 'Champagne Aria' from *Don Giovanni*, 'Fin ch'han del vino,' was incorporated into the Spanish soldier Francesco's effective potpourri on a soldier's life, set to the martial text 'The drums are calling, bullets are falling.'[28] Later, in a comic number adopted by Andersen from Nestroy's delightful farce *Der böse Geist Lumpazivagabundus*, 'Eduard and Kunigunde,' in which these three words were sung repeatedly with changing expression to various operatic melodies, the formula was 'sung tearfully' to 'In diesen heiligen Hallen' from *Die Zauberflöte*.[29] This musical sacrilege 'called forth disapprobation,' according to the critic for *Dagen* (19 April 1836), and

---

27 *Samlede Skrifter*, XI, 14
28 *Ibid.*, 55. Heiberg criticized this potpourri for inept musical transitions:

see Collin, *H.C. Andersen*, p. 219
29 *Samlede Skrifter*, XI, 84

was 'to be dropped from the next performance.' In *The Invisible Man* Blomme's song of indecision before swallowing the 'magic' potion, 'I will, oh no I will not,' was a broad parody of the duet from *Don Giovanni*, 'La ci darem la mano,' and Zerlina's reply 'Vorrei e non vorrei.' This irreverent treatment of the classics again shocked reviewers, however, who found it too gross a travesty of Mozart's music.[30]

Despite Heiberg's relatively valid criticism that the songs in *Parting and Meeting* were undramatic, and the highly prejudiced criticism by Andersen's longtime adversary Christian Molbech that he 'under no circumstances understands how to write a *Danish* vaudeville such as we have become accustomed to that dramatic genre in Professor Heiberg's works,'[31] he obviously displayed both considerable wit and dramaturgical finesse in this genre. One of the better-known examples from his plays of a scene which succeeds perfectly in capturing the elusive 'vaudeville tone' is the celebrated *tour de force* by Theodor, man-of-the-world and matchmaker in *The Invisible Man*, in which he describes his international experience in affairs of the heart. 'It would be odd if I wasn't able to do for others what I have so often done for myself – reach the goal in the kingdom of love,' he boasts to the audience. 'But here it's a question of arranging a wedding – it's true I've never tried that, but the preliminaries ... yes, in most countries I've made acquaintances!' An engaging, Maurice Chevalier lead-in is hereby provided for the international catalogue of amorous escapades which follows. Theodor describes the girls he has known in a witty medley of 'national' songs: 'Lovely Minka,' Weyse's 'Dannemark! Dannemark!,' a Swedish folksong, 'God Save the King,' 'La Parisienne,' 'Of Spanish Girls' from the comedy *Farinelli*, and a Tyrolese melody; the medley is framed by the untranslatably charming verse:

> *To all the world's four corners,*
> *My heart with me I brought,*
> *I left it with the lovely girls,*
> *You give them what you've got.*[32]

It was mainly in the 1830s that Andersen was occupied with the topical, lyrical vaudeville. A letter written from Leipzig and dated 3 July 1841 is

30 *Ibid.*, 134, and *Portefeuillen for 1839*, IV, 42

31 Collin, *H.C. Andersen*, p. 218, and Hetsch, *H.C. Andersen*, pp. 50–1

32 *Samlede Skrifter*, XI, 128–9

indicative of his growing disinterest in this genre; 'this evening I was in the theatre,' he observed, 'to see the first and undoubtedly the only vaudeville ... on my entire trip; I have almost forgotten this genre.'[33] The following year saw his final vaudeville effort produced at the Royal Theatre. By then, however, he had already contributed in large measure to popularizing in Denmark the form which Heiberg had succeeded in proving, by a specious application of Hegelian dialectics, was the most suitable type of dramatic art for the stage of the day. Ibsen would subsequently dwell at length, in his student newspaper article *The Hostel in Greenland*, on this relatively 'unimportant' form of drama, and would adapt the conflicts of the popular vaudeville to his own needs in *Midsummer Eve* and *Love's Comedy*.[34]

OPERA AND SINGSPIEL

Andersen's enthusiasm for dramatic music induced him to produce a total of six opera and singspiel libretti, most of which likewise stem from the 1830s. A sensitive and imaginative personality made him naturally receptive to music and explains the significance of the musical element in his dramaturgy. 'He loved music,' notes Gustav Hetsch in his perceptive study, 'and, without having an actual knowledge of it, he often perceived it with a fresh immediacy which led him by way of instinct to the same results which professionals reached.'[35] Andersen's close personal acquaintance with opera manifests itself in his selection of vaudeville melodies, in his innumerable commentaries on a long life of theatregoing, and particularly in the musical 'entertainments' he prepared for the Royal Theatre, such as *Wandering through the Opera Gallery / Vandring gjennem Opera-Galleriet*, in which a cicerone conducts the audience on a 'tour' of the great operas, and *The Soprano / Sangerinden*, an unpublished dramatic situation in which an opera singer wins her freedom from a band of robbers by performing Donizetti's aria 'Perchè non ho del vento' from *Lucia di Lammermoor* – Jenny Lind's greatest number – for them.[36]
    Andersen's choice of operatic subjects illustrates both his own artistic

33 Topsøe-Jensen, *Brevveksling med Jonas Collin*, I, 185
34 See Tennant, *Ibsen's Dramatic Technique*, p. 38
35 Hetsch, *H.C. Andersen*, p. 141

36 *Samlede Skrifter*, XIII, 195 ff, and 'Det Kgl. Teaters Sufflørarkiv' 650 (Royal Library). Both were produced in 1841.

intentions and the theatrical trends of the time. Walter Scott ranks among the most important influences on romantic theatre, especially in the field of opera. Both the Waverley novels and Scott's poetical romances were seized upon by dramatists as quickly as they appeared for presentation in innumerable adaptations on the English stage.[37] Their popularity was equally great on the Continent. As early as 1819 Rossini's *La donna del lago* appeared in Naples, followed by a host of copies. In 1825 *Guy Mannering*, the first of the Waverley novels to be adapted in England, was combined with *The Monastery* and dramatized by Scribe in his most famous opera libretto, *La dame blanche*. The themes of Scott's novels, combining colourful romantic settings, piquant figures, and picturesque milieu descriptions, were readily transferred to the stage and acclaimed by nineteenth-century theatre audiences. 'Walter Scott romanticism' came to mean an entire genre of picturesque romantic operas depicting moonlit landscapes, mediaeval ruins, forest mystique, musty castles, and the entire minutiæ of the Gothic tradition.

With this background in mind, it is hardly surprising that Andersen's first opera libretto was an adaptation from Walter Scott. Since his boyhood Andersen had cherished a strong predilection for Scott's writings, and in February 1831 he completed a singspiel text based on the popular novel from 1816, *The Bride of Lammermoor*. Indeed the Royal Theatre's report dated 2 March 1831 expressed surprise that an adaptation of Walter Scott had not been attempted in Denmark sooner.[38] The young composer and future Royal Theatre conductor, Ivar Bredal (1800–1864), completed the score in December of the same year; the first of eight performances was given with considerable success the following May.

The action of Scott's novel and of Donizetti's celebrated opera is presumably familiar. Andersen's treatment of these picturesque incidents and boldly drawn figures was in no sense selective. 'I have tried to include the entire novel in this brief theatre evening,' he wrote in his preface, 'and have used everything I thought could be used.'[39] An inevitable result of this approach was a series of unrelated and extraneous details. In addition, his arrangement of the libretto was clearly influenced by the fact that the dramatic actress Anna Wexschall, for whom the leading role

37 For surveys of Scott's influence on drama, see Nicoll, *History of English Drama*, IV, 91–6, and White, *Sir Walter Scott's Novels on the Stage*

38 *Det Kgl. Teaters Censur Protokol*, I, 97

(Rigsarkivet); reprinted in Hetsch, *H.C. Andersen*, pp. 18–19, and Bredsdorff, *H.C. Andersen og England*, pp. 18–19

39 *Bruden fra Lammermoor*, p. 1.

was intended, no longer possessed a strong singing voice. As a result he was forced to avoid arias in Lucie's part and instead to maintain many of the dramatic high-points, such as Edgar's entrance in the wedding scene and his confrontation with Lucie, in dialogue – a method thoroughly criticized by the reviewer for *Den danske Bi* (18 Nov. 1832). Nevertheless, the text provided a substantial framework for the theatrical presentation of a picturesque Scottish milieu, which was also carried through in the folk elements of the score and the gothic style of the stage settings.

Andersen's treatment of *The Bride of Lammermoor* won the warm approval of the established composer C.E.F. Weyse (1774–1842), who asked the young dramatist to prepare an adaptation of another of Scott's best-known novels, *Kenilworth*. This work was among Scott's most frequently adapted novels; before Andersen's text appeared, no fewer than twelve stage versions had seen the light in England, and in 1825 Scribe and Auber's opera comique, *Le Château de Kenilworth*, was produced in Paris. Andersen completed his libretto in less than a month, but the Royal Theatre returned it for revision and did not accept it until March 1833.[40] In April of that year, having delivered his text to the composer, he left on his first great journey through Europe. This gave him the opportunity to see with his own eyes the Walter Scott rage in Paris, where he attended the opening of Scribe, Planard, and Carafa's opera adaptation of *The Heart of Midlothian* entitled *La prison d'Edinburg*.[41]

The long delay before *Festival at Kenilworth / Festen paa Kenilworth* was finally produced in January 1836 was the result of extensive revision and rewriting of the libretto by the composer, a fact which caused Andersen to repudiate the text and publish only the songs from the opera. The complete text, with blank verse substituted for the prose dialogue, was not published until after Andersen's death. Although he had followed Scott's novel closely in his adaptation, Weyse had insisted on adding a happy ending in which Amy Robsart and Leicester are united. 'All the additions and changes Weyse has *demanded*,' wrote Andersen bitterly, 'are exactly those which do not work; but with this piece *I* have been only an obedient servant.'[42]

40 See Collin, *H.C. Andersen*, pp. 163-4, Hetsch, *H.C. Andersen*, p. 22; for a summary of events pertaining to this opera's composition, see Topsøe-Jensen, *H.C. Andersen og Henriette Wulff*, v, 21 -2

41 Topsøe-Jensen, *Brevveksling med Jonas Collin*, I, 90

42 Bille and Bøgh, *Breve fra H.C. Andersen*, I, 322. See also Thrane, *Weyses Minde*, pp. 40-2, and Hetsch, *H.C. Andersen*, pp. 28-30

Although the opening was followed by a stormy newspaper debate in which the adaptation was criticized for its unselective and episodic nature, the production was praised and Weyse's score was declared a masterpiece. 'Every number was accorded an ovation which one could almost say was carefully measured according to the worth of the music,' commented *Dagen* (7 Jan. 1836) enthusiastically. By far the most informative of the *Kenilworth* reviews is that in *Musikalsk Tidende*, which occupied three issues (III–V, 1836) and included a thorough score analysis. In recognizing the lyrical function of a singspiel text in which 'the action progresses and characters develop during the musical numbers,' as distinct from vaudeville where music stops the action and opera where arias are connected by recitatives, this critic had considerable praise for Andersen's libretto. His dramatic disposition was particularly admired in preparing for an effective quintet allegro con spirito in the first act; Tressilian seizes Amy's arm ('I order you to follow me'), she cries out 'Oh, help!' and Lambourne and Foster rush in with drawn swords while Varney dashes in from the background ('You are a dead man'), thereby creating a bold theatrical introduction to a masterful quintet in which each part maintains independence and contrasts with the threatening tones of the accompaniment. Weyse's rich score remains the element of greatest interest in *Festival at Kenilworth*, however, and includes some of his finest music: the lovely minor duet in the second act between Leicester and the astrologer Alasco, and the Minstrel's pastoral romance in 6/8 time in the second act finale, enriched by one of Andersen's most celebrated lyrics, 'The Shepherd grazes his Flock.'[43]

It was not only the novels of Walter Scott which supplied Andersen with suitable material for his early opera libretti. In 1830 he submitted to the Royal Theatre an adaptation of Carlo Gozzi's *Il corvo*, a play which E.T.A. Hoffmann had once suggested as an appropriate operatic subject.[44] In his preface to *The Raven*, Andersen recalled that when he read Gozzi 'the entire romantic world appeared to me in a clearer light, many fairytales became more meaningful for me, the figures in the old paintings

---

43 Weyse's score has been published by
  Samfundet til Udgivelse af dansk Musik
  (1875).
44 Andersen read the play in his former

headmaster's translation, in Meisling,
Dramatiske Eventyr af Carlo Gozzi.
Hoffmann refers to it in 'Der Dichter
und der Componist' (*Die Serapions-
Brüder*, I, 1819).

came alive and appeared dramatically real.'[45] While the action of this adaptation follows Gozzi's original closely, certain technically practical concessions had to be made regarding the fantastical elements. Three mermaids appeared to warn Jennaro instead of the talking doves in Gozzi, the incident of disabling the horse and the falcon was not shown but merely retold, and a chorus of vampires was substituted for the dragon which confronts Jennaro outside Millo's bedchamber. Least successful among Andersen's modifications was his handling of the comic commedia dell'arte figures; in Gozzi they work from a traditional scenario rather than from written dialogue, but in *The Raven* they tended to become undramatic and unnecessary appendages. For a revival of *The Raven* in 1865 Andersen tried to circumvent some of the problems of the original libretto by eliminating the commedia dell'arte element entirely and by rendering the dialogue wholly in recitatives, but he was nevertheless criticized for the fact that a number of the principal events were not shown on stage.[46]

The production of *The Raven* in October 1832 was most notable, however, for its lavish staging and costuming as well as for its fine score by Denmark's foremost romantic composer, J.P.E. Hartmann (1805–1900).[47] In a significant six-page review in *Neue Zeitschrift für Musik* (1840) of the publication by Musikforeningen of piano selections from *The Raven*, Robert Schumann warmly praised both Hartmann's music and Andersen's text.[48] While all of Hartmann's music is permeated by depictions of the sea, *The Raven* in particular can basically be called an opera of the sea.[49] Violent storms and ocean waves were vividly portrayed both in Hartmann's score and in the staging. Perhaps the most effective musical highpoint was the climactic theatrical *melodrama* (in the German sense of dialogue spoken to orchestral accompaniment), in which Jennaro, having out of fraternal affection disobeyed the mermaids' dire warning, undergoes in the third act a three-step transformation into a marble statue. The moment was brilliantly underscored by Hartmann's maestoso tones, laced with dramatic tremolos and culminating in a double forte at each partial transformation.

In addition to Scott and Gozzi, yet another romantic subject source for

45 *Ravnen eller Broderprøven* (Copenhagen 1832), p. 1
46 *Mit Livs Eventyr*, II, 283–4
47 See the reviews in *Allernyeste Skilderie* *af Kjøbenhavn* (23 Nov. 1832) and *Dagen* (2, 5 Nov. 1832)
48 Hammerich, *J.P.E. Hartmann*, p. 59
49 Cf Hove, *J.P.E. Hartmann*, p. 17

Andersen's libretti was Alessandro Manzoni's *I promessi sposi*. In 1836 he submitted a dramatization of this work, entitled *Renzo's Wedding | Renzos Bryllup*, which, interestingly enough, he felt to be his 'first theatre piece displaying real familiarity with the stage.'[50] After several delays and difficulties in securing a willing composer, the project was shelved; it was first produced as an opera, under the present title of *The Wedding at Lake Como | Brylluppet ved Como-Søen* and with a score by the German composer and conductor Franz Gläser (1798–1861), in 1849.

In general, *Wedding at Lake Como* follows the main action of *I promessi sposi*: two peasant lovers are prevented from marrying by a tyrannical robber baron who wants the girl for himself. The libretto, however, with the exception of the extraneous character Pater Christophorus, is far more selective and less episodic in technique than any of Andersen's previous adaptations. The romantic subject matter and the picturesque Italian setting were squarely in the popular vein of the period. The production afforded effective dramatic situations for Gläser's simple and expressive score, particularly successful in the character of the lyrical cleric Abondio, and a piquant theatrical milieu for Bournonville's imaginative mise-en-scène. 'The criticism was warmly appreciative of [Gläser's] music and Bournonville's staging was especially praised, I however was not mentioned,' Andersen declares;[51] but a glance at the review in *Folket* (9 Feb. 1849) shows that his wounded sensibility had no basis in fact. 'When an opera is unsuccessful, one is apt to blame the author of the libretto; if it succeeds, however, he is hardly mentioned, although it is not seldom that he deserves his true share of the praise it is afforded ... Andersen deserves ... much recognition for the libretto of this justly applauded opera.' *Berlingske Tidende* (30 Jan. 1849) praised only the music and the production, but *Fædrelandet* (6 Feb. 1849) also singled out the lyricism and the dramatic texture of Andersen's dialogue.

Andersen's work in the genre of opera and singspiel also includes three libretti which derive their subject matter from Nordic folk material. These folk texts represent, moreover, his best known as well as his least successful endeavours in this field. Belonging in the latter category, *The Nix | Nøkken*, an opera libretto in recitatives which draws on Swedish folklore, was first submitted to the Royal Theatre in 1845. When it finally did secure a hearing in 1853, the score was once again by Franz Gläser. The theme of

50 In a letter dated 15 June 1836,   51 *Mit Livs Eventyr*, II, 80
   Collin, *H.C. Andersen*, p. 243

this one-act opera, a familiar one in Andersen's dramaturgy, treats an affair of the heart; in fact the dramatic situation might be seen as a sentimentalized version of the student parody *Love on St Nicholas Tower*. Although Hedda, the daughter of a wealthy landowner, loves Oluf the minstrel, she is promised by her father to the castellan Pehr Laurin. Fortunately for all concerned, Queen Christine of Sweden herself intervenes, and proves to the assembly that she is the nix, or protecting spirit, of the title who unites the lovers and makes all end well. A listless and undistinguished performance did nothing to ameliorate the banal and expository text. Reviewers for *Berlingske Tidende* and *Flyveposten* (14 Feb. 1853) were 'polite,' but *Dagbladet* (14 Feb.), *Kjøbenhavnsposten* and *Fædrelandet* (16 Feb.) deplored the production as totally static.

Another folk theme dramatization, *Agnete and the Merman | Agnete og Havmanden*, is not strictly an opera or a singspiel, although it does comprise a number of sung lyrics and a musical score by the gifted composer Niels V. Gade (1817–1890). This play, a scenic version of Andersen's dramatic poem of the same name from 1834, was a resounding failure in 1843 in spite of Gade's music and Johanne Luise Heiberg's portrayal of Agnete. Received coldly by *Berlingske Tidende* (21 April, 1843), wickedly by *Corsaren* (28 April), and with hostility by Heiberg in *Intelligensblade* (xxix–xxx, 1843), the production disappeared from the repertory after two notorious performances, leaving no theatrical archives behind to document the debacle. Only two divergent elements have rescued the event from total oblivion, Gade's lovely, idyllic cradle-song which was sung by Agnete, and Andersen's outraged letter from Paris when he had learned of the fate of his play ('I hate Denmark, which hates and spits upon me!'), certainly the most monumental outburst of fury extant from his frequently furious pen.[52]

In shining contrast to these failures, meanwhile, stands Andersen's libretto for *Little Kirsten | Liden Kirsten*, whose 310 performances to date place it as the most frequently performed of all Danish operas. The early seeds of a nationalistic romanticism which eventually flowered in this folksong dramatization were sown during Andersen's stay in Rome in 1833; on 10 November he noted in his diary: 'A princess became a nun; [the poet Ludvig] Bødtcher told me of a young girl he had seen, how they laid the shroud over her and rang the bells; I read the folk ballads and found an opportunity for a similar situation for the stage in the Romance

---

52 Topsøe-Jensen, *H.C. Andersen og Henriette Wulff*, 1, 330–1

"Herr Sverkel," which I will use for a drama. The folk ballads are a gold-mine of subjects.'[53] In 1835 Andersen submitted a libretto on this subject, for which Ivar Bredal was to arrange a score based on existing folk melodies. This plan failed to materialize, however, and it was not until 1844 that J.P.E. Hartmann began work on the score for this opera. In October, 1845 he wrote to dissuade Andersen from presenting their new opera too soon after the recent triumphant visit of Jenny Lind to Copen-hagen.[54] When it finally opened on 12 May 1846, this delicate scenic picture of the romance of Sverkel and Kirsten was hailed as the perfect expression of the fervent romantic interest in the national-idyllic, the mediaeval, and the atmosphere of folksong and balladry. It fulfilled, in the view of the critic for *Fædrelandet* (23 May 1846), the desire for the creation of a truly 'Nordic opera'; and *Kjøbenhavnsposten* (25 May 1846) proclaimed it as 'the loveliest painting we long have seen on the Danish stage, a picture which leaves a deep and beautiful impression on the spectator.' Far from waning with time, moreover, its popularity gained momentum. In a letter dated 29 December 1855 on the occasion of the forthcoming production of *Klein Karin* in Weimar, for which Andersen provided the German translation, Franz Liszt wrote enthusiastically to Hartmann that 'Ihre Oper für mich von wahrhaft künstlerischen und musikalischen Interesse ist.'[55] Perhaps the most eloquent characterization of the work's atmospheric charm and of the search for a romantic ideal to which it appealed is found in a review by Clemens Petersen after its revival in 1858; writing in *Fædrelandet* (2 Nov. 1858) he called *Little Kirsten*:

... a true poem, an inspiration, *un rêve de l'idéal au milieu des tristes réalités de la vie.* A world stands written on these pages, such as it perhaps has never been, and such as it perhaps never will be. But that does not matter, for there is beauty in it which touches our hearts, like something for which we yearn.

Hence, Andersen's opera libretti brought him into collaboration with some of the leading Scandinavian composers of the age – Weyse, J.P.E.

53 Rubow and Topsøe-Jensen, *H.C. Andersens Romerske Dagbøger,* pp. 18–19
54 Bille and Bøgh, *Breve til H.C. Andersen,* pp. 167–8
55 'Your opera is, to my mind, of true artistic and musical interest': *Mit Livs Eventyr,* II, 439; see also Topsøe-Jensen, *Brevveksling med Jonas Collin,* III, 257–9, and Torben Krogh, *Musik og Teater* (Copenhagen 1955), p. 128. The opera was performed in Weimar on 17 Jan. 1856, but not under Liszt's baton.

Hartmann, Niels V. Gade, and Franz Gläser – and included, as seen in the comments of Robert Schumann and Franz Liszt, examples of his theatrical writing known outside Denmark as well. In addition, these opera productions provide some of the best illustrations of the 'living picture-gallery,' flavoured with gothic, exotic, or national-idyllic elements, which constituted the nineteenth-century theatre ideal. It was upon opera and the more complex romantic dramas that the greatest amounts of money and concern were normally expended in an effort to achieve an illusory and picturesque atmosphere in all aspects of production. Conversely, Andersen's choice of operatic subjects was conditioned by the romantic desire to present on the stage a piquant situation in a picturesque theatrical milieu.

ROMANTIC DRAMA AND FAIRY-TALE FANTASY

In the 1830s Andersen's concern as a playwright was chiefly with vaudevilles and with opera libretti featuring the gothic elements of Walter Scott romanticism. In the 1840s he took a new direction, as he consciously turned toward French romantic drama and the style of Victor Hugo. These two apparently found much in common on a personal basis as well. In March 1843 Andersen was a welcome guest of Hugo in Paris, attending *Les Burgraves* with the French dramatist only a few days after its tumultuous première.[56]

The strong interest during this period in local colour and ethnographic details spurred the popularity of 'exotic,' far-away environments and peoples on the stage. It is in direct relation to this theatrical convention that Andersen's two romantic verse dramas, *The Mulatto | Mulatten* and *The Moorish Girl | Maurerpigen*, must be seen. The increasing number of books which appeared on national customs, costumes, and mores served as an important stimulus for early nineteenth-century playwrights in presenting more convincing exotic surroundings and details in the theatre; Andersen's remark that in writing *The Mulatto* he 'swallowed all the available books on Africa and America' is characteristic. Moreover, in such dramas music was frequently included as accompaniment or as background to strengthen and deepen the impact of the romantic pathos and picturesque localities depicted.

The Mulatto, which Andersen himself felt would mark an epoch in his

56 *Mit Livs Eventyr*, I, 274

career, quickly became his greatest scenic triumph when produced at the Royal Theatre in February 1840. Audiences greeted the play with a storm of enthusiasm, and five sold-out houses were registered in the course of the first eleven performances.[57] Much of this popular success was the result of the drama's piquant subject matter and the illusionistic presentation of its exotic milieu on the stage. The subject of *The Mulatto*, which Andersen clothed in lyrical rhymed verse 'in order to subjugate the theme to the music of language,'[58] is reminiscent of Hugo's French romanticism and of numerous popular romantic dramas of the time. The play was adapted from a story by Fanny Reybaud, 'Les épaves,' which the dramatist read in the *Revue de Paris* (Feb. 1838).[59] Both Eleonore and Cecilie, the wife and the ward of La Rebelliere, wealthy planter on Martinique, meet and fall in love with the young, cultivated mulatto, Horatio. However, La Rebelliere plots vengeance on the hero and, by unscrupulous means, has him imprisoned and offered for sale at a slave auction. Disaster seems imminent until a legal deus ex machina, in the form of Cecilie's declaration that she will marry Horatio, frees him from slavery and disgrace. Never far beneath the surface of the conflict is Andersen's perpetual preoccupation with the 'ugly duckling phenomenon,' his running apologia for the gifted but poor, persecuted, or 'different' individual, excluded from polite society but ultimately triumphant. The moral of *Cendrillon* was carried forward by Andersen as a banner and a challenge.

Critical regard for *The Mulatto* was high. 'This widely admired author has,' wrote *Dagen* (4 Feb. 1840), 'again managed to grasp the tones which find response in the audience's breast.' In addition, fine acting by Johanne Luise Heiberg, for whom Andersen had written the role of Cecilie, and an exciting scenic representation of the exotic atmosphere, particularly in the dramatic juxtaposition of Horatio's dank prison with a glittering ballroom in the fourth act and in the sensational slave-auction scene of the last act, substantially aided the success of the play.

In marked contrast, generally wretched acting and apparent indifference toward the exotic Spanish setting in Andersen's romantic drama *The Moorish Girl* resulted in a disappointing run for this play of only three performances in December 1840.[60] Countless difficulties prior to the

57 Overskou, *Den danske Skueplads*, v, 405

58 *Mit Livs Eventyr*, I, 219

59 This provoked a hefty debate on originality in *Fædrelandet* (16 Feb.

1840); see P. Høybye, 'H.C. Andersen og Frankrig,' *Anderseniana*, ser. 2, II (1951–4), 146–7

60 *Fædrelandet*, 28 Dec. 1840

opening of *The Moorish Girl*, including Johanne Luise Heiberg's pointed refusal to play the 'masculine' leading role, led to an open breach between the playwright and the powerful House of Heiberg. The apologia which the tormented author added as a preface to the play was particularly ill-timed. The 1840s marked the beginning of a new development in Danish theatrical criticism, characterized by the rise and eventual predominance of newspaper 'reviews' at the expense of the more sober evaluations of the critical journals. The domination of newspaper reporting in theatrical matters brought with it a wave of glib, slashing polemics, as publications like *Figaro* and *Corsaren* (The Corsair, which sported a Barbary marauder delivering a cannon salvo on its masthead!) spearheaded a reign of terror from which no dramatist or actor was safe. Seeking to vindicate *The Moorish Girl*, Andersen introduced it with a jeremiad which reproached such hostile treatment and which began: 'It is rather well known that I have suffered a miserable childhood, and even though the good God has since led me forward, I have, however, at each step had to survive many battles.'[61] This document, judiciously omitted from his collected works, bore its own punishment in the form of devastating ridicule in the columns of *Corsaren* (1 Jan. 1841) and other papers.

Separating evidence from outraged sensibilities, however, *The Moorish Girl* is clearly inferior to most of Andersen's other plays. Although the dramatist styled this five-act verse drama a 'tragedy,' its theme and use of background music composed by Hartmann bring it closer to the category of conventional melodrama. Raphaella, a Spanish Saint Joan-figure who wins the love of the King of Cordova after saving his life in a battle against the Moors but who flees from his proposal of marriage on patriotic grounds, is basically a stock melodramatic heroine with 'ugly duckling' overtones. Although Raphaella discovers that she is in reality the daughter of the enemy King of the Moors, the King of Cordova nevertheless renews his proposal. She pretends to agree, only to take her own life on rather vague grounds of honour and decency. The play should, however, be seen from a theatrical rather than a literary vantage point; 'all is and must be calculated for the stage, for performance, thus it must be judged,' Andersen insisted in his preface.[62] In this context, the picturesque exoticism in costuming, landscape, and architecture suggested in the text provided the concrete means by which the dramatist sought to invest the

61 Topsøe-Jensen, *Omkring Levnedsbogen*, p. 216   62 *Ibid.*, p. 217

melodramatic story with an interesting and evocative atmosphere. His conference with the stage manager, the scene designer, and the costume designer which followed Heiberg's reading of the play in the greenroom on 20 Sept. 1840 was undoubtedly aimed at clarifying this objective.[63] Hence when the Royal Theatre succumbed to the negative attitude of the Heibergs and neglected to provide a suitable physical exoticism in the production, the disappointing result was a foregone conclusion.

After the florid exoticism of *The Mulatto* and *The Moorish Girl*, Andersen turned closer to home and explored the areas of Danish history and Danish folk material for romantic subjects. Moreover, following the failure of his ballad dramatization, *Agnete and the Merman*, he sought refuge in anonymity, a common practice in Denmark during this decade marked by the 'reign of terror' of the newspaper polemic. The first of Andersen's anonymous productions was the one-act romantic drama performed in 1844, *Dreams of the King*, which treats the historic imprisonment of King Christjern II in Sønderborg Castle. In many ways this short play ranks among Andersen's most interesting theatrical productions; in his critique as dramaturge Heiberg praised the work for its originality and inventiveness – causing Edvard Collin to remark: 'Anonymity already begins to have its interesting sides.'[64]

Dreams of the King is based on Samsøe's eighteenth-century historical tragedy, *Dyveke*, and on Andersen's own youthful studies of Christjern II conducted in connection with an unfinished historical novel.[65] The play depicts, by means of a 'flashback technique' which was effectively supported in production by Henrik Rung's dramatic music, Christjern's dreams of his mistress Dyveke, whom he meets in Bergen and subsequently allows to be poisoned in Copenhagen. The play's national-historical subject, verse treatment, and poetic-psychological contrast between the realms of fantasy and reality all make it a typical representative of the genre of romantic drama. The critical debate which greeted the produc-

---

63 Two and a half weeks before the actual reading rehearsal on 8 Oct.; see Andersen's letter of 16 Sept. in Topsøe-Jenson, *HCA og Henriette Wulff*, I, 276, and his diary for 20 Sept. Heiberg was dramatic consultant for the Royal Theatre and also led the reading of new scripts for the actors. See Borup, *Johan Ludvig Heiberg*, II, 163–4

64 Bille and Bøgh, *Breve til H.C. Andersen*, p. 93

65 Cf Høeg, *H.C. Andersens Ungdom*, pp. 271–304

tion became essentially an aesthetic discussion of 'dramatic rules'; critics of the play's romanticism opposed its 'lack of dramatic action' and its violation of correct classical versification through an overabundance of caesura and hiatus.[66] It was Heiberg, meanwhile, who, in a brilliant review in his *Intelligensblade* (1 March 1844), cut through the foggy theoretical discussion to demonstrate the effective theatricality of the play's situation, and the visually striking manner in which the dreams become a part of reality. The scenic treatment of these dream transitions, foreshadowing more modern techniques, comprises the essential core of *Dreams of the King* as theatre.

The *Blossom of Happiness* / *Lykkens Blomst*, which appeared the following year and which Andersen designated a 'fairy-tale comedy,' similarly transfers the main character to two dream situations, thereby poetically contrasting the realms of fantasy and reality. Although the basic tones of *Dreams of the King* and *The Blossom of Happiness* are very different, the subject matter of the latter play is again national-historical. Henrik, a forester, 'becomes,' by means of an elf's magic pearls, first the eighteenth-century Danish poet Johannes Ewald and next the mediaeval Prince Buris at the castle of King Waldemar. However, once he discovers that 'wishing will make it so' and experiences the terrible sorrows of the poet and the torments of the prince, the forester of Andersen's fable is happy to find that true happiness – the 'blessed peace of mind' of the wise Alidor in *Cendrillon* – is to be sought in his humble cottage together with his little family.

If the moral of the play was thus reminiscent of Andersen's own fairytales, its immediate theatrical model was most probably Heiberg's historical dream-play, *Day of the Seven Sleepers* / *Syvsoverdag*, first produced in 1840. In his role as the Royal Theatre's consultant, Heiberg charged (unjustly) that *The Blossom of Happiness* was a direct copy of the three spheres in his own play, the realistic as represented by Henrik and his wife Johanna, the fantastic as represented by the mischievous elf and the good fairy Kirsten Piil, and the ideal, depicted in the worlds of Johannes Ewald and King Waldemar. Heiberg found Andersen's unusual treatment of the material, particularly the fact that Henrik actually *becomes*

---

66 For the various viewpoints see *Kjøbenhavnsposten* (15 Feb 1844), *Berlingske Tidende* (15 Feb.), *Fædrelandet* (17 Feb.), *Journal for Litteratur og Kunst* (1844), p. 129, and *Ny Portefeuille for 1844*, I, 187

Ewald and Prince Buris, 'absurd.'[67] Andersen studied and followed historical reality closely in the Ewald episode, and the actor who played the poet tried to achieve 'a portrait likeness,' thereby discarding the character of Henrik entirely.[68] Although the play was finally accepted in spite of Heiberg's hostile attitude, the difficulties were thereby far from being overcome. Andersen's utter disregard for 'rules' of form and propriety distressed his contemporaries greatly. Bournonville refused on the grounds of decorum to choreograph a scene in which Kirsten, Prince Buris's sweetheart, is forced to dance herself to death.[69] Johanne Luise Heiberg temperamentally turned down the part of Kirsten; 'Fru Heiberg suggests that Kirsten's role be given to a dancer and not to her,' wrote Andersen in his diary on 10 Oct. 1844. 'In a furious rage! Would like to leave Denmark forever!' Finally, although the acting proved to be a strong point in the Royal Theatre's production in February 1845, the staging of the demanding poetic contrasts and transitions in this fantasy was beset by severe technical problems in performance.[70] 'The entire structure [of the play] conflicts with the existing and customary dramatic rules governing an ordinary (eg, Scribean) play,' declared the unimaginative reviewer for *Dansk Album* (23 Feb. 1845). While the play 'reveals a poetic genius' and 'a truly brilliant eye for scenic effect,' this critic advised Andersen to concentrate on a stricter and more 'well-made' construction.

In contrast to other prominent Danish authors such as Heiberg or Henrik Hertz, H.C. Andersen was immediately responsive when Casino Theatre, the first private theatre authorized in Copenhagen, opened in 1848 under the direction of W.H. Lange. Andersen was attracted from the outset by the idea of a smaller, popular theatre, and at Casino he found consolation for the unresponsiveness and high-handed treatment he was often forced to endure at the Royal Theatre. He became Casino's unofficial house dramatist, and for a time also functioned as its literary consultant and served on the board of directors. During the early 1850s he achieved

67 Heiberg's hostile report is reprinted in Topsøe-Jensen, *Brevveksling med Edvard og Henriette Collin*, v, 116–17. For Andersen's description of the production of *Day of the Seven Sleepers* see Topsøe-Jensen, *H.C. Andersen og H. Wulff*, 1, 274

68 *Dansk Album*, 23 Feb. 1845. For the Ewald episode Andersen studied F.C. Olsen's 'Digteren Johannes Ewalds Liv og Forholdene i Aarene 1774–77,' published in 1835 in *Kjøbenhavns flyvende Post*.

69 Bille and Bøgh, *Breve til H.C. Andersen*, p. 43

70 *Berlingske Tidende*, 17 Feb. 1845

considerable fame as a playwright at Casino with a series of fairy-tale fantasies similar in form to *The Blossom of Happiness*. His success in turn attracted other established dramatists to the new popular theatre and helped greatly to increase its prestige.

Following the production, five months after Casino's opening, of Andersen's one-act adaptation of Warin and Lefevre's *Une chambre à deux lits*, called *A Night in Roskilde | En Nat i Roskilde*, he turned for inspiration to the type of popular fairy-tale play perfected by the Austrian actor and dramatist Ferdinand Raimund, whose fantasies he later recommended for careful study to the young director Henrik Ibsen during his visit to Copenhagen in 1852.[71] During his first trip to Vienna in 1834 Andersen had had an opportunity to see the special Viennese *Zauberpossen* at first hand. He was particularly enthusiastic about Karl Meisl's *Das Gespenst auf der Bastei*, which he saw at the Theater an der Wien on 2 July, noting in his diary that 'the whole light fantastic humour delighted me,' especially Johann Nestroy as the ghost 'who very humorously haunts the Bastei.'[72] In 1838 Andersen tried unsuccessfully to secure a production at the Royal Theatre for his rather undistinguished translation of *Der Verschwender*, Raimund's saga of a reckless spendthrift. At Casino, however, he succeeded in capturing the unique style and flavour of the Viennese fairy-tale comedy. 'The talent which the world acknowledges in me as an author of fairy-tales must surely also bear some fruit in this direction,' he reasoned.[73] His prediction proved correct. His fairy-tale fantasy *More than Pearls and Gold | Meer end Perler og Guld*, produced for the first time at Casino on 3 October 1849, played to a succession of capacity audiences in the 2500-seat playhouse and enjoyed no fewer than 162 performances in the repertory until 1888. The play is an adaptation of Raimund's *Der Diamant des Geisterkönigs*, the story of a young man promised a statue of diamond if he can find a girl who has never told a lie. The technique is pure Raimund, presenting a fantastic mixture of realistic scenes from contemporary life and frankly unreal, supernatural situations in order to demonstrate the worth of good, honest, simple integrity. A sincere and honest girl is 'the finest diamond,' worth 'more than pearls and gold.' To Raimund's play Andersen added ideas from *The Arabian Nights* and a piquantly localized Copenhagen flavour. The audience was treated to a stream of

71 Neiiendam, *Gennem mange Aar*, p. 99   *Studier*, p. 169
72 Topsoe-Jensen, *H.C. Andersen og andre*   73 *Mit Livs Eventyr*, II, 111–12

3 Drawing by H.C.C. Ley of scenes from
Andersen's *More than Pearls and Gold*. Danish Theatre Museum

topical details woven into the action: Tivoli with Lumbye's popular orchestra, the amazing wonders of the new railroad to Roskilde, a balloon ascent, the newly formed Parliament, and even Andersen's publisher were mentioned.

No reliable source documents comparable to the Royal Theatre archives have survived to clarify the manner in which these Casino productions were actually staged. However, four drawings by H.C.C. Ley depicting scenes from *More than Pearls and Gold* hang in the Theatre Museum in Copenhagen; shown in Fig. 3 they present a charming pictorial impression of the fairy-tale tone of Andersen's play.[74]

In concluding his review of *More than Pearls and Gold*, the novelist and critic M.A. Goldschmidt remarked on Raimund's 'flirtation' with the notion of fantastic wealth: 'Many a spectator of such a folk-comedy perhaps goes home to his simple parlor and finds it poorer than before, is even more dissatisfied with life than before going to the theatre. We believe that H.C. Andersen, when he creates an original play, will offer the public healthier nourishment for its imagination.'[75] The play to which Goldschmidt alluded was *Ole Shuteye / Ole Lukøie*, which appeared at Casino five months later and became Andersen's most solid success in the genre of fairy-tale fantasy. It is based on one of his own fairy-tale characters, Ole Shuteye, the Nordic sandman or god of sleep. Its moral is that implied in Goldschmidt's remark and dramatized by Raimund in, for example, *Der Bauer als Millionär* – 'health, good humour, and peace of mind' are worth more than the world's riches. The method used to demonstrate this optimistic message was, of course, the technique of the Viennese *Zauberpossen* – the free intermingling of topical reality and supernatural fantasy – presented with calculated naïveté and witty dialogue.

The specific literary influences in *Ole Shuteye* are many.[76] Raimund and Andersen's own fairy-tales have been mentioned. The basic dream structure of the play is clearly related to the framework of the powerful *Der Traum, ein Leben* by the Viennese dramatist Franz Grillparzer, a close friend of Andersen. In *Der Traum*, the Eastern hero dreams in such a way that his real life is influenced by what he has experienced when asleep.

74 All four drawings are reproduced in Robert Neiiendam, 'Omkring H.C. Andersens dramatik,' *Anderseniana*, ser. 2, II (1954), 327–41

75 *Nord og Syd*, I (1849), 411

76 Topsøe-Jensen presents a perceptive analysis of this play in *H.C. Andersen og andre Studier*, pp. 153–72.

In *Ole Shuteye*, Christian, the honest but discontented chimney-sweep, wishfully dreams of acquiring limitless wealth – a dangerous fantasy in the fairy-tale genre! On Østergade in Copenhagen Christian encounters, in the dream which forms the play-within-the-play, the ghost of a vagabond 'dressed all in white with white cane and white cigar,' who allows the chimney-sweep the traditional three wishes. The genealogy of the figure in white is not difficult to discern: the very same character haunted the Bastei, the favourite promenade in old Vienna, in Meisl's *Das Gespenst auf der Bastei*, which Andersen had seen sixteen years earlier at the Theater an der Wien. Finally, Christian's plight closely resembles that of the charcoal-burner Peter Munk in Wilhelm Hauff's popular fairy-tale, *Das kalte Herz*. Both young heroes relinquish their hearts to the powers of evil in order to attain riches; the evil junk-dealer Blake replaces Christian's heartbeat with the tick of a costly gold watch. The ultimate moral of Hauff's tale is fully equivalent to the gospel of *Ole Shuteye*: 'Es ist doch besser, zufrieden sein mit wenigem, als Gold und Güter haben, und ein kaltes Herz' [Far better to be satisfied with little, than to have gold and goods and a cold heart].[77]

In the Viennese *Zauberpossen* the machinist was the dramatist's closest collaborator, and thus in *Ole Shuteye* spectacular theatricality played a major role. The audience was treated to surprising scene changes, lavish dance numbers, sudden transformations, and, not least, a scene of black magic in the second-hand shop of the wicked Blake, in which the furniture danced, portraits moved, and the fireiron performed pirouettes! Although no production records have survived, Andersen found that his spectacular fantasy was staged 'as properly as possible' on the 'small, narrow, oppressive stage at Casino.'[78]

Least successful of Andersen's fairy-tale fantasies was his one-act dramatization of another of his own tales, *Mother Elder / Hyldemoer*. Its production at Casino in December 1851 convinced him that most Danes had 'little appreciation for the fantastic,' preferring 'to nourish themselves honestly on wretched dramatic recipes right out of the cookbook.'[79] Conservative critics found it difficult to accept Andersen's loosely structured and frankly impressionistic fantasy. 'The play lacks nearly all the conditions for being called a drama,' asserted *Berlingske Tidende* (2 Dec.

77 *Wilhelm Hauffs sämtliche Werke in sechs Bänden* (Stuttgart: Cottasche Bibliothek der Weltliteratur, nd), VI, 322

78 *Mit Livs Eventyr*, II, 112

79 *Ibid.*, 144

1851). 'Instead of a plot, the author gives us a series of isolated scenes which, since they lack all inherent connection, he has found necessary to paste together by means of "Phantasus," who at every turn must support poet and public with opinions and explanations.'

COMEDY

In marked contrast to the complexities of his fairy-tale fantasies, Andersen's charming short comedy, *The New Maternity Ward | Den nye Barselstue*, provided the Royal Theatre with an uncomplicated and immediate success when first performed there anonymously in March 1845. The popularity of Andersen's best-known play has also been permanent, and to date it has been given a total of 116 performances in the Royal Theatre repertory. The inspiration for this comedy was undoubtedly a capricious little publication by Søren Kierkegaard entitled *Foreword | Forord*, which had appeared the previous June and which suggested that someone should write a new, literary version of Holberg's classic comedy, *The Maternity Ward | Barselstuen*.[80] Hence Andersen's comedy is a 'new' *Maternity Ward* in literary terms, written in the classical manner and presenting a cavalcade of amusing caricatures from the Copenhagen of Christian VIII. Its action follows Holberg's model. Doctor Wendel returns home after many years in America to find that his old friend Jespersen has just had a great success as the author of a comedy called *Love*. A group of foolish visitors therefore flocks to the 'maternity ward' – Jespersen's study – to pay homage to the new 'child.' Unlike Holberg's play, however, Jespersen is ironically *not* the father of the child, and it rapidly emerges that Doctor Wendel himself wrote the play as a poem of unrequited love for Jespersen's sister Christine, and gave it to his friend before going away. However, to the 'poet's' relief Wendel agrees to keep the secret, the latter decides to renew his suit to Christine, and the curtain falls on an ovation by the guests for the chastened Jespersen. If several of the comic portraits and coups de théâtre, such as Christine's opening speech about the guest list, were patterned directly on Holberg's play, Andersen's satire nevertheless had a sharp topical and contemporary edge. 'Taken from raw reality' was Heiberg's phrase, but this fact by no means hampered its sweeping popularity as he had implied it would.[81] The play's piquant

80 Billeskov Jansen, *Danmarks Digtekunst*, III, 195

81 Heiberg's official report appears in Collin, *H.C. Andersen*, p. 371.

salon tone represented a particular forte of the Royal Theatre personnel, led by its dominant spirit and chief artist Johanne Luise Heiberg, and the comic character portraits in the classical tradition afforded rewarding acting material.

Andersen's attempt a year later to reduplicate the witty tone, comic characterizations, and 'mistaken parenthood' intrigue of *The New Maternity Ward* in a comedy entitled *Herr Rasmussen* led, however, to his most resounding failure as a dramatist. *Herr Rasmussen* received a single, anonymous performance, after which it was, for very good reason, banished from the repertoire, ignored in Andersen's autobiography, and expunged from his collected works.[82] Reviews of the debacle are short and to the point; 'this evening the audience in the Royal Theatre was obliged to hiss a new play off the stage,' wrote the critic for *Kjøbenhavnsposten* (20 March 1846), 'which would never have been put on the stage if the Royal Theatre management was not – the Royal Theatre management.' It is no surprise to find that production records for this play are few and meagre. 'Everything functioned in the proper order. The play was completely hissed off,' recorded the Theatre's *Regiejournal* tersely.[83]

Apart from his libretti for *Wedding at Lake Como* and *The Nix*, and the short prologue play *The Bulwark of Art | Kunstens Dannevirke*, a patriotic panegyric of Danish arts and letters commissioned for the Royal Theatre centennial on 18 December 1848, eighteen years passed after *Herr Rasmussen* before Andersen was represented by another new play at the theatre on Kongens Nytorv. This was the romantic comedy *He is not well-born | Han er ikke født*, which was produced in April 1864. In that year the attention of Andersen and of the Danish nation was focussed on the war with Germany in Slesvig-Holstein rather than on the stage of the national theatre. Under the circumstances, however, the production was relatively successful, due largely to the acting of romantic idol Michael Wiehe, whose tragic death in October put an end to further performances of the play. Although he found the plot of this comedy 'very slender,' Bjørnstjerne Bjørnson regarded *He is not well-born* as 'a delightful little work,' written with 'elegance and psychological, adept refinement.'[84]

---

82 Edvard Agerholm first edited the play, with a short introduction describing its bizarre history, in 1913. It might be noted that Andersen earned only 70 Rdl. for his labours (*Theaterkassens*

Regnskaber, 7 April 1846, Rigsarkivet).
83 *Regiejournal Jan. 1837–April 1848*, 16 March 1846 (Royal Theatre library)
84 Cf Bille and Bøgh, *Breve til H.C. Andersen*, p. 637

The play contrasts the nobility of blood, of money, and of intellect, a contrast effectively conveyed in the dialogue and the characterization. Gathered within a rather loose framework of mistaken parenthood, a gallery of amusing character portraits surrounds the two lovers, Frederik and Elisabeth. The topicality of this romantic comedy lent itself to effective realization on the stage. Particularly the caricature of a sensitive and temperamental poet named Kluhd (Rag), author of an 'apocalyptic comedy in nine acts' entitled *Death and Damnation*, was drawn by Andersen with fine self-irony; 'they shall be all rotting in the ground when I am ripe fruit on the public tongue!' cries the vexed Kluhd vindictively, and when told that the company was concerned after he had rushed out in a rage he strikes an injured pose which epitomizes the Andersen whimsy: 'Let them worry! Let them torment themselves! Have they dragged for me in the canals?'

By this time Andersen's world renown had at last won him immunity from the vituperous domestic criticism that had previously dogged his steps as a dramatist. 'The public has realized,' wrote critic Erik Bøgh in *Folkets Avis* (29 April 1864), 'that although [Andersen] has never succeeded in forming a work for the stage according to the accepted rules of the art, he is a far greater poet than someone possessing the most complete talent for dramatic construction, and when he leaves his limitless realm in the world of the fairy-tale to visit the narrow stage with the slanting floor, upon which each step must be measured, he should be considered as a guest who brings rich gifts from another land, where art makes other demands.' In the eyes of the younger critics representing a new generation, Andersen's genius had already passed into legend. Yet their praise of his 'innocent-satirical, naïve-ingenious dialogue' tends somewhat to neglect his insights as a dramatist and the purely theatrical merits of his later comedies.

When the Spaniards were here / *Da Spanierne var her*, Andersen's last play, was a romantic comedy produced in April 1865 and written with his customary awareness of contemporary theatrical taste. Based on a re-writing of his vaudeville *Parting and Meeting*, the popular historical theme of the Spanish troops stationed in Odense in 1808 provided the scenic milieu. 'His picture has a large and brilliant ornamentation,' remarked the reviewer for *Berlingske Tidende* (7 April 1865), 'conveyed through scenic effect, the use of music, and the illumination of the spoken word. The scene is set in Middelfart and southern Jutland ... the spectator has the Great Belt before him, where British warships cruise.' Andersen's diary entries for 15 and 16 June 1864 indicate that historical studies were made for the play, and the contemporary interest in historical 'accuracy' was also the basis for the rather pedantic objection, raised by the critic for *Tilskueren* (9 April 1865), that the Marseillaise heard at the end of the play had in reality been forbidden under Napoleon's emperor-ship from 1804 to 1814.

The Spanish element in this scenic environment was, however, pro-jected through the ear rather than the eye: the sound of Spanish songs and castanets is heard but the Spaniards themselves are never shown, with the exception of three children dressed in uniform who appear at the close of the first scene. Unlike Francesco in *Parting and Meeting*, Hermania's Spanish soldier, Don Juan de Molina, never actually appears on stage; only his serenades are heard in the distance. Against this dim, idealized outline of the Spanish soldier, the character of the strong-willed and spirited Hermania stands out in yet bolder relief to dominate the action. Her attraction to and pursuit of the unseen Spanish lover assumes an added dimension and becomes in the play a flight towards a romanticized ideal which echoes the richest strains in Andersen's art:

I need to cross the rolling water! I have the swan's nature – I won't stay in this stagnant pond, nice enough for geese and ducks to swim in.[85]

Hence the sharply etched character portraits, the love affairs, happy or otherwise, the intrigues of mistaken parenthood, the fairy-tale transforma-tions, and the quests for a romantic ideal which pervade Andersen's dramaturgy received expression in a wide variety of styles and an assort-ment of dramatic forms that included vaudeville, opera, singspiel, roman-tic drama, fairy-tale fantasy, and comedy. This chapter has tried to suggest some of the more significant influences on Andersen's plays – the Heiberg vaudeville, Walter Scott romanticism, exoticism, Danish history, and folk material. In each of the genres he attempted, he registered popu-lar successes – *The Invisible Man*, *The Mulatto*, *Dreams of the King*, *Little Kirsten*, *Ole Shuteye*, and *The New Maternity Ward*, to mention the more ob-vious examples – although the myth of his totally fruitless career as a play-wright prevails, nourished no doubt by his own misleading accounts. In

85 *Samlede Skrifter*, XXXII, 46

reality, Andersen's plays were generally written with an acute awareness of the practical theatre of his time and a concrete image of that theatre constantly in mind. As such, they are remarkably informative reflections of the nineteenth-century theatrical context, the interplay of styles, methods, conventions, and techniques in staging, costuming, and acting which preceded the emergence of naturalism.

THREE
Scene Design and Staging

THE OBJECTS OF THEATRE HISTORY – stage productions – are best characterized in a terminology which is reconstructive, because the work of the theatre historian is recreative: it must focus on the stylistic peculiarities which in turn bear witness to, or clarify, 'artistic intentions' in the work of art.[1] 'Intentions' (*Kunstwollen*) can only be formulated in terms of alternatives: a situation must be supposed in which the dramatist – but *not* the characters in his plays, as frequently suggested in literary analyses – is confronted with a possibility of choice between various procedures or modes of emphasis. To evolve a historical reconstruction of the productions of H.C. Andersen's plays, the main features of scene design and staging, costuming, and acting style in these productions must be identified and considered. Such a production history is, in turn, a reflection of the history of theatrical style in the given period, a reflection often surpassing its original in clarity of outline. It may further be argued, moreover, that such a history can frequently express the perplexing problem of the playwright's *Kunstwollen* in clearer or, at least, more tangible terms than the dramas themselves.

Among the source documents which enable us to reconstruct the staging of Andersen's plays, the most important are the extraordinary folio volumes known as *maskinmesteroptegnelser*, containing ground plans and invaluable descriptions of all aspects of the décors used for opera, comedy,

---

1 These remarks, and the method they espouse, are indebted to Erwin Panofsky's *Meaning in the Visual Arts* (New York 1957), particularly 'The History of Art as a Humanistic Discipline' and 'The History of the Theory of Human Proportions as a Reflection of the History of Styles.'

tragedy, and ballet at the Danish Royal Theatre. This series of hand-written volumes was begun by F.C. Gynther when he assumed the post of *maskinmester*, or stage manager, at the Royal Theatre in 1824. At this time information concerning older productions was found on loose sheets, and Gynther set about to transfer this data to the ponderous folio volumes, thereby preserving considerable valuable source material from the eighteenth century. After Gynther's death in 1851, he was succeeded by A.P. Wedén, who continued the work with the collection and expanded it to include several hundred plays, operas, and ballets comprising the Royal Theatre's entire repertoire between the 1820s and the opening of the new building in 1874.[2]

In addition, an interesting series of miniature, pocket-size *maskinmester* books, probably carried about on the stage itself and frequently containing useful supplementary information about a particular setting, exists in a private collection. It has been useful to include a number of relevant details from this collection, referred to here as Series B.

Complementing the *maskinmester* journals is a series of *regieprotokoller*, also kept by the stage manager and maintained up-to-date to the present day. The pages of these protocols are divided into vertical columns for dramatis personæ, actors, costumes, props, settings, dates played, music and sound cues, and, on occasion, position directions for supernumeraries. The remarks about sets are, however, often a mere transcription of the author's stage directions, and as such are of less inherent interest than the *maskinmester* journals. These principal sources are supplemented, meanwhile, by a wide variety of scenery inventories, unbound protocol pages, financial accounts, prompt copies, letters, and similar documents housed n the Royal Theatre library and the Danish State Archives.

In contrast to the wealth of written source material, however, pictorial documentation of Andersen's productions at the Royal Theatre is scarce. Five rather impressionistic drawings by the artist Edvard Lehmann hang

2 This collection, from which all information presented in this chapter concerning specific sets is drawn and to which repeated individual references would serve no useful purpose here, is divided according to genre and includes the following volumes: For opera and singspiel: *Decorationer til Syngespil* and *Decorationer til Opera*,

Syngestykker, mm. (ca 1860); For tragedy: *Decorationer til Tragedier*; For comedy, romantic drama, etc.: *Decorationer til Comedier*; For ballet: *Fortegnelse over Decorationer til de paa det Kongelige Theater givne Balletter, Divertissementer og Entréer.* All volumes are in the Royal Theatre library.

4 Drawing by Edvard Lehmann:
The Bride of Lammermoor, I, 3. Theatre Museum

5 Drawing by Edvard Lehmann:
The Bride of Lammermoor, IV, 2

6 Drawing by Edvard Lehmann:
The Festival at Kenilworth, I

7 Drawing by Edvard Lehmann:
The Festival at Kenilworth, I

in the Danish Theatre Museum (Figs. 4–8), but no actual scene designs have survived. This fact does not, however, present as great an obstacle to the reconstruction of these productions as might be imagined. In actual fact very few new settings were created for Andersen's plays; the majority of these productions were mounted by combining a number of appropriate elements from already existing décors. Since a considerable number of the designs for these 'parallel' settings, reused for Andersen's plays, are extant, the available ground plans for the productions can be supplemented with illustrations of related décors borrowed and named in the particular plan.

In the light of this system of borrowing stock décors, the scene-painter exerted a major influence on the style and appearance of the entire repertoire. The effect of romanticism, as James Laver has remarked, was to depose the architect in favour of the landscape painter. 'Instead of the formal recession of baroque pillars there were wide stretches of blasted heath or distant vistas of town and village. Even architecture itself was treated in a purely pictorial way.'[3] Laver sums up the development of scene design in the first half of the nineteenth century by observing that the backcloth eventually absorbed the side-wings and finally swallowed the whole stage picture. The gallery of such backcloths presented on the nineteenth-century stage still included, moreover, work of genuine artistic merit; it had not yet become a virtue for the scene designer to be *neither* an artist *nor* a decorator *nor* an architect but simply a 'craftsman' having, in the terminology of modern training schools, 'a working knowledge' of these arts. The importance of the nineteenth-century scenic artist is emphasized by the fact that in playbills and reviews of the period his name is often the most prominent one. Hence it seems appropriate to pause before proceeding in order to introduce the three Danish designers whose work during this period at the Royal Theatre had a profound influence on the production of Andersen's plays there.

Aron Wallich, the Royal Theatre's designer for nearly three decades from 1814 to 1842, received his initial training at the Royal Danish Academy of Fine Arts and made study trips to the traditional artistic meccas of France and Italy. In the towns of northern Italy Wallich discovered countless examples of the favourite gothic subjects of contemporary scene design – murky cathedrals, barren churchyards, vaulted monastery passages, and sombre grave monuments. Later, as the Royal

3 See his *Drama*, pp. 198–9

Theatre's scene-painter, this perceptive and sensitive artist carried on the eighteenth-century traditions of Peter Cramer and Thomas Bruun. Despite studies under the renowned Ciceri and a few designs in the romantic vein, Wallich maintained a predilection for eighteenth-century Italian traditions, grandiose lines, and deep perspectives. His work is characterized in general by a fine, light style; art historian Christian Elling has happily described his sketches as 'enchantingly musical, sparkling, as it were, in tone, a spiritual accompaniment to the melodies of Cimarosa and Rossini.'[4]

Wallich was succeeded in 1842 at the Royal Theatre by two scenic artists, Troels Lund and C.F. Christensen. Lund, like his predecessor, attended the Academy of Fine Arts, where he specialized in architecture and the study of perspective, and travelled extensively to the accepted artistic centres, where he studied under Ciceri and Simon Quaglio. With utmost enthusiasm he drew inspiration from the stage painting of masters like Sanquirico and Ciceri, and from the amazing atmospheric effects of Daguerre's Diorama in Paris. Regarding the significance of the latter phenomenon, Allevy's summary of Diorama effects reads like a catalogue describing the full range of nineteenth-century scenic milieux: 'Paysages nocturnes, souterrains aux éclairages blafards, clairs de lune sur des chapelles en ruines ou des palais antiques, obscurs ermitages entourés de rochers abruptes, toiles de fond noyées de ténèbres ou de lumière, effets de clair-obscur si goûtés dans ses tableaux à double présentation de jour et de nuit, spectacles terrifiants: incendie, éruption volcanique, inondation &c.'[5]

Lund continued until 1864 as scene designer for the Royal Theatre, where his chief duty was to serve as an architecture painter and an occasional adviser in sceno-technical affairs. As an artist, his designs were frequently influenced by an early ambition to paint historical subjects. Two of his most successful Danish-historical décors were executed for Bournonville ballets: a design of Viborg Cathedral for *The Youth of Erik Menved | Erik Menveds Barndom* (1843) and an earlier gothic hall for *Waldemar* (1835), reused the following year in Andersen's *Festival at Kenilworth*.

Christensen, who was employed as a scene designer at the Royal Theatre until 1869, was an imaginative and highly gifted artist widely conceded to be more talented than Lund. While Lund's speciality was architecture, Christensen's strength lay in finely wrought romantic land-

4 See his *Breve om Italien*, pp. 76–7   5 Allevy, *La mise-en-scène en France*, p. 49

8 Drawing by Edvard Lehmann: *The Festival at Kenilworth*, II, I

9 Design by Aron Wallich for a gothic dungeon, coloured in contrasting browns, with blue sky and green trees visible through the perspective arch.
Royal Theatre library

10 *above* Design by Troels Lund for a gothic hall in Bournonville's ballet *Waldemar* (1835). This design, Lund's project for admission to the Royal Academy of Fine Arts, was altered somewhat in actual practice. The original water-colour hangs in the Academy. *below* Lund's gothic hall still in use in the background in the 1866 revival of *Waldemar*. Engravings from *Illustreret Tidende*

scapes executed in bright, warm, and genial tones. After training under Wallich and exhibiting early water-colour views of Copenhagen, Christensen undertook the customary study trip to France and Italy. On his return to Denmark in 1839, he achieved one of his greatest successes with his much-admired Italian décor for Bournonville's romantic ballet, *Festival in Albano*, a décor which also figured prominently in the staging of Andersen's plays.

The work of Wallich, Lund, and Christensen, together with earlier designs by Thomas Bruun, Cocchi, and Anders Poulsen, constituted the artistic tone and style which dominated the stage picture at the Danish Royal Theatre during the first half of the nineteenth century. In addition to the designs which survive by these artists, a Royal Theatre décor inventory in the form of a small album of miniature drawings (entitled *Fortegnelse over Tepper*), probably prepared about the time of the opening of the new building in 1874, gives an added impression of the large number of scene designs no longer extant in actual sketch form and is therefore useful as a supplementary source of information.

The basic framework of the eighteenth-century stage, consisting of loose wings mounted on carriages which could slide in and out and separate backdrops and overhead borders which could be raised or lowered by means of ropes and winches, remained essentially unaltered for the production of Andersen's plays. During the nineteenth century there were eight parallel wing positions at the Royal Theatre, numbered on floor plans from number one farthest downstage to number eight farthest upstage. This framework was then filled out with a wide variety of groundrows and three-dimensional set-pieces arranged in various combinations to produce the desired illusion.

The continued use of the wing-and-border set was closely related to the subject of stage lighting, which profoundly influenced the nineteenth-century stage picture. Gas lighting was not introduced at the Royal Theatre until 1857-8, a surprisingly late date compared to other European theatres – Drury Lane and Covent Garden had introduced gas in 1817, followed by the Paris Opéra five years later; the Royal Theatre in Stockholm was equipped with gas lighting in 1854. Consequently, in the glow of the oil-burning Argand lamps at Kongens Nytorv the wing setting afforded the best solution for combining satisfactory illusion with maximum visibility and illumination. When the Argand lamps replaced candle lighting at the Royal Theatre in 1819, it became possible to burn oil more completely than before without smoking, owing to the cylindrical lamp walls and the introduction of lamp glass.[6] Several additional improvements of significance were made in the theatre's lighting equipment in 1826. At this time the row of footlights was made longer and wider 'so that more lamps of greater calibre could be accommodated.' Moreover, 'coloured and shaded taffetas [were placed] before the lamps in the footlights and wings in order to produce coloured lighting.'[7] A further modernization was achieved by installing 'mechanical arrangements with rollers and windlasses, whereby all lamps on the wings can simultaneously be darkened or made brighter, whether this is required quickly or slowly, and which is managed by only one man in the machine cellar where the equipment is placed.' This arrangement, representing respectably advanced scenic technique for its time, is the basis for the lighting cues which are usually appended to each ground plan – 'lamps on the wings are in red taffetas, dark in the drapes [ie, overhead borders],' 'the red taffetas are slowly lowered from the footlights and it thereby becomes light,' and so on – and which allow us to include stage lighting in our visualization of the total stage picture.

Changes of scene, which normally took place in full view, were also facilitated in 1826 by the addition of a third set of wing chariots which made it possible to mount as many as three settings simultaneously. In addition, scene changes were usually implemented by the venerable technique of alternating shallow and deep scenes. While a shallow 'carpenter' scene was played on the forestage, a larger scene might be prepared undisturbed behind the backcloth. With his practical theatre sense Andersen fully recognized the need for such 'carpenter' or front scenes in his own plays. Thus in *The Mulatto* a brief front scene between Cecilie and Kadu, her faithful overseer, was inserted in the last act to allow for a change to the complicated slave-auction finale which followed; the short scene was staged as simply as possible, comprising two wings from the previous scene in Eleonore's bedroom and using no furniture. Although well aware of its practical function, however, Andersen was nonetheless careful to make such a scene artistically palatable. For this particular scene he reserved one of Cecilie's richest and most poetic speeches, the charming fable of the prince who erected a bell which anyone might ring who

6 Cf Krogh, *Oehlenschlägers indførelse*, p. 15

7 'Fortegnelse paa Ombygninger, Foran- dringer og Forbedringer ved Det Kongelige Comediehus, 1824–1851,' MS, Royal Theatre library

suffered injustice in his kingdom and which is finally pulled by an old, maltreated horse which is then given redress for its grievances. 'Probably everyone familiar with the scenic capacity of our theatre,' noted one reviewer, 'recognizes this little scene as an addition for the sake of the following scene change. But it is treated by the playwright with love and enthusiasm, and is played so brilliantly by Fru Heiberg that it becomes one of the highpoints of the play.'[8]

Despite technical and dramaturgical provisions for scene changes, however, they frequently represented the weakest point in this system of staging. Highly illusory scenery was marred by clumsy set-shifting techniques: thus in Andersen's complex fairy-tale comedy *The Blossom of Happiness*, which depends heavily on smooth machinery for the effectiveness of the hero Henrik's transformations to the poet Ewald and Prince Buris, 'the poetic transformations were reduced to mere prosaic changes.'[9] 'The machinist is in no way able to function as the interpreter of poetry,' complained the critic for *Berlingske Tidende* (17 Feb. 1845), 'whereas the scene-painter has, in the second act's finely executed and magically illuminated décor, proven himself worthy to be.'

Difficulties in changing scenery arose, as Richard Southern has demonstrated, as the scenic apparatus began to outgrow the mechanical practices of the older system. There is no reason to assume, however, that scene changes in the Danish theatre were much inferior to those at other European playhouses at this time. When a review of Andersen's *Dreams of the King* in *Fædrelandet* (17 Feb. 1844) castigated 'the unsuitably poor machinery of our theatre,' remarking that 'the wings, which should change as with a magic wand, move in the same tempo as sacks of flour being hoisted in a warehouse,' Denmark's most influential man-of-letters, J.L. Heiberg, wrote a reply which endeavoured to place the situation in its proper perspective:

[Such criticism] strengthens the widespread misunderstanding that scene changes at our theatre are so far behind those of foreign theatres. But anyone acquainted with the best foreign theatres knows that no great miracles in this respect are seen at any of them. At the Paris Opera, which no doubt must be considered the model theatre for the entire external scenic apparatus, the décors themselves are amazingly effective, but the changes are certainly no magic tricks and are therefore

8 *Portefeuillen for 1840*, I, 161–7   9 *Dansk Album for Litteratur og Kunst* (23 Feb. 1845)

avoided as far as possible. The set changes in *Dreams of the King* satisfy all reasonable expectations.[10]

Yet in spite of such shortcomings, a wealth of romantic illusion was conjured forth within the conventional nineteenth-century wing set lit by oil lighting. The playwright of this period was, moreover, often in close contact with the conventions and techniques of the practical theatre. Not infrequently a dramatist wrote his play with a specific style of décor and costume in mind, and occasionally, as was the case with Andersen's *The Invisible Man*, he even wrote for a specific set of wings already in existence. Countless references in Andersen's writings and correspondence reveal his lively professional interest in the scenic techniques and styles of his day. His plays represent, more fully than those of any other single contemporary classic examples of each of the significant theatrical styles of the period. Although numerous variations within each style occur in any given production, it is possible to identify principles governing major types of décor, and to relate these principles to the artistic intentions of the author.

GOTHIC

The style of stage setting employed in Andersen's three early operas, *The Bride of Lammermoor*, *The Raven*, and *The Festival at Kenilworth*, was termed gothic, an epithet which during the seventeenth and much of the eighteenth century had implied something barbaric, disharmonious, and planless, but which in the late eighteenth and far into the nineteenth century became synonymous with the mediaeval atmosphere and environment representing the highest fashion in the romantic theatre. The scenic mood pictures, the standardized romantic milieu of which audiences never seemed to tire in opera, musical drama, and *genre sombre*, consisted of the same spellbinding elements that flavoured the novels of Mrs Radcliffe, 'Monk' Lewis, and Walter Scott: mediaeval fortifications with walls, towers, moats, and drawbridges, gothic ruins, landscapes shrouded in darkness, churchyards bathed in moonlight, and forest mystique replete with secret grottoes and robbers' dens. A page of such gothic elements taken from the sketchbook of Troels Lund in the Royal Theatre library is shown in Fig. 12. Particularly the gothicism of Scott, whose colourful and explicitly detailed depictions displaced classical strictness of composi-

10 *Intelligensblade* (1844), IV, 248–9

11 Backdrop design by C.F. Christensen for Bournonville's ballet
Festival in Albano (1839). Royal Theatre library

12 Nineteenth-century gothic style, from the sketch-book of Troels Lund,
depicting impressions of his travels in Germany, Austria, and Italy.
Royal Theatre library

tion with an exquisite picturesque charm, fostered an entire genre of 'picturesque' romantic operas. It is in relation to this gothic tradition that Andersen's adaptations of *The Bride of Lammermoor* and *Kenilworth* must be regarded.

Some conception of the popularity of gothic staging at the Royal Theatre may be gained by analyzing the list of the theatre's shop inventory dated 1824–31. It mentions seventy-odd complete settings; of this number, no fewer than eleven are described as 'gothic,' while eight others depicted locales related to this style: prisons, cloisters, ruins, and the like. Hence nearly one-third of the available settings at this time belonged to the gothic-romantic category; of the remaining two-thirds, nine décors depicted 'exotic' locales – Indian, Moorish, Egyptian, American, Mexican, Italian, and Isle de France – and thereby reflected the parallel popular interest in picturesque scenery and landscapes representing far-off lands. The remainder of the inventory consisted on the whole of general utility stock settings.

The gothic style is vividly illustrated by the opening scene of Andersen and Bredal's *The Bride of Lammermoor*. With strong overtones of traditional forest mystique, Annie and Ailsie are discovered gathering magical herbs in their aprons, and they prepare the mood for Edgar's impending tragedy with an eerie song of prophecy that at once recalls the weird sisters in *Macbeth*. Stage directions call for a woodland scene in moonlight at the so-called Knight's Spring; the gothic front and vault of the spring are dilapidated, and a stream winds among the ruins and the scattered stones. It is possible to reconstruct in detail exactly how this mood picture was conveyed and amplified in the theatre. As seen in the ground plan (Fig. 13), the stage was arranged as a forest set in seven wings; a blue gauze drop, or scrim, was hung just below the eighth wing position, in front of which a cliff riser and set-piece were erected. Behind the gauze drop a 'moon-rise apparatus,' no doubt similar to that shown in Fig. 14, was placed.

The Knight's Spring with its accompanying set-pieces was erected at mid-stage, leaving the downstage area open to play in. A large, high bush, a set-piece representing a dilapidated, walled spring, and a rocky cave ran diagonally from the fifth wing stage right to behind the sixth wing stage left. In front of the spring, also running diagonally across the stage, a stretch of lake and a low groundrow depicting grass and bushes were placed. Of these set-pieces all but the new walled spring were borrowed

13 Ground plan, *The Bride of Lammermoor*, I, I:
'lamps on the wings are in red taffetas, footlights up full in red taffetas,
but dark in the drapes.'

14 Detail from Lund's sketch-book showing application of a 'moon-rise
apparatus.' In the mechanism at right, the 'moon' (a) is a transparency on
canvas painted with clouds, and is raised by means of a rope. In the sketch,
left, the moon is in place in a design for Wolff and Weber's *Preciosa*

directly from the existing inventory. The function of the tree stump conspicuously positioned downstage left first becomes apparent when, inflamed with thoughts of revenge on Lord Ashton, Edgar of Ravenswood stumbles on to the fatal spot and the stump provides him, on an otherwise barren stage, with a convenient support on which to lean in his distraction.

The lighting of this scene was designed to contribute to the scenic mood picture. Although the text specifically indicates moonlight, the first light cue reads: 'Lamps on the wings are in red taffetas, but dark in the drapes' – ie, sunset lighting. It is not until after Annie and Ailsie's song that the sunset red disappears and the moon rises as the red taffetas over the footlights shift to blue for moonlight. (Presentation of a moonlight scene had been a great novelty in the Stockholm production of P.A. Wolff's popular lyric drama *Preciosa* in 1824; in the second act in the gypsy camp, the audience had been startled, in the words of *Stockholms-Posten* (30 Oct. 1824) by a 'new and amazingly natural tableau of a moonlit night.') Provided with a blue scrim and a moon-rise machine in the Andersen production, the *maskinmester* thus elected to use them to present a picturesque effect of sunset, nightfall, and the rising moon. Later in the scene, during a revenge cavatina sung by Edgar, Bredal's dramatic music was further highlighted by thunder clouds, reminiscent of de Loutherbourg's Eidophusikon, which crossed and partially obscured the moon. During the final terzette Edgar-Lucie-Lord Ashton which closes the scene, the clouds were re-emphasized by thunder claps at the end of each chorus.

Hence the rich gothic atmosphere which pervaded a single scene such as this was highly dramatic and illusory. Aided by imaginative lighting and the uncommon diagonal placement of set-pieces, a convincing perspective view was presented to the audience, which saw a foreground of grass and rushes, beyond them a lake, on its far shore ruins and a rocky cave, and in the distant background the threatening sky and the rising moon. Such a scenic mood picture remained, however, an independent entity, in the sense that no stage director was present to co-ordinate and blend the separate elements of scenery, costuming, and acting into a conscious and harmonious whole.

The Royal Theatre inventory included a number of gothic settings originally designed for earlier productions but reused continually, in varying combinations and with occasional set-pieces added to disguise their appearance, whenever 'gothic' atmosphere was required. An inventory dated 1831 lists the following stock gothic interiors which were drawn upon for the productions of Andersen's early operas:

A gothic Knight's Hall in ten wings for Galeotti's ballet *Macbeth* (1816)
A gothic room with spiral pillars, in four wings, for Oehlenschläger's *Sons of the Forest* [*Skovens Sønner*, 1823]
A gothic hall in eight wings for Kuhlau and Boye's singspiel, *Hugo and Adelheid* (1827)
A chamber in gothic style, in eight wings, called 'Dyveke's Chamber,' for Samsøe's *Dyveke* (1796)
A chamber in gothic style, in six wings, called 'The Castellan's Chamber,' for *Dyveke*

Particularly the latter settings designed by Thomas Bruun for Samsøe's historical tragedy *Dyveke* (Figs. 15–16) played a prominent part in the productions of *The Festival at Kenilworth* and *The Bride of Lammermoor*, as they did in innumerable other pieces in the gothic vein far into the nineteenth century. The third scene of *Lammermoor*, for example, which is set in a barren hall with a crumbling fireplace suggesting the humble state to which the hero has fallen, was played in the first three wings and backdrop for 'Dyveke's Chamber.' It is obvious from Bruun's scene design in Fig. 15, however, that the elegant interior of Dyveke's chamber, even allowing for considerable wear since 1796, corresponded poorly to Andersen's description of a ruined hall in disrepair. The discrepancy was resolved, meanwhile, by an interesting but simple expedient: the grandiose background with its central doorway was concealed behind a new setpiece painted as a 'dilapidated fireplace with a practicable mantel and a painted mirror which is cracked.'[11] An appropriate note of disrepair was thus sounded by adding, with no basis in the text itself, the shattered mirror over the fireplace to symbolize the despair and misery of Edgar's position.

Although Edvard Lehmann's drawings from *Lammermoor* and *Kenilworth* tell us little about the stage settings in the scenes which they depict, his sketch of this particular scene (Fig. 4) does reveal something about the construction of the fireplace in question. The value of Lehmann's pictures

11 *Inventarii-Regnskab for Decorationer,*   (Royal Theatre library)
Meubler m.m. 1838–1843, p. 18

15 Design by Thomas Bruun for Samsøe's *Dyveke* (1796):
'Dyveke's Chamber.' Royal Library

16 Design by Thomas Bruun for *Dyveke*: 'Castellan's Chamber.' Theatre
Museum

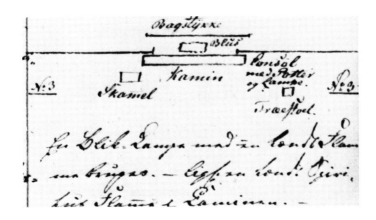

17 Ground plan, *The Bride of Lammermoor*, I, 3:
'a tin lamp with a lighted flame is used, also a lighted alcohol flame in the
fireplace.'

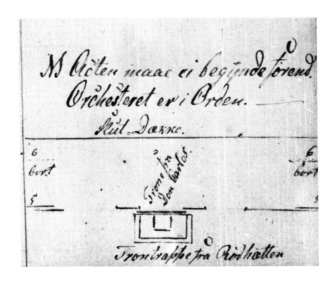

18 Ground plan, *The Festival at Kenilworth*, II, 1:
'NB The act must not begin before the orchestra is ready.'

as documentation is undermined, however, by numerous inaccuracies. In this case Fig. 4, depicting the actor C.M. Foersom explaining as the servant Caleb how all the kitchenware happened to get smashed at the bankrupt castle, shows the servant woman Mysie, left, in the improbable situation of standing with her back to the audience. In reality this character was not onstage for Caleb's song; nor did the little boy seen seated on the fireplace in the background appear at this time. As for the fireplace itself, its position in Lehmann's drawing is clearly contradicted by the ground plan for the scene (Fig. 17), which shows that it was placed to cover the centre door in the rear wall of 'Dyveke's Chamber.'

Both of the Thomas Bruun designs for *Dyveke* shown here reappeared in the last act of *The Festival at Kenilworth*. 'Dyveke's Chamber' in three wings with its corresponding backdrop and centre door saw service in a brief scene with Elizabeth, Leicester, and Burleigh in the Queen's chamber prior to the dramatic gallery finale, the climax in which a plot is launched to murder Amy by means of a hidden chain which can cause a threatening gothic gallery to collapse with its victim. The scene in the Queen's chamber, although omitted for some reason in Andersen's collected works,[12] contains both the dramatic motivation for the attitudes of Elizabeth and Leicester in the subsequent scene and a charming and melodious terzet by the composer Weyse. Queen Elizabeth is at first furious with Leicester for his deception and the arrival of his wife, but is reminded by Burleigh of her station, regains her self-control, and forgives her favourite. Its inclusion in the *maskinmester* journal and in a promptbook containing Andersen's own corrections[13] assures us that the scene was actually performed. It was staged with no alteration whatever of the *Dyveke* set; since it functioned as a carpenter scene prior to the change to the gallery, no furniture was used.

The absence of furniture and the fact that Elizabeth, Leicester, and Burleigh were alone on the stage refutes the assertion that Edvard Lehmann's sketch in Fig. 8 is an illustration of this scene.[14] In actual fact Lehmann's drawing depicts the first scene of Act II, set at the Queen's Castle in Greenwich, and it corresponds closely to the description in the *maskinmester* records. Elizabeth's throne was placed, as shown in the ground plan for the scene (Fig. 18), before the centre arch of Lund's backdrop

12 Andersen, *Samlede Skrifter*, XXXII, 123 ff

13 Det Kgl. Teaters Sufflørarkiv 883,

pp. 114–16 (Royal Library)

14 Put forth in Neiiendam's 'Omkring H.C. Andersens dramatik,' 332

for Bournonville's ballet *Waldemar* (Fig. 10). One of the finest examples of Lund's art, this setting was characterized by its deep perspective illusion achieved by the effect of a long, light room running diagonally to the left beyond the cut drop. Like Bruun's *Dyveke* designs, Lund's *Waldemar* enjoyed a long life on the Danish stage: an engraving from the 1866 revival of Bournonville's ballet clearly reveals Lund's gothic hall still in use in the background, and the theatre's inventory album of miniature sketches (*Fortegnelse over Tepper*, 267) prepared in the 1870s also catalogues the setting, whose paint and canvas had, after some forty years of use, become by this time 'dull and dry.' Erected against Lund's impressive backdrop in Andersen's *Kenilworth*, Elizabeth's throne (likewise borrowed from the stockroom) was draped with red velvet and decorated with gold braid and ornaments. The platform on which it stood was covered with a blue carpet with gold braid; the royal seat itself was an antique white armchair with gilded ornamentation and blue upholstery. In Lehmann's drawing of this scene (Fig. 8), Leicester and Sussex are standing before the throne of the Queen, while their retainers – sixteen members of the chorus, according to the *Regieprotokol* – are seen in the background. Leicester is presumably speaking his line: '*(bowing deeply)* My heart remains more open to Your Highness! / I owe Your Highness all, my life and my position.' The sword in Elizabeth's hand seems to be the artist's invention.

Similar instances of the use of stock gothic settings recurred frequently. It would be erroneous to assume, moreover, that these standard wing-and-backdrop sets disappeared with the advent of gas lighting in 1857. On the contrary, they continued to see service, either disguised by new set-pieces or else repainted so as to suggest satisfactory local colour. Hence the *Dyveke* settings went on functioning in productions not strictly in the gothic category but merely requiring 'old-fashioned' halls or chambers. This was the case in Andersen's *Dreams of the King* in 1844; indeed as late as 1864 we encounter 'Anna Møenstrup's Chamber,' the only *Dyveke* design which is not preserved, in use to represent a large, old-fashioned banquet hall with rococo furniture in the first act of *He is not well-born*. In 1873, only six years before the world premiere of Ibsen's *A Doll's House* at the Royal Theatre, all of the traditional gothic interiors named above – including the venerable *Dyveke* sets, which by then had already celebrated their diamond jubilee – were still to be found in the Royal Theatre inventory of active décors.

Just as in the Walter Scott adaptations, the staging of *The Raven*, Andersen and Hartmann's singspiel adaptation of Gozzi's *fiabe*, *Il corvo*, also utilized stock gothic décors for interior scenes. Thus, the Italian designer Cyprian Pelli's royal hall, used in 1786 for Lessing's *Emilia Galotti*, reappeared half a century later in the second act of *The Raven* as Millo's royal palace. Similarly, Wallich's gothic hall for Oehlenschläger's *Sons of the Forest* was joined to a backdrop from Hérold's *Zampa, ou La fiancée de marbre* to provide the décor for the third-act scene in which Jennaro rescues his brother from the vampires, only to find himself transformed to 'le frère de marbre.' The most interesting scenic element in *The Raven*, however, is its gothic-romantic presentation of exterior localities, where most of the opera takes place. One example of a typical gothic landscape with ruins and moonlight has already been provided by *The Bride of Lammermoor*. Two more indispensable elements in the nineteenth-century outdoor milieu were the cave and the storm-tossed sea, both of which played a prominent part in *The Raven*.

The natural cave or grotto populated with spirits, fairies, nymphs, will-o'-the-wisps, and other preternatural creatures of romanticism was a favourite and traditional ingredient of gothicism, just as the artificial man-made cave or underground dungeon, offering possibilities of prisons, secret tribunals, sacrificial altars, and bloody deeds, also exercised a wide appeal. The first scene of *The Raven* takes place in the former type of deep mountain cave. Opening with Hartmann's impressive chorus *allegro con fuoco* in F major depicting the busy activity of the gnomes, sylphs, elemental spirits, salamanders, and other preternatural beings in the service of the mighty magician Norando, the scene engaged no fewer than fifty-five supernumeraries from the chorus and ballet personnel.[15] The arrangement of this large natural cave is a highly effective instance of this type of décor, and was accomplished through the adroit combination of a series of borrowed drops and cliff wings. As the ground plan reproduced in Fig. 19 illustrates, a total of four drops were hung to convey the desired illusion of great depth. The backcloth for the setting was the standard 'desert drop.' Between the fifth and sixth wings a cut drop from Galeotti's popular comic 'magical pantomime' *The Washerwomen and the Tinker / Vadskepigerne og Kjedelflikkeren*, representing a comparable enchanted cave, was placed. In the two openings in this cut drop stood two alcohol lamps burning with red flame, presumably to heighten the suggestion of

15 *Regieprotokol 24. April 1828*, p. 149 (Royal Theatre library)

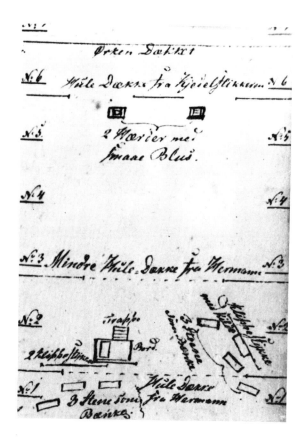

19 Ground plan, *The Raven*, I, I:
'All lamps are in the red taffetas, footlights up full in red taffetas.'

20 Drawing by Andersen of the opening scene of *The Raven*,
from the sketch-book of Otto Zinck. H.C. Andersen Museum, Odense

an underworld atmosphere created by the hellish brood of sprites and gnomes gyrating in the red glow of the wing lamps and footlights. Two additional cave drops were hung much farther downstage, both borrowed from A.P. Skjöldebrand's drama *Herman von Unna*, which in 1800 became the first real pièce à spectacle on the Danish stage.[16] Both cave drops had originally been designed for the sensational, blood-chilling highpoint of Skjöldebrand's mediaeval melodrama, a 'secret tribunal' in the fourth act in which its author's knowledge of free masonry and secret orders brought the whole symbolic machinery of glittering daggers and clanking chains, burning torches and blazing altars, robed figures, oaths, and initiative rites into play. Little wonder, then, that the scenery for this gothic ritual continually reappeared in the caves of gothicism and romanticism.

The furniture of Norando's cave in *The Raven* consisted of six stone benches from *Herman von Unna* arranged on the forestage in a kind of semicircle around Norando. Stage left was a three-dimensional cliff piece with a practical waterfall in which the water nymphs might cavort. Two high cliff pieces were erected at the entrance to the cave stage centre, behind which stairs and an elevated platform were concealed to provide the seat upon which the wizard Norando was enthroned at the beginning of the first act.

Andersen was understandably delighted with the bold and picturesque effects achieved in the staging of *The Raven*, and an enthusiastic sketch which he drew in the childhood album of actor Otto Zinck (Fig. 20) provides a delightfully vivid impression of the cave scene.[17] As Deramo rushes in to tell the wizard the dreadful news of the abduction of his daughter, the entire stage picture just described looms up behind the outraged Norando. The deep, murky cave filled with preternatural beings in motley costumes dancing in the red glow of the inferno formed a dramatic, atmospheric background emphasizing Norando's magical power to work the wonders he does in the course of the opera.

The next exterior scene in *The Raven*, which takes place in a harbour a short distance from the palace of Prince Millo of Frattombrosa, illustrates the use of a storm-tossed sea. A large boat with Pantalone, Jennaro's retainer, and a group of sailors carrying a tent appear from the left,

16 Overskou, *Den danske Skueplads*, III, 748
17 The sketchbook is in the H. C. Andersen Museum in Odense. Cf Zinck, *Fra mit Studenter- og Teater-liv*, pp. 26–8

between the seventh and eighth wings in Fig. 21 (marked *Baad*); Pantalone and some of the crew disembark, and the boat is then drawn across the stage and out of sight. The landing takes place during a violent storm, vividly expressed both in Hartmann's score, which is distinguished for its depictions of the sea, and in the staging, which supplied thunder, lightning, a clouded horizon, and a storm-tossed ocean.

The technique of presenting waves in motion on the stage is venerable and was familiar already in the Renaissance. The practice enjoyed wide popularity at the Danish Royal Theatre during the eighteenth century, particularly in the numerous, often identical scenes of shipwreck which often occurred in ballet.[18] For Ewald's *The Fishermen / Fiskerne*, where a shipwreck is the dramatic highpoint of the play, stage manager Christoffer Nielsen constructed in 1780 a new 'movable sea' so convincing and effective in operation that its designer was presented with a medal of honour. The popularity of such devices remained unabated in the nineteenth century. One senses Andersen's fascination upon witnessing the scenic legerdemain of a typical *féerie* at the Théâtre de Porte St Martin in Paris: 'We saw a piece which in its staging surpassed anything I have seen; first a primaeval forest appeared, then a wondrous oriental churchyard, and then the open sea in a storm, the waves seemed to rush out upon us!'[19] Led backstage by Alexandre Dumas, who assured him that the chorus girls 'were in their short petticoats by now,' Andersen saw, among other delights, the sea machine for this production, Cogniard's *Mille et une nuits*, at close range.[20]

Such a sea machine, which because of its demanding nature was usually employed only when absolutely necessary at the Royal Theatre, consisted of a number of rollers placed across the stage to represent waves (marked *Bølge* in the ground plan in Fig. 21). By rotating these rollers at different speeds the sea could be shown in all its phases, from gentle rocking to storm-lashed waves. In addition the theatre also possessed a storm horizon on rollers painted with dark clouds, some of which were transparent. In *The Raven* this storm horizon was hung at the rear wall and was rolled so that the portion with clouds was visible. Two-thirds of the stage lighting was also covered with these transparent clouds. Canvas

18 Cf Krogh and Kragh-Jacobsen, *Den kongelige danske Ballet*, p. 135

19 Topsøe-Jensen, *Brevveksling med Jonas Collin d. Ældre*, I, 198–9. Andersen's diary for 9 March 1843 also describes this production.

20 *Mit Livs Eventyr*, I, 277

breakers concealing the roller mechanism (marked *Dynning*) were placed across the stage in front of the horizon and at the eighth wing position. This background picture of a stormy harbour was framed by a low balustrade across the stage at wing seven, decorated with lions and divided in the middle by a platform and two steps. The remainder of the stage, which was flanked by palm wings, was an open playing area where the sailors could pitch a tent as shelter for the kidnapped princess Armilla.

Following the sailors' chorus the thunder and lightning abate, the sea subsides, and the storm clouds roll back on the movable horizon. A calm is created in which Jennaro and Armilla, who arrive in a gondola from stage left, can sing their first duet without interference from the elements. The function of the curved grass bank placed downstage left in the ground plan is obviously that of the place where Jennaro may sink into a reverie following his cavatina, 'Why can I not express / The thought within my happy heart.' His contemplation is rudely interrupted by the appearance of three mermaids who prophesy the dreadful fate in store for his brother Millo at the hands of Norando and his own peril if he seeks to interfere. The mermaids make their appearance through three small upstage traps behind the first row of breakers, labelled *Lem* in Fig. 21. In the second act, when the mermaids return to remind Jennaro of the curse after he has unsuccessfully tried to save his brother from the mistake of marrying Armilla, a similar technique is repeated. This time the mermaids come up through the large central trap and stand in the positions marked *x* in Fig. 22. A row of movable waves on rollers erected in front of this trap together with canvas breakers and a horizon drop in the background sounded the proper nautical note. The middle section of the backdrop from Pelli's gothic hall could simply be hoisted at the proper moment, when Jennaro has been left alone in his despair, to reveal the prophetic mermaids in the rolling waves. The area between the castle drop and the horizon was brilliantly illuminated to allow the audience to see them clearly.

By now it is apparent that the scenic components in *The Raven* represented a strange mixture of gothic and exotic styles – a mixture which became a major object of criticism when the opera was revived in 1865. Side by side with Pelli's gothic hall one finds the balustrade decorated with lions and the gondola in the harbour scene, both of which would seem to suggest Venice; the balcony of Millo's palace seen at the beginning of the second act was a new drop expressly designed in *Moorish* style.

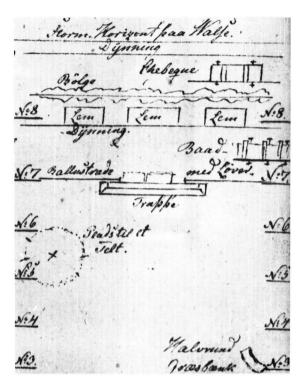

21 Ground plan, *The Raven*, 1, 2: 'during the chorus the red taffetas are slowly lowered from the footlights and it becomes light. Occasional thunder and flashes of lightning.'

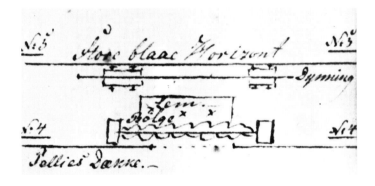

22 *The Raven*, II, 2: 'strong illumination between both drops.'

The final tableau, which features a fairy castle conjured out of the air by Norando in the twinkling of an eye for the union of Armilla and Millo, introduced yet another stylistic element: atop a large staircase taken from August Klingemann's Mexican drama *Ferdinand Cortez* stood a Grecian temple with Ionic columns outlined against a background of rose bushes. Palm wings flanked the setting, and *réverbères* (lanterns with reflectors) and calcium lighting added a further touch of exotic theatricality. 'The final scene was lit with Greek fire which had a superb effect,' wrote Andersen enthusiastically to a correspondent, oblivious of the nonchalant mixture of Venetian, Moorish, Grecian, and other elements which characterized the production.[21]

The scenic conventions of gothic staging lie at the very roots of romanticism in the theatre, and their influence on Andersen's work as a playwright is clear. Typical romantic-gothic landscapes, such as those in *The Raven* or *The Bride of Lammermoor*, favoured picturesque scenes of ancient ruins and enchanted springs bathed in moonlight or cloaked in shadow, storm-tossed seas, or mountain crags and deep caves inhabited by nymphs, trolls, and other creatures of the vivid romantic fancy. Interior scenes depended upon mediaeval walled fortresses with moats and drawbridges, vaulted dungeons in sombre colours, or the borrowed architectural elegance of eighteenth-century gothic designs for the proper atmosphere. It was to the last vestiges of this once vigorous tradition that Zola scornfully referred when he sought, in his celebrated Preface to *Thérèse Raquin* in 1873, to sweep away 'the decayed scaffoldings of the drama of yesterday ... the mediaeval scrap-iron, the secret doors, the poisoned wines, and all the rest.'[22]

EXOTIC

The importance of the picture in the romantic theatre and especially the strong popular interest in local colour, geography, and ethnographic detail gave rise to a second important scenic style in the nineteenth century, the depiction of far-off, exotic places on the stage. A comparable interest in folk scenes and ethnographic studies is reflected in contemporary travel books such as Andersen's *A Poet's Bazaar / En Digters Bazar* (1842) and enlivens the many drawings made by Andersen on his travels, depicting such objects as whirling dervishes, a Mohammedan girl,

21 *Anderseniana*, IX–XIII (1941-6), 52
22 Quoted in John Gassner and Ralph

Allen, *Theatre and Drama in the Making* (Boston 1964), p. 556

23 Design by C.F. Christensen for Halévy's *La juive* (1838).
Inventory description: 'German town with church towers, surrounded by a
wall. Light, bright colouring.' Royal Theatre library

24 Design by C.F. Christensen for a tropical rain forest. Royal Theatre library

Turkish graves at Istanbul, an Athenian street, Pompeii, and the temples of Paestum. More or less simultaneously with the appearance of Walter Scott romanticism at the Danish Royal Theatre, a parallel movement toward a geographical, rather than historical, depiction of folk life and mores arose. A Swedish review of the 1828 production of *La muette de Portici* at the Paris Opéra provides a taste of the atmospheric, picturesque milieu which the Scandinavian theatre was anxious to emulate: 'There are no décors, no views of certain cities, no groups of persons clad in Neapolitan costumes; one is *in* Naples, visits its loveliest spots, witnesses its folk festivals, hears its national songs, sees its happy folk dances, the lazzi of Pulcinella, and so on.'[23]

Three of Andersen's plays from the 1840s, the romantic dramas *The Mulatto* and *The Moorish Girl* and his libretto for *The Wedding at Lake Como*, are direct products of this wave of exoticism, which quite naturally on the Scandinavian stage frequently favoured southern European milieu depictions. Hence southern Spain between Cordova and Granada provides the setting for *The Moorish Girl*, the action of *The Wedding at Lake Como* is set in an Italian village in that district, while *The Mulatto* takes place on Martinique.

A poem written to Andersen by the actor Wilhelm Holst, who played the title role in *The Mulatto*, immediately following the reading rehearsal of the play is an enthusiastic summation of the kind of exotic milieu that the drama sought to convey:

> *I heard – and yet I seem to hear it still,*
> *Strange sounds of clanking as though I stood*
> *Where gentle breezes through the lofty palms*
> *Can lift but a corner of the broad leaf.*
> *I seem to see the jungle's fertile nature,*
> *And the fields of straw burnt by the sun;*
> *I seem to see the parrot nesting there,*
> *And here the rabbit, behind the sugar cane.*
> *I seem to see the hut with the black brothers*
> *Who lie in rags – but close the door again!*
> *I seem to hear the clatter of the mill,*
> *The keeper's whiplash and the sigh of slaves.*[24]

23 *Heimdall* (Stockholm), 21 May 1828   24 *Portefeuillen for 1840*, I, 145; reprinted in *Mit Livs Eventyr*, I, 221-2

A similar preoccupation with the play's exotic milieu flavours Andersen's own correspondence. 'Human passions are the main character,' he wrote to C. Høegh-Guldberg, 'and all of the tropical nature with its snakes and flowers twines around it.'[25] Shortly after starting work on *The Mulatto* he wrote to Henriette Hanck describing the principal settings he visualized: a log house, the jungle, a garden house, a manor, and a slave market. 'The tropical sun which burns in my breast illuminates the whole picture with all the exotic plants, slender palms, and flowers of the imagination,' he added somewhat later.[26]

However, the transition from mere ethnographic accessories and exotic details of the imagination to a convincing and stylistically co-ordinated milieu picture on the stage remained difficult so long as designer, stage manager, and ballet master were independent and decentralized authorities functioning without a stage director. Occasionally this system led to rather disturbing stylistic inconsistencies, particularly in the exotic genre.

The production of *The Mulatto* was nevertheless an excellent example of highly complex staging successfully employed to convey exotic illusion. Although Andersen states that new settings were to have been designed for the first and second acts,[27] no new wings or drops were actually painted for the production. However, a large number of new set-pieces were built which added to the illusion of West Indian plantation life. The character of these pieces is reflected in Andersen's recollection of the day of the opening, which had been postponed because of the death of King Frederik VI: 'I was up at dawn and watched from my windows as the grips carried the new palm trees, Paléme's hut, Eleonore's bed, and the market stalls into the theatre.'[28]

The setting for the opening scene, depicting Horatio's home in the forest, was particularly convincing. The dramatist's stage directions call for a large room resembling a gallery and containing dried plants, wild animal skins and skeletons, stuffed birds, a large book collection, and two portraits, all of which were calculated to suggest the hero's breeding, sympathetic background, and intellectual interest in natural history and philosophy. In addition, the stage directions indicate a bedroom in the background concealed by drapes and two candles burning in large glass containers. A one-page preliminary outline of the staging of *The Mulatto*, evidently drafted prior to the final *maskinmester* protocol, suggests that

25 Collin, *H.C. Andersen*, pp. 111–12
26 *Anderseniana*, IX–XIII, 241–2, 337
27 *Ibid.*, 375
28 *Ibid.*, 403

this entire setting might be borrowed from Scribe and Auber's oriental opera, *Le cheval de bronze*, provided the original Chinese accessories were masked by the portraits, animal hides, and bookcases just mentioned.[29] In its final form, however, the set was constructed from the French décor for Mélesville's *La berline de l'émigré*, which had the added advantage of containing a large drawing of the Palais Luxembourg appropriate for Horatio's reminiscences of Paris. Nonetheless, the same technique of masking any distinguishing French traits in the borrowed set with appropriate tropical set-pieces was generally followed.

The floor plan for Horatio's house in the midst of the tropical rain forest is reproduced in Fig. 25. Two flats painted as glass cases, one containing animal skeletons and the other stuffed birds, stand on either side of the background door. On the wall to one side of the door, two bows, two arrow sheaths, two lances, and other hunting equipment are hung; the opposite side is draped with animal hides, described in a costume list for the play as 'one cat skin' and 'one bear skin.' Behind the background door, which was hung with white curtains, an Indian hammock was arranged into which Cecilie retired at the end of the act. Two bookcases along the right wall served to conceal two small doors in the original décor from *La berline de l'émigré*. On either side of the door in the left wall a cloth painted to resemble green wooden blinds masked the original door and window and suggested a tropical atmosphere.

The convincing illusion of this setting was heightened not only by means of the evocative collection of exotic objects, but also to a large extent by the appearance of a closed, walled room which this arrangement of flats and set-pieces conveyed. The result was hardly a box set in the modern sense, however, since the furniture continued to be painted on flats and loose overhead borders were still necessary so long as oil lighting was employed. In this respect Danish theatre lagged somewhat behind the general course of development elsewhere. In spite of Bournonville's having introduced the box set to Denmark in 1829, its use had remained limited. In France and Germany, however, experiments with a closed room had begun, in line with Diderot's theories, toward the end of the eighteenth century. By the 1820s the box set was in common use in Paris and Berlin; the London and New York productions of Dion

29 Det Kgl. Teaters Arkiv, Rigsarkivet, under 'N. Diverse, 13.' Although a pencil notation reads 'written by H.C. Andersen,' the document is unfortunately not from Andersen's hand.

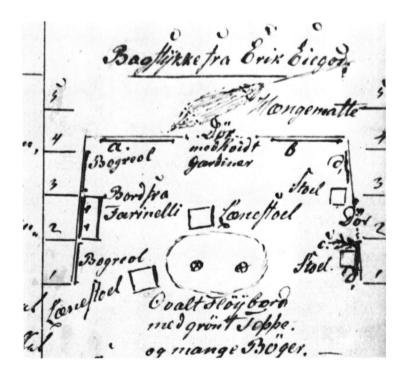

25 Ground plan, *The Mulatto*, 1: 'a cabinet with painted skeletons, b cabinet with painted birds, c a branch or plant painted on cardboard, dd two pieces with cloth painted as green wooden blinds, ++ two male portraits above the table right, ⊗⊗ two footed glass spheres with lighted yellow candles. Oval drop-leaf table with green baize and many books.'

6 Ground plan, *The Mulatto*, ii, using a desert backdrop similar to Fig. 27.
a large high palm tree with very large leaves, *bb* two set-pieces as treetops,
ccc three palm bushes.'

27 Desert backdrop by C.F. Christensen for C. Hauch's *A Desert Tale* (1855).
Royal Theatre library

Boucicault's *London Assurance* in 1841 brought the set with three complete walls and realistic furnishings to England and the United States as well.[30] Nevertheless, the *Mulatto* setting does represent a technical advance, emphasizing more elaborate and picturesque background constructions in conjunction with the barest minimum of loose side wings. Despite this new approach, however, the action continued to be held downstage as much as possible, and was played in front of, rather than within, the atmospheric background. Hence the ground plan indicates an oval table, on which books and two candles were placed, downstage centre and somewhat outside the frame of the décor. Beside this table stand two oriental armchairs, borrowed from *Le cheval de bronze*, in which Eleonore and Cecilie could comfortably play their long, expository scene together.

The reviewer for *Portefeuillen for 1840* criticized the fact that no new settings had been designed by Christensen, comparable to his previous designs (Figs. 23 and 11) for *La juive* (1838) and *Festival in Albano* (1839), to convey the specific tropical milieu which Andersen described in his play. Particularly the second act of *The Mulatto*, which takes place in a tropical jungle where Cecilie and Eleonore stumble upon the hut of the run-away slave Paléme, was deficient in this respect:

The dramatist conveys us to a 'wild tropical forest region'; we say the *dramatist* because nothing in the setting indicates that the scene takes place in surroundings which cause Cecilie to exclaim involuntarily: 'Oh, what an arch woven of bananas ...' etc. What a wonderful project it would have been for our talented scene designer Christensen to depict such a tropical region on our stage, where we have not since he designed the setting for *Festival in Albano* had the pleasure of seeing new samples of his fine talent. The playwright poured such atmosphere and richness into this act, however, that one soon forgot the inferior scenic production.[31]

The arrangement of the ground plan for this act (Fig. 26) suggests interesting staging possibilities, despite the lack of tropical atmosphere in the décor. At the back hung the 'desert drop,' comparable to Fig. 27, and the side wings were a haphazard mixture of stock cliff and forest wings. The chief 'atmospheric' elements therefore included three palm trees, three palm bushes, a flowering bush, and a prominent new piece repre-

30 Bergman, *Regi och Spelstil*, pp. 26–7;   *Theatre*, p. 140
    Nicoll, *History of English Drama*, IV, 38;   31 *Portefeuillen for 1840*, I, 161
    Hughes, *A History of the American*

senting 'a large poison tree with a loose branch' which Paléme lops off in the opening scene. The preliminary staging outline already referred to remarked: 'All the palms and other tropical plants that the Theatre possesses must be utilized to make the whole picture as lush as possible.' A winding path in the cliff was represented by means of a complex arrangement of platforms covered with green carpet, running high across the back, descending along the stage right side, extending across the front, and disappearing again upstage into a large trap. With this elevated, three-dimensional background occupying the greater portion of the stage, the action around Paléme's hut was clearly relegated to the far foreground on a relatively small strip of playing area. Although the stage may be said to have been effectively arranged in terms of space and perspective, however, the scene picture itself suggested only very vaguely and abstractly the exotic, tropic atmosphere which animates *The Mulatto*, relying largely on the reuse of stock materials rather than the creation of an original ethnographic milieu.

The fourth act of Andersen's most successful play featured the transition from Horatio's imprisonment in a gloomy dungeon to a glittering ball scene. 'By letting us hear the distant music in the prison,' observed the enthusiastic reviewer for *Fædrelandet* (16 Feb. 1840), 'and by suddenly conveying us at the conclusion of the act from the dark prison to a brilliant ballroom, which like a fireworks display rises up out of the dark night and just as suddenly disappears, Andersen achieves a gripping contrast.' Horatio's dank prison, 'a vaulted stone chamber in the Sugar Mill,' appeared as shown in the ground plan in Fig. 28. On a very dark forestage, where details of the setting were barely distinguishable, a walled arch resembling the upper part of a sewer and reaching six inches over the floor was placed across the stage, directly over the forward trap which was open but concealed by a pile of loose stones. Horatio's cot stood stage right. The front wings – the only ones visible on the darkened stage – were from the Egyptian vault for *Die Zauberflöte*. Contrasting with the gloom of the dungeon, gay dance music from the ballroom was heard in the distance – played by an orchestra in the greenroom.

The entrance of Paléme, the renegade slave who tries to rescue Horatio, was appropriately theatrical: carrying two knives the fugitive appeared dramatically in the low sewer opening and then crawled forth, thrusting aside loose stones and gravel as he spoke.

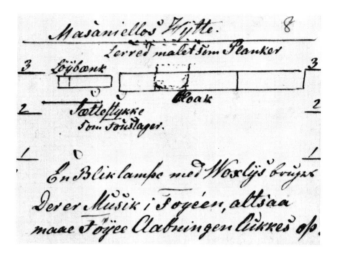

28 Ground plan, *The Mulatto*, IV, 6: 'dark in wings and drapes,
half dark in the footlights with gray taffetas. A tin lamp with candle is used
Music in the greenroom, hence the greenroom-door must be open.'

29 Ground plan, *The Mulatto*, IV, 9: 'full illumination;
a six candelabra with lighted white candles in glass spheres. 13 white lacquere
stools.'

PALÉME: (*raises his head*) Are you asleep, mulatto!
HORATIO: What? Paléme!
PALÉME: You long for freedom? I bring it with me!

Following Horatio's noble rejection of Paléme's escape plan and the departure of the latter through the sewer, the ballroom suddenly 'rose up out of the dark night,' brightly illuminated by the customary light sources supplemented by six candle holders, each bearing a glass globe containing six lighted candles and marked *a* in the ground plan in Fig. 29. This quick scene change, which according to *Dagen* (4 Feb. 1840) was 'striking in the highest degree and aroused much admiration by everyone,' was accomplished by means of the venerable but effective technique of a front 'carpenter' scene in the prison followed by the deep scene farther upstage. The candle-holders and a semicircle of thirteen white stools in the ballroom had been positioned beforehand behind the backdrop; the single set of candle-holders which overlapped the prison scene, between the third and fourth wings on the ground plan, was pushed out on to the stage on a groove chariot at the proper moment.

Conventionally decorated with lighted lamps, flags, and open colonnade drops, this ball scene represented an indispensable fourth-act tradition in romantic drama. Yet its effectiveness was increased immeasurably by two theatrical devices: the *coup* of the sudden shift from the gloomy Sugar Mill dungeon, and Andersen's innovation of counterpointing and interweaving the loud dance music and the dialogue of the scene. The latter was achieved, according to *Dagen*'s critic, 'in a hitherto unfamiliar but thoroughly tasteful manner, which will certainly win even greater applause in subsequent performances when the audience has become accustomed to the novelty.'

It was, however, the climactic finale of *The Mulatto*, a slave market in which the hero is placed on the auction block as a Negro, which, Andersen wryly asserted, was the exotic touch that persuaded theatre manager Frederik v. Holstein to accept the play. 'A slave market, I don't think we've had that yet!' the business-minded aristocrat supposedly exclaimed. 'I'll be perfectly honest with you. That slave market appeals to me!'[32] In presenting this new attraction on the Royal Theatre stage, atmospheric set-pieces were strategically deployed. At the far back of the stage the 'horizon drop' was hung, the nineteenth-century equivalent of the cyclorama. Placed in front of this drop was a standard set-piece depicting a 'still' sea (as opposed to the rotating waves on rollers); a groundrow at the eighth wing completed the perspective. Three newly designed set-pieces 'painted as market stalls on Martinique' were distributed as indicated in the ground plan in Fig. 30; the two stalls farthest upstage were obviously smaller in order to create an illusion of depth. Tropical vegetation was supplied by the palm trees and bushes used earlier in the play. A number of new palm pieces had been painted for the production of *The Mulatto*, including a 'very high palm tree' and two set-pieces representing palm bushes, but these could then be reused in countless 'exotic' productions to follow, including Andersen's own play *The Moorish Girl*.

In front of this broad and deep perspective background of palm trees, market stalls, and the open sea, within which no one played because of the reduced size of the perspective, the picturesque action of the slave auction was enacted. A bamboo table covered with record books and writing materials and two straw stools for the auctioneer and the extra who played his clerk stood downstage left. On an unpainted barrel beside this table stood a Negro slave being offered for sale. To satisfy Andersen's stage directions calling for 'a milling picture of life in a tropical climate,' an impressive array of supernumeraries, including ten soldiers and an officer, ten sailors and an officer, twenty Negro slaves, six planters, twenty women as Negresses and planters' wives, and twelve children, were grouped around the action.

However, despite the individual efforts of the dramatist, the designer, the stage manager, and the ballet master who choreographed such an arrangement, the lack of a unifying hand is evident in the stylistic inconsistencies which marked an otherwise effective stage picture. Thus while the background scenery and the colourful folk groupings suggested a tropical plantation milieu, the first and third wings stage right, borrowed from Scribe and Auber's *Le Dieu et la bayadère*, depicted *Indian* buildings, whereas the second and fourth wings on the *same* side, borrowed from the same two artists' *La muette de Portici*, represented a piazza in Naples. All such scenery, regardless of which part of the world it was intended to suggest, was broadly classified in the inventory as 'exotic.'

One of the most versatile décors in this category at the Danish Royal Theatre was Christensen's immensely popular design for Bournonville's ballet *Festival in Albano*, a setting which turned up in countless exotic productions including *The Mulatto*, *The Moorish Girl*, and *The Wedding at*

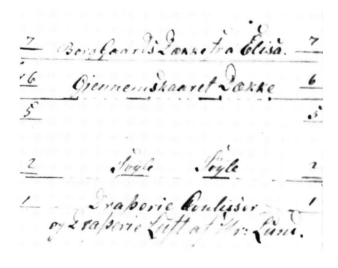

30 Ground plan, *The Mulatto*, v, 8

31 Ground plan, *The Moorish Girl*, iii, 1:
'Drapery wings and drapery border by [Troels] Lund.'

Lake Como. In the opening scene of Andersen's *Moorish Girl*, depicting a Spanish camp in the wild, mountainous region between Cordova and Granada, the panorama for Christensen's *Albano* décor, with its green vegetation, high blue sky, and view of the gray Campagna with Rome in the distance, formed the background. The wings represented an unlocalized, stock 'cliff' setting, and several non-practical tent flats placed at various angles filled out the background. The guitar players, the two dice players, and the man kneeling with his rosary with whom Andersen populated this folk-scene were grouped in the foreground around a lighted transparency representing a watch fire and a 'number tree' (the latter was a perspective flat with a large number on the back corresponding to the wing number at which it stood, the smallest at the back of the stage; there was a series for each kind of tree.) Although the background of canvas tents and Christensen's drop (Fig. 11) conveyed a certain vaguely 'exotic' flavour in the dim gray stage lighting, obviously no effort was made on the theatre's part to suggest a specific ethnographic milieu in southern Spain.

Andersen was bitterly disappointed with the inferior production of his play: 'the stage arrangement was enough to kill everything, poor, tasteless, and distracting,' he recorded.[33] It was particularly a short but crucial scene in the Alhambra in the third act which he found 'completely clumsy and ridiculous, which the public naturally blamed on the author.' The Royal Theatre archives (specifically Series B) bear out this opinion. Intended as a scene in the Alhambra, in a hall rich with pillars and ornate galleries, the actual setting displayed a stiff and haphazard combination of borrowings, arranged in a highly unimaginative floor pattern (Fig. 31). The first wing and border represented red drapery painted on flats by Lund (the so-called *manteau d'Arlequin* used to reduce the proscenium opening); behind this hung a new cut drop 'painted as a gate with two loose columns which stand stage centre.' The remainder of the open, rather barren stage exhibited 'oriental' wings and Wallich's 'kitchen or chimney drop' taken, like many other components in *The Moorish Girl*, from Oehlenschläger's exotic fantasy *The Fisherman and his Children | Fiskeren og hans Børn*.

The theatre's apparent indifference to geographical realism in *The Moorish Girl* and its utilization of inappropriately borrowed stock sets should not be ascribed to mere technical naïvety. One possible difficulty

33 *Ibid.,* 236

may have been the large number of scene changes, twelve in all, which *Corsaren* (1 Jan. 1841) whimsically alleged was 'a new, happy parody of the rage for scene changes dominating many plays.' More damaging, however, was Johanne Luise Heiberg's refusal of the role of Raphaella, the 'Moorish' girl. This influential actress's ridicule of the play before anyone who cared to listen had its inevitable effect on the zeal with which it was produced at the Royal Theatre, and her absence from the cast left the tragedy at the mercy of its own built-in bathos. The reception accorded the heroine's climactic suicide is suggested by the remarks in *Berlingske Søndagsblad* (27 Dec. 1840): 'She climbs up on the railing of the well from the first act [an octagonal structure filled with functional pillows and cushions], scratches out a few words to the King with an arrow, and then leaps into the abyss, with no regard whatsoever for the damage which the decomposition of a corpse will do to the nice, clear water.'

In a more positive vein, one of the best co-ordinated examples of exoticism on the Danish stage is to be found in the production of Andersen's operetta, *The Wedding at Lake Como*, which takes place on the outskirts of a village in northern Italy. The author's remarkably explicit stage directions provide a veritable mise-en-scène, on the basis of which Bournonville created a highly successful and much admired stage arrangement. Typically pastoral-exotic elements of the palmy couleur locale popular in romantic ballet and opera permeate both the theme – the complications attending the Arcadian wedding of Lucia and Ranzo – the village setting of *Wedding at Lake Como*.

The ground plan seen in Fig. 32 follows Andersen's own disposition of the stage in this complex unit setting closely. The same illustration sketches the magical tree with its traditional Madonna picture, upon which the village girls hang their love charms – 'a large plane-tree trunk' decorated with 'one wreath with red flowers, two wreaths without flowers, two silver hearts of wood each hung in a red ribbon, and two hearts of tin pierced by an arrow, likewise of tin and hung in a red ribbon.' Around this ethnographic and highly significant property, placed downstage centre, the remainder of the scenery was grouped. Illusion was heightened by means of an interesting technique: side wings were replaced by an essentially closed set with a filled atmospheric background of set-pieces. A number of newly designed pieces of scenery were combined with appropriate borrowings from H.P. Holst's Neapolitan drama *Gioacchino* and from Bournonville's ballets *Festival in Albano* and *Toreador*.

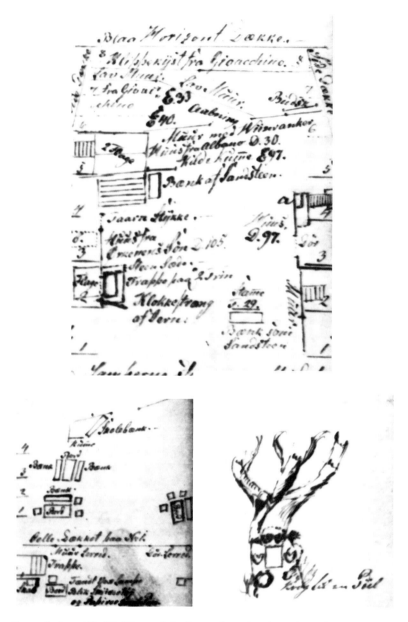

32 Ground plan, *The Wedding at Lake Como. above* plan for unit setting;
below left changes for the third act; *below right* sketch of a new set-piece
depicting a large plane-tree; the text reads: 'Hook for an arrow.'

In front of the standard horizon drop and its side pieces – the equivalent of the unlocalized cyclorama – a perspective background was built up of walls placed at various angles to form an alley (called *aabning* in the ground plan), from which the three bandits could appear when they surprise the priest Abondio and threaten his life if he weds the lovers. The wall across the stage presented a colourful facade overgrown with grape vines. Although two long flats placed at the eighth wing position represented the high Neapolitan coast, cleverly masked as they were by the other pieces they undoubtedly gave a perfect impression of the shores of Lake Como.

Most of the loose side wings were removed, and the left side of the stage was closed in by new set-pieces painted as a wall and as Agnese's house, a rustic building in southern character with practical door and balcony above.' The latter construction, actually only a new facade for a house from an earlier play, included a high platform and stairs behind the balcony, upon which Agnese appears in the third act to summon help by lighting a signal torch. The right side of the stage in this carefully arranged ground plan completed the village square. The two principal buildings were similarly practical, with concealed stairs and upper levels; upstage stood an Italian inn, downstage the cleric Abondio's house. The latter building was equipped with two steps and a practical window in which Abondio's housekeeper Perpetua appears in the third act when Tonio and Gervasius ring to rouse the priest. Outside the inn an atmospheric stone basin with a spring was placed beside a sandstone bench.

The widely travelled H.C. Andersen's detailed stage directions for *The Wedding at Lake Como* were closely adhered to by the theatre in evolving a vivid Italian milieu for this opera. The unit set was designed to remain standing throughout. In the second act a long table with place settings, a school bench, and two brown chairs were (typical of general nineteenth-century stage practice) carried in to accommodate the villain Roderigo and his henchmen. For the third act the square was turned into a festive outdoor café, with chairs and tables placed outdoors for the bandits and for Renzo and his guests. For a short scene in the same act inside Abondio's house, a 'cell drop' was simply lowered at the second wing and the action was played on the forestage.

A series of lighting changes, not suggested in Andersen's stage directions, contributed richly to the atmosphere of the final act. Beginning in evening red, it became slowly dark after the bandits left their table, with the footlights 'in gray taffetas.' Towards the end, when extras appear carrying torches in response to the sounding of the alarm bell, the gray taffetas are first lowered and then raised again when the glow of the torches disappears. At last, following a climactic duel between hero and villain, wing and border lamps are slowly raised in red taffetas because, as the *maskinmester* recorded, 'the play ends in the glow of early dawn.'

HISTORICAL ROMANCE

A third distinct group of Andersen's productions, embracing some of his most characteristic themes and taking for their backgrounds nationalistic or idyllic settings, represents a scenic style in nineteenth-century Scandinavian theatre which may be placed under the broad heading of historical romance. Plays dealing with subjects of Danish history had, of course, been popular already in the eighteenth century and were often linked to 'gothic' scenery. However, the performances of Andersen's historical romances in the 1840s at the Royal Theatre reflect a new popular interest in picturesque details of history or folklore and in national personages, landscapes, and prints, parallel to the interest in exotic places and surroundings.[34] To satisfy this thirst the theatre became a kind of historical picture-book. The popular desire for historical detail was met either by new stage décors which reflected a certain degree of historical realism, or else by more effective and selective borrowings from older sets.

Obviously no very radical changes in established staging techniques occurred at this time. Hence in the first production of Andersen and Hartmann's *Little Kirsten*, the most celebrated example of Danish romantic opera, the idyllic mediaeval setting for Kirsten and Sverkel's poetic romance was presented on the stage in a patently conventional manner. This conventionality was epitomized by the attitudes of reviewers; 'the scenic production contained nothing particularly disturbing,' noted *Fædrelandet* (23 May 1846) and 'the scenic arrangement as a whole leaves nothing to be desired,' echoed *Kjøbenhavnsposten* (25 May). The second scene in the castle hall presented a familiarly symmetrical arrangement of candle-holders, white stools, and gothic chairs combined with 'King Skiold's Hall' in five wings from the prologue to J.L. Heiberg's national Danish drama *Elves' Hill / Elverhøj*. Although the opening scene in the

---

34 See Bergman, *Dramaten 175 År*, pp. 48 ff on the introduction in Sweden of such national-romanticism with Böttiger's *Ett nationaldivertissement* in 1843.

33 Ground plan, *Little Kirsten*, I, I: 'all lamps are in the light red taffetas and red taffetas raised slightly in the footlights.'

34 Sketch of the first scene in *Little Kirsten* in a production about 1881. Royal Theatre Music Archives score copy

castle yard was also staged simply, as the ground plan in Fig. 33 testifies, some effort was nevertheless made to localize the action. The scenery was selected from among the charming and appropriate settings painted by Troels Lund and C.F. Christensen in 1843 for Bournonville's national-historical ballet *The Youth of Erik Menved*. A cut drop placed at the fifth wing was Christensen's castle yard from this ballet, with an open gate through which the backcloth with 'a painted view of Skanderborg Castle and Lake' could be seen. An impression of this castle yard is gained from the later sketch shown in Fig. 34.

While the background offered a view of a localized Danish landscape in Jutland, however, the remainder of the stage was arranged conventionally with a combination of stock forest and castle yard wings. A projecting balcony, the bower described in the folksongs on this theme, where Kirsten sits while Etie braids her hair in preparation for entering the convent, was placed as far downstage as possible because of the opening duet which is sung there. It consisted of a simple platform onto which one long, narrow flat and four smaller ones, painted for this opera to represent 'the bay or covered balcony of an ancient castle,' were fastened. The original scenic framework for Andersen's most beloved and most performed opera was thus an abstractly simple one, flavoured however with a specific touch of mediaeval Danish landscape provided by Christensen's pictorial backdrops. Later stage plans indicate that a remarkably similar pattern persisted in subsequent nineteenth-century revivals of the work.

Frequently, however, the historical romance was distinguished by entirely new décors painted to enhance illusion. Thus, although no other records exist for the ill-fated *Agnete and the Merman*, the 1838–43 inventory list does indicate that new scenery was painted to portray the mediaeval Danish-mythological background of the play, including 'a backdrop painted as a limestone cave with figures.' Two of the best examples of more effective staging in this genre are Andersen's two 'dream' plays, *Dreams of the King* and *The Blossom of Happiness*, in each of which the central character is conveyed in his imagination to two dream situations. *Dreams of the King*, which depicts King Christjern II's dreams of his mistress Dyveke during his imprisonment, is strictly historical in its subject matter. *The Blossom of Happiness* is a fairy-tale fantasy in the manner of Raimund in which a forester is magically transported to two 'historical' situations. In terms of staging styles, however, both plays belong in the broad category of historical romance.

It is interesting that in each case the main setting, in which the action begins and from which the dreams develop, consisted of new scenery designed for that production, while the dream sequences were played in partially borrowed décors. In addition, *Dreams of the King* demanded a complex and unusual technique of 'dissolving,' with the aid of Henrik Rung's background music, from reality to dream. The result was an integrated, artistic, and highly atmospheric scenic arrangement, supervised according to Andersen by J.L. Heiberg.[35] The clear-sightedness and theatrical acumen of Heiberg's analysis of the play speak for themselves. The technique of drawing the dreams into reality of the action, he writes in a review in his journal *Intelligensblade*, 'was already evident in the ground plan, which with all its faults nevertheless demonstrates how the prison foreground, with the alcove in which the King sleeps, the fireplace where Benth lies, and the marble table, is drawn into the dream and becomes part of the settings in which it appears. For this reason also, the characters in the dream step forward into the proscenium so that the dream quite sheds its frame and blends with immediate reality, not only for the King but for the spectators who ... assume entirely the same viewpoint as he.'[36] Despite difficulties in scene changing discussed at the beginning of this chapter, an effective stage picture, as Heiberg's comments suggest, aided the production of *Dreams of the King*. Rich source material makes it possible to reconstruct this picture in considerable detail.

The Spartan arrangement of the King's prison in Sønderborg Castle is clearly indicated in Andersen's stage directions, which call for a small vaulted chamber with a niche on each side, one of which forms a fireplace and the other an alcove covered with curtains in which the King sleeps. The door is walled up and the only means of entrance is through an opening in the ceiling by means of a ladder. Stage centre stands the traditional round stone table around which the restless monarch walked unceasingly, the original of which, with a groove worn into the surface by the pacing King's thumb, may still be seen at Sønderborg.

Both the *Regieprotokol* and the ground plan (Fig. 35) followed Andersen's directions closely. The set for the prison consisted entirely of new scenery. Both the fireplace stage right and the alcove left were large set-pieces, furnished with mattresses on which Benth and King Christjern could lie;

35 *Mit Livs Eventyr*, I, 324   36 *Intelligensblade* (1 March 1844), XLVII–XLVIII, 237

35 Ground plan, *Dreams of the King*: Sønderborg Castle. '*aaa* mattresses,
bb wedge mattresses, *c* green divided curtain. A tin lamp with lighted candle.
Dark in drapes and wings, half dark in the footlights with gray taffetas.'

the King's alcove was covered by a green curtain. These set-pieces were arranged behind the first wing on either side, which represented red drapery, to suggest a closed room. The background of this short set consisted of a cut drop painted as a stone arch, above which hung a large border representing a stone vault with a practical opening. Behind the stone arch a wall with stone pillars was seen, consisting of two flats stretching across the stage to form a shutter. The round stone table stood close to the backdrop stage centre.

In what could be called 'flashback' scenes, during which the King first dreams of his meeting with Dyveke and then of her poisoning, the round table was effectively incorporated into the dream sequences (cf Figs. 35–7). As Heiberg observed, the stage was arranged so that the foreground was drawn into the dream, the actors came downstage and the dream stepped out of its frame and blended with reality. For the flashbacks, Rung's dramatic music was heard, the stage darkened, and the back shutter representing a wall opened to reveal the dream scene *through* the stone prison arch. This procedure was simpler than the almost cinematic one envisioned by Andersen, in which the stage was to be 'veiled in mists which little by little become transparent.' Notwithstanding the complaint of the critic for *Fædrelandet* (17 Feb. 1844) who felt that the changes should have taken place 'as if by a magic wand,' it was intentional that they happened slowly to emphasize the dream-like atmosphere. 'When the music begins, complete blackout and in the dark change slowly the large border above, and both flats are drawn slowly to the side,' were the instructions in the *maskinmester* journal. Hence it was basically the venerable and useful technique of a back shutter opening to 'discover' a scene behind that formed the basis for the staging of this play. The critic for *Berlingske Tidende* (15 Feb.) vigorously opposed this technique, objecting to 'the visible division of the entire background into several sharply divided pieces.'

The first 'discovery' revealed a large, old room in Madame Sigbrith's house in Bergen, where the King met Dyveke. Through the stone arch in Christjern's prison a Norwegian farmhouse in three wings and a backdrop appeared, borrowed from an Oehlenschläger tragedy. It is obvious that the floor plan (Fig. 36) sought to create the effect of a closed room by covering the side wings with two practical doors, a cabinet containing pitchers, goblets, and a platter, and a window where Mother Sigbrith can stand and describe the mob outside. Brown wooden chairs with

cushions for Dyveke, Walkendorf, Prince Christjern, and Mother Sigbrith were grouped in a semicircle around the table from the prison, a
good indication that much of the scene was played upstage, in contrast
to the earlier tradition of forestage acting. The second dream is particularly interesting in terms of staging:

> *In Copenhagen was built a wondrous house,*
> *Of stone with high gables and balconies,*
> *And here he set his little turtledove.*

In staging the 'wondrous house' built for the King's mistress and described
here by Benth, the servant, the *maskinmester* appropriately turned again
to the familiar settings from Samsøe's *Dyveke*. Through the stone arch
Thomas Bruun's design, the 'Queen's Chamber' in three wings and a
backdrop, appeared. The imaginative selection of a traditional décor
which Royal Theatre audiences would readily be expected to associate
with the character of Dyveke is significant. As the floor plan in Fig. 37
indicates, the backdrop was arranged in the customary way with backings
behind each of the two practical doors and 'brilliant gothic chairs' flank-
ing them on either side. A window with a protruding bay, on which Sigbrith could lean for her taunting line, 'There stands a whole flock! The
high council / At Mother Sigbrith's door! Well let them wait,' was a
new addition to Bruun's design. The round stone table from the prison
was again drawn into the action as in the previous dream.

Following the second dream the music blends into a morning hymn
from outside, a long ladder is thrust down through the opening in the
border over the stone arch drop, and a knight descends from the flies into
the prison. This is King Christian III in disguise, who brings greater freedom to the imprisoned monarch – the distinction in spelling is maintained
by Andersen and suggests the transition from the mediaeval absolution
of Christjern to the new impulses of the Reformation and the Renaissance.
Three lamps were placed on the high scaffolding which was rolled in
behind the open border, apparently to create an impression of daylight
streaming in from above, and a 'tower room' flat backed the opening.
Critics are not always easy to please, however, and *Fædrelandet* (17 Feb.)
objected that it would have been better to sacrifice the historical accuracy
of placing the entrance to the prison in the ceiling, on the grounds that
it was offensive to public decorum to witness King Christian III crawling

36 Ground plan, *Dreams of the King*, first scene change

37 Ground plan, *Dreams of the King*, second scene change

down a ladder! Historical realism was, however, an aesthetic goal of this kind of play. Andersen's principal source of historical background information was in all probability his own notes gathered for an uncompleted novel about Christjern II, based on the research and writings of historian Vedel Simonsen.[37] But while the atmospheric new scenery, combined with selective borrowing from traditional décors, lent the production a certain historical colouring, it should be obvious that such 'colouring' cannot be equated with absolute historical accuracy or realism.

The Blossom of Happiness, a dramatized fairy-tale typical of the most generally familiar side of Andersen's authorship and exemplifying the Casino productions as well, combined dream transitions and historical personages in a very different spirit. The aim in this case was to demonstrate that 'it is not the artist's immortal name, not the glory of a royal crown, that makes man happy. Happiness is found where a man, satisfied with little, loves and is loved in return. The scene is typically Danish, an idyllic life of sunshine, upon the sky of which is cast, as in a dream, two dark pictures – the unhappy life of [the Danish poet Johannes] Ewald and the tragic fate of Prince Buris in the folksongs.'[38]

This chapter began with a discussion of the reviews of *Blossom* in *Berlinske Tidende* and *Dansk Album*, which agreed that while the scenery itself was quite convincing, particularly the 'perfectly executed and magically lighted décor' in the second act, the scene changes were ragged, slow, and 'unpoetic.' Three specifically Danish localities are indicated in Andersen's fantasy: Jægersborg Deer Park, the game preserve outside Copenhagen; Rungsted, the home of Ewald on the Sound; and the mediaeval castle of Waldemar. Despite this specificity, however, we find that in the Royal Theatre production the stock forest wings and borders remained unchanged throughout. Similarly, standard and unlocalized backdrops served in all three sets: 'Christensen's woodland drop' in the first set, the stock horizon drop and side pieces in the second, and a light forest drop in the third. Obviously, then, it was not these stock wings and drops which won praise from the critics for creating illusion.

On the contrary, the new staging technique at this time emphasized filled-out backgrounds and three-dimensional set-pieces, rather than side wings and borders, in the creation of the desired atmospheric illusion. Regarding this de-emphasis of the side wings, the influential Swedish

37 See Harald Hatt in *Anderseniana*, VIII   38 *Mit Livs Eventyr*, I, 321
  (1940), 31–3

theatre personality Gustaf Lagerbjelke asserted that they were 'the least functional element in the arrangement and co-ordination of the stage picture' and were furthermore 'the least important for the audience, since *everyone* sees the background but only a few see *every* wing.'[39] In this he echoes J.B. Pujoulx's criticism of the wing system in France at the turn of the century. In a chapter entitled 'Illusion théâtrale, Décorations,' Pujoulx supports the box set, deplores, as Strindberg did nearly a century later in his Preface to *Miss Julie*, the unnatural quality of light from below, and rejects the use of wing sets which can be seen in correct perspective from only one point in the auditorium: 'C'est ainsi qu'une décoration, bien conçue dans son point de vue, n'offre plus que des lignes sans ordre, des corniches qui se confondent, des entablements sans correspondance, enfin, une architecture grotesque, semblable à celle qui résulterait d'un déplacement général dans toutes les parties d'un salon.'[40] The de-emphasis of wings and the introduction of a kind of 'set' scenery had occurred in England as early as the Kemble era. In the gothic chapel erected by William Capon for the opening of Drury Lane in March 1794, *Thespian Magazine* noted that 'the *wings* to the side scenes [were] removed for a complete screen ... thereby perfecting the deception of the scene.'[41] Another Capon church designed for Joanna Baillie's *De Montfort* at Drury Lane in 1800 was called by Percy Fitzgerald 'one of the earliest specimens of "set" scenery.'[42] This development toward three-dimensional 'practicables,' architectural and natural, reaches its culmination in England in the work of Charles Kean and his scenic artists in the fifties.[43] In a somewhat more primitive fashion, perhaps, the ground plans for *Blossom of Happiness* are clearly examples within the Danish theatre of the same growing emphasis on free-standing set-pieces at this time. These plans should also help to dispel the erroneous notion of Ibsen as a single-handed reformer who 'overcame the false perspective' of flat wings in the Scandinavian theatre and 'introduced three-dimensional scenery with walls and solid properties.'[44]

The familiar stock forest wings, drops, and borders used throughout

39 Bergman, *Regi och Spelstil*, p. 242
40 Pujoulx, *Paris à la fin du* xviiie *siècle*, p. 130
41 *Thespian Magazine* (March 1794); see also Odell, *Shakespeare from Betterton to Irving*, ii, 91
42 Fitzgerald, *The Kembles*, ii, 19

43 See Muriel St. Clare Byrne, 'Charles Kean and the Meininger Myth,' *Theatre Research*, vi (1964), 149–50; cf Laver, *Drama*, pp. 200–10
44 Tennant, *Ibsen's Dramatic Technique*, pp. 60n, 64, 66, *et passim*.

Blossom of Happiness can, moreover, be said to have functioned simply as a stylized framework within which atmospheric set-pieces were manoeuvered, a conventional framework to which the audience no doubt paid as little attention as modern audiences devote to the familiar black drapes or flats of a current 'stylized' production. If this is true, the nineteenth-century theatregoer merely accepted and 'looked past' the conventional forest décor to concentrate on particular set-pieces forming the core of the scenic picture and giving it its specific charm or atmospheric character.

Thus in the set for Henrik's first transformation to Johannes Ewald, which takes place in Rungsted, the five pieces placed at various perspective angles in Fig. 40 localized the action. In the background within the horizon enclosure, a new set-piece 'painted as the sea and with a distant view of the island of Hveen above' specified the locality. A farmhouse flat, a set-piece painted as a wood pile, and a three-dimensional grass bank added pastoral flavour to the scene. The key piece in the constellation was, however, 'Ewald's Hill,' a new piece representing the actual knoll overgrown with brush and bushes which is still to be seen in Rungsted.

The opening scene, depicting the forester's Arcadian residence in Jægersborg Deer Park, combined a similar group of set-pieces: sunflowers, bushes, a cradle, and especially a charming rustic cottage with a practical door and an opening in the roof where the play's mischievous elf first appears (Figs. 38 and 39). However, the setting which earned the greatest applause was unquestionably the mediaeval castle of Waldemar in the second act. As evident in the ground plan (Fig. 41) the most prominent aspect of this set was the castle itself, which stretched horizontally across the entire width of the stage and consisted of a large three-dimensional construction of wooden platforms masked by a facade of flats. This facade, beginning stage right, displayed transparent windows above and open windows below through which the spectator saw a busy kitchen 'in which the cooks are hard at work with casseroles etc.' On a level with the transparent windows above, a castle drawbridge with an iron railing extended over to a bridgehead stage right which was masked by two flats representing a wall. A groundrow painted as a wall ran under the bridge. Steps led up to this construction from both sides, and it naturally heightened the effect to see the characters and the processions moving on several levels. Stage left, at right angles to the imposing castle structure, stood the 'sinister tower' where Prince Buris was imprisoned.

Several other aspects of the mise-en-scène underscored the illusion

38 Ground plan, *The Blossom of Happiness*, I, I: 'all lamps are in the red taffetas, footlights up in red taffetas.'

39 Design by C.F. Christensen for a Danish peasant cottage, comparable to the set-piece placed downstage left in Fig. 38. Royal Theatre library

40 Ground plan, *The Blossom of Happiness*, I, 2:
Henrik's transformation to the poet Ewald

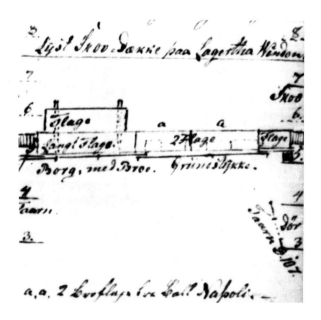

41 Ground plan, *The Blossom of Happiness*, II, 2:
Henrik's transformation to Prince Buris

created by this picturesque castle background. Henrik Rung's dramatic music was especially effective; 'particularly all the numbers in the second dream gave a very beautiful impression of mediaeval spirit and tone,' remarked *Dansk Album* (23 Feb. 1845). In addition, the lighting of this scene cast a magic, dream-like atmosphere over the décor. Andersen, with his customary eye for scenic effect, placed the entire second act in moonlight, and blue lamps and foots shed the properly enchanted 'gothic' hue on Waldemar's castle. Against this romantic, dream-like background Waldemar's legendary dance (cf Fig. 10), a colourful procession of twelve couples led by six torch bearers, moved across the drawbridge, out on to the stage, and then disappeared again, providing an effective highpoint in the visual display.

The difficulties involved in shifting a set consisting of many set-pieces evoked much adverse comment. Although the settings for *Blossom* conveyed sufficient illusion in themselves, particularly when viewed in the dim stage lighting, the *a vista* scene changes which accompanied Henrik's transformations were unequal to the poetic demands of the play. Rapid, *visible* changes were naturally the very core of the appeal of a fairy-tale comedy like *Blossom of Happiness*, the whole charm of which relied on exciting visual transformations. The changing of scenes was meant to be seen and transformations were part of the spectacle. The stage manager's notes also confirm the fact that *a vista* changes were used throughout, accompanied, when the mischievous elf crushed his magic pearl to start the process, by 'a terrible crash and underground roar.' Andersen's concept of enveloping the stage in mist and darkness during the changes was, however, not realized.

Changing of the background was necessarily handled in practice by means of the conventional alternation of shallow and deep scenes. Thus the forest backdrop in the opening scene of Andersen's fantasy was hung between the fourth and fifth wings, allowing the three-dimensional castle in the Prince Buris scene and the horizon background in the Ewald transformation to be brought into position beforehand, and then revealed simply by hoisting the drop at the proper moment. However, downstage set-pieces presented a different kind of problem. The majority were flown with the help of the high overhead grid, and the remark, 'Signal only the flies,' recurs continually in the stage manager's journals.[45] In the first

45 The statement by Tennant (*ibid.*, p. 6on) that the Royal Theatre possessed no fly gallery at this time is simply misinformed.

42 Design by C.F. Christensen for a comedy setting, described in the *Tepper* inventory as 'little Holberg street, old-fashioned.' The design is an accurate copy of an old engraving of Amagertorv in Copenhagen

scene, moreover, both a dock-leaf bush in which the elf hides and a bench outside the forester's house were mounted on wheels, so they could be pulled offstage. The child's cradle, in contrast, was carried offstage into the cottage by Henrik and his wife. The large grass bank on which Ewald casts himself in his misery was hidden during the opening scene behind a bush. Nevertheless the obvious difficulty involved in shifting the multitude of set-pieces grew in step with the continual growth of built sets and three-dimensional constructions, leading eventually to the passing of the visible scene change and the lowering of the curtain instead.

COMIC

It was usually for opera, ballet or pantomime, and the more complex romantic dramas that new settings were created and involved staging techniques employed in the nineteenth century. The lighter comic genre, however, was most frequently mounted in standard décors or in surroundings previously created for opera or drama. The staging of Andersen's comedies and vaudevilles reflects an unmistakable relationship with the traditions and conventions of the eighteenth century, particularly in the presentation in the topical vaudevilles of local scenes which the audience delighted in recognizing from daily life. From the earliest days of the perspective stage the delight in local scenes had been exploited in theatrical décor.

In Andersen's first vaudeville, *Love on St Nicholas Tower*, the scenic picture of Copenhagen was augmented by a picturesque new backdrop 'painted as a view of Nicholas Tower seen from the corner of Viingaardsstræde and Holmensgade,' a novelty which *Dagen* (28 April 1829) informs us 'was greeted with applause.' This view of a specific streetcorner appeared in the second scene of the play, where it served as the backdrop for four rows of the theatre's stock 'street wings.' An interesting descendant of this backcloth is Christensen's design for a 'Holberg street' (Fig. 42), an offspring of the taste for historical realism, depicting Nicholas Tower from Amagertorv and reproducing in almost every detail an old engraving by Jacob Brun from 1756. The street décor in Andersen's vaudeville was further supplemented by two practical houses borrowed from Hertz's comedy of Copenhagen, *Moving Day*, and placed, as customary in such a comedy setting, far downstage at either side of the action.

The flavour of eighteenth-century conventions permeated other aspects

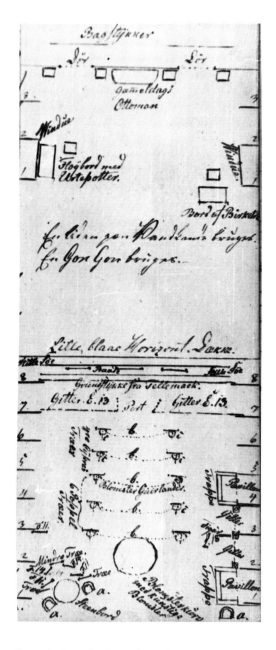

43 Ground plans, *Parting and Meeting*, parts one and two

44 Production plan, *When the Spaniards were here*

of the staging of *Love* as well. A strong link with older traditions is found in the lively dance scene at the Tailors' Inn, which was presented in one of the earliest of all the Royal Theatre's basic interiors, 'the simple cabinet' in three wings. Also known as 'Holberg's room,' this set was a stock Holberg comedy décor belonging to the small collection of interiors surviving from the previous century. In the Andersen vaudeville it appeared unaltered except for four gilded candle arms attached to the wings and a chest painted on the backcloth. One is reminded of Tate Wilkinson's felicitous remark about a stock setting in use at Covent Garden for half a century: he never saw those wings glide forth without the feeling of having 'unexpectedly met with a very old acquaintance.'[46]

In the vaudevilles of Andersen, Heiberg, and their contemporaries, these older traditions persisted; it was not until the close of the century that the naturalistic director William Bloch introduced a fresh approach that rescued the classical Holbergian comedy from the doldrums. In Andersen's time major parts of a vaudeville set, including touches of local life, were generally acquired from the older ballet and French singspiel repertoire. *Spaniards in Odense*, the first section of *Parting and Meeting*, was set in a room taken in its entirety from Devienne and Picard's operetta *Les visitandines* (1797). The floor plan in Fig. 43 follows, down to the positioning of the chairs and tables, the plan for the original set exactly, except that a barred window in the original convent background was masked in *Parting and Meeting* by a map and a candy-striped ottoman. Similar traditional patterns can be recognized in the scenic arrangement of other Andersen comedies. It is evident from the stage plan for his last play, *When the Spaniards were here* (Fig. 44), which reworked the theme of *Parting and Meeting*, that the staging underwent little substantial change in the thirty years that had elapsed since the original vaudeville. The interior of Madame Prip's manor in the first and second acts, a borrowed set with the standard arrangement of wings, backdrop, chairs placed against the wall, and a window between the first two wings, bears a striking resemblance to the earlier floor plan for *Parting and Meeting*. A drawing-room scene in the third act utilized Lund's décor known as 'Holberg's green drawing-room' (Fig. 45) – green walls were the tradi-

46 Wilkinson, *Memoirs of his own Life*, IV, 91. A century later, however, the Brandes brothers were far less patient in their caustic remarks about the

Royal Theatre's stock interiors: cf Marker, 'Negation in the Blond Kingdom,' p. 508

45 Rough sketch from the Royal Theatre *Tepper* inventory, showing
'green Holberg drawing-room painted by Lund.'

46 Lund's unusual rendering of the same 'green Holberg drawing-room':
actor Rudolph Waltz's shooting target in the Royal Copenhagen Gun Club.
The original, an oil painting on wood about two feet in diameter, depicts
a scene from Act 1 of Holberg's *Jean de France*

tional indication of lower-class milieu. This much-used comedy interior, preserved in the unique 'target' painting rendered by Troels Lund in 1845 on the occasion of actor Rudolph Waltz's membership in the redoubtable Royal Copenhagen Gun Club and Danish Brotherhood (Fig. 46),[47] was a direct lineal descendant of the older 'Holberg room' used in *Love on St Nicholas Tower*. The presentation of Miss Hagenau's living-room in the second act of *Spaniards* provides one further fact of interest. Although the interior itself was a common stock décor known as 'the violet room,' the backdrop glimpsed through the windows was no local view of Middelfart as might be expected, but none other than the same view of Nicholas Tower originally painted for *Love on St. Nicholas Tower*. The circle of H.C. Andersen's productions from 1829 to 1865 had come full swing!

The lasting success and frequent revivals of his most popular comedy, the Holberg imitation entitled *The New Maternity Ward*, makes the staging of the original production in 1845 particularly noteworthy. Andersen's description of the fraudulent dramatist Jespersen's drawing-room, in which the entire play takes place, calls for a conventional comedy interior. A door right leads to the hall, a door left to Jespersen's study, and in the rear wall is the entrance to the dining room. The classic drawing-room set (Fig. 47) utilized three pairs of wings and the backdrop from a stock décor known as the 'yellow grooved hall,' listed in the inventories as a modern interior in eight wings with grooved columns. The doors were placed according to the conventional pattern, on either side between the second and third wings. The stiff arrangement of chairs and tables along the rear wall is reminiscent of a host of other ground plans from this period. The frontal placement of the two ottomans and the round pedestal table in the floor plan thrust the action downstage to face the audience. The furnishings of the plagiarist's living room were pointedly smart and comically festive, comprising white painted tables and chairs with red seat covers. Through the centre door upstage the audience saw a long table surrounded by six leather chairs to accommodate the stream of 'well-wishers' who come to dine, and who flock out again at the end to drink a toast to the chastened Jespersen.

The arrangement of this setting undoubtedly afforded a satisfactory and appropriate framework, a gay salon in keeping with Andersen's gallery

47 Cf Anker, *Den danske teatermaleren Troels Lund*, pp. 73–83

of amusing character portraits and with the Holberg tradition which he imitated. The remarkable continuity of this traditional arrangement for *The New Maternity Ward* at the Royal Theatre is indicated, moreover, by a subsequent production plan which dates from around the fiftieth performance of the play in 1862. A 1903 production, in contrast, exemplifies the advent of richly detailed naturalism and the *Regieprotokol* lists a variety of new, realistic props that included a small piano, a book of music, a real sewing basket on the table, real ham on a platter, eleven glasses, and a (hopefully real) bottle of champagne.

Side by side with such conventionalized comedy drawing-rooms, outdoor settings were naturally important in the staging of comedy and vaudeville. For Andersen, however, the outdoor counterpart of the drawing-room interior was not the classical street setting but, typically enough, the garden. The gardens of his vaudevilles are, moreover, far removed from the stiffly clipped parks of classicism; here are to be found festoons of flowers, pear-trees, cabbage stalks, and washlines, combined with the dashes of local colour so much a part of this genre.

The garden setting for *25 Years After*, the second half of *Parting and Meeting*, is a characteristic instance (Fig. 43). Rosebuds, dandelions, and an array of other flowers that cause the visiting Spanish ambassador to exclaim his admiration created an appropriate atmosphere for this sentimental vaudeville. In addition to the floral element, the garden needed hidden silvan nooks where the overhearing that causes much of the ado in the action could take place. An alley of cypress and poplar, across which were hung festoons of flowers, decorated the centre axis of the stage and was terminated by a large, round container of flowers. Still more wreaths of flowers were brought in by a chorus of servants in a musical number which culminates in the *Lumpacivagabundus* parody. To the right of this colourful alley, 'number trees,' rose bushes, and creeping roses formed a 'leafy hut' containing a stone table and garden chairs, in which the characters later conceal themselves. Obviously in such a garden setting, however, the trees, bushes, flowerbeds, and flora remained as a rule painted canvas flats arranged in perspective.

The background for the bucolic scene in *Parting and Meeting* was meant to suggest the local flavour of Elsinore. The stage directions describe 'a gate and a view of the Sound and Kronborg,' and later in the act the traditional cannon salute for passing vessels is heard. While the staging afforded no such specific view, some impression of the Sound was created

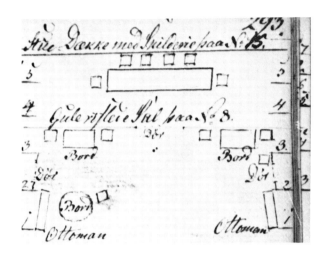

47 Ground plan, *The New Maternity Ward*

48 Ground plan, *The Bird in the Pear-Tree*

by means of a series of set-pieces placed in front of the horizon backdrop. Through a garden fence the spectator saw a groundrow from Galeotti's shipwreck ballet *Telemak on the Isle of Calypso* / *Telemak paa Calypsos Ø*, behind which stood three ships with tall masts and the so-called 'still sea' (ie, without wave rollers). Apparently the 'optical view of Kronborg' mentioned in an older inventory for 1763–4 was no longer usable.

A yard is the setting for two of Andersen's most delightful plays, *The Bird in the Pear-Tree* and *The Invisible Man*. In both these vaudevilles unit settings provided maximum opportunity for the arrangement of a fuller and more convincing stage picture composed of numerous set-pieces and properties. In the effective split set which Andersen envisioned for *Bird*, many of these set-pieces were of necessity new. Indeed, much of the effect of this 'dramatic jest' depends directly on the original setting, which depicted two neighbouring backyards divided by a board fence. The garden of Councillor Arents, stage right in the ground plan (Fig. 48), is distinguished by exotic plants and luxurious vegetation; the plan reveals the symmetrical arrangement of set-pieces painted as rose bushes and tubs (marked *Ballietræer*) containing orange trees and 'foreign plants' which were used to convey the proper impression. In marked contrast to this finery stood Captain Petersen's down-to-earth backyard on the other side of the fence. The most prominent objects at the rise of the curtain were a clothesline strung from the first wing to the fence and four wooden sticks downstage, on which white stockings were hung to dry. Cabbage leaves and stalks, over which the servants in this parody of warring households and star-cross'd lovers quarrel as they take in the wash, covered the forestage on both sides of the fence. Petersen's garden house, in which the lovers take shelter during a rain storm, was furnished with practical windows facing the audience, an octagonal writing table, a leather chair, and a sea-chart.

The two contrasting gardens, divided by a board fence, effectively characterized their owners' respective dispositions. The object which both dominated and united the stage, the point of dispute between Arents and the Captain, and the central plot device was the towering pear-tree 'richly hung with fruit' which stood in Captain Petersen's yard near the fence. This tree, like the board fence a new construction, consisted of a flat representing a large pear-tree trunk and a corresponding border that hung above it to form the crown. The downstage position of this tree, the garden chairs, and the garden house drew most of the action to the front of the stage. Obviously, however, special attention had to be paid to the trysts between Petersen's son Herman and his 'bird' which take place in the top of the pear-tree. 'Behind the trunk a little platform is placed corresponding in height to the board fence,' instructed the *maskinmester* plan:

On the platform itself is a step like a stool, see *e.* in the ground plan. At the upper end of the platform stands a large case on end, see *f.*, and behind the same a smaller case placed upright, see *g.* Beside the platform, but on the other side of the fence, stands a small step with the help of which Henriette can go from the platform, over the fence, and down into the garden stage right and back again in order to place herself in the tree.

This construction of steps and platforms was masked by bushes, and in the comparatively dim oil lighting the treetop rendezvous was doubtless a charming and credible scenic effect. On the whole the two contrasting gardens in *Bird,* representing vivid visual characterization and divided by the board fence running downstage to the prompter's box, created a functional and descriptive environment for Andersen's vaudeville intrigue.

In a similar way the island of Sprogø afforded a charming and piquant setting for *The Invisible Man,* which takes place, according to the *Regieprotokol,* 'outside the inn on Sprogø; the telegraph is seen right; the trees are covered with frost, the earth with snow, and the lake is completely frozen.' This play is remarkable for the fact that it was written specifically to fit a discarded décor designed for Henrik Hertz's unsuccessful *Flight to Sprogø.*[48] This setting, Andersen remarked in the Danish draft for *Das Märchen meines Lebens,* 'is excellently designed, but represents a specific place, a specific winter scene' and would hence 'be unusable for other plays.' It is impossible to determine what alterations were made in the décor to accommodate Andersen's play, however, since no theatre records have survived for *Flight to Sprogø.*

The ground plan for *The Invisible Man* (Fig. 49) reveals, behind a proscenium of red drapes, a large building left with practical stairs and a door and a barn right which enclose the stage to form the yard where the action takes place. A trough and a barrel downstage right are 'covered with snow,' and 'snowballs of cotton wool lie here and there.' The upstage end of the yard was closed off by a red fence and a gate stretching across the stage at the fourth wing, behind which a filled background

49 Ground plan, *The Invisible Man*; the backdrop was the heath décor in Fig. 50

50 Rough sketch from *Tepper* inventory of the backdrop for Christensen's heath décor in *Waldemar*: 'Grathe Heath, large cloudy sky-piece.' Series B adds that the same backcloth was used in *The Bird in the Pear-Tree*. The extra section, right, was added to make the drop suitable for the wider stage of the new Royal Theatre

depicted an atmospheric winter landscape with splashes of local colour. The background was a heath, and the upstage wings and backcloth were borrowed from the brilliant décor, Grathe Heath, designed by Christensen for Bournonville's ballet *Waldemar* four years earlier (Fig. 50). Christensen's backdrop was rendered more suitable, however, by concealing the heather on the original cloth with three groundrows eight inches high and painted as ice. The resulting impression of a wintery landscape was continued in a descending cliff path masked by a snowy set-piece, and in the floor-cloth 'painted as snow' and covering the floor down to the fence – but no further 'on account of the dance' which was performed in the yard. Contemporaneity was added to the background in the form of a high flat representing a telegraph pole, replacing the fifth wing left in the heath décor. This localized, wintery perspective view constituted the realization on the painted stage of Andersen's vision of snow-bound Sprogø, where the characters in his vaudeville farce are stranded.

The styles of staging which are so graphically represented in the productions of Andersen's plays – gothic, exotic, historical, and comic – represent popular tastes as well as modes or choices of expression directly related to the artistic intentions of the playwright in the nineteenth century. Andersen's painstaking and highly practical stage directions often constitute a physical mise-en-scène which, in the absence of a director in the modern sense, served as a guide for mounting the production. Although his plays exemplify several different stylistic tendencies running side by side and sometimes intermingling, one common emphasis characterizes them all: the emphasis upon the stage picture. The evocation of a picturesque scenic mood, expressed in piquant locales viewed in the flickering glow of the dim stage lighting, is an objective which was pre-eminent in the *Kunstwollen* of Andersen and his contemporaries. Often the desired picture was a montage, comprising a strange mixture of newly designed elements combined with stock items plucked from a wide variety of older productions. However, new techniques and developments – closed sets, realistic details, greater consistency of style, and increasingly deeper and more three-dimensional backgrounds – were also emerging within the limits of the traditional wing-and-border system, as a result of efforts to portray more effectively on the painted stage the vaulted dungeons and moonlit landscapes, slave markets and storm-tossed seas, Italian village squares and neighbouring backyards of the romantic theatre.

FOUR

Costuming

THE COSTUMING AND MOVEMENTS of the actor on the romantic stage contributed in large measure to its predominantly pictorial quality. An impressive quantity of untreated source material, in the form of sketches and hand-written costume lists preserved in the archives of the Royal Theatre, illuminates the wide subject of costuming on the Danish stage during the prenaturalistic period.[1] Most of the salient features and important stylistic tendencies in the theatrical costuming of this period are exemplified in the numerous productions of Andersen's plays at the theatre on Kongens Nytorv.

The lighter genre requires little detailed attention regarding costume, however, since comedy and vaudeville at this time were usually performed in contemporary clothing. In return for a stipulated payment, the actors themselves frequently provided their own garments as costumes. Two costume lists which have survived intact for Andersen's vaudevilles, for *Bird in the Pear-Tree* and *Love on St Nicholas Tower*, both illustrate the principle that contemporary garments were used for this type of play. For this same reason specific costume descriptions are not generally pro-

[1] The written sources contained in the Royal Theatre library, from which all information presented in this chapter is drawn and to which repeated references would serve no useful purpose, are of three main kinds: Individual, unbound costume lists, usually called *Paaklædningsregulativer* Wardrobe inventories: *Garderobeinven-* *tarium 1825, Systematisk Fortegnelse over Det Kgl. Theaters Garderobe 1830–4*, and *Continuation til Det Kgl. Theaters Garderobe Inventarium*, 1 June 1845–31 May 1846; 1 June 1846–31 May 1847 Tailor protocols and records of new acquisitions: *Protokol over Skrædderarbejde 1835–45, 1845–74; Protokol over Garderobe Anskaffelser 1833–5, 1835–6*.

vided in the stage directions of these vaudevilles. Moreover, the use of ordinary street clothing corresponded nicely to the topical tone so vital to the vaudeville genre. Hence, for example, the costume list drawn up by J.C. Ryge for *Love on St Nicholas Tower* prescribes contemporary domestic clothing for most of the characters. The town watchmen wore 'real watchmen costumes' complete with the familiar morning-stars and whistles. Maren, the confidante in this mock tragedy, appeared in a realistic folk costume, partly borrowed from an eighteenth-century Galeotti ballet and partly made for the occasion. To exaggerate the farcical element in this parody, the two 'neighbouring knights,' Ole and Peer Hansen (the suitor), both wore 'old-fashioned' bourgeois costumes. Ole was dressed in an out-moded brown coat, motley vest, black breeches, and Herman von Bremen's cap from Holberg's classic comedy *The Political Tinker*. Peer's 'knightly' costume consisted of an old-fashioned round hat, dark blue coat, motley vest, gray breeches, and peasant boots. By contrast, however, the heroine Ellen's costume was typically contemporary – a plain white cambric dress, plaid apron, white stockings, and black shoes – and free from farcical elements. Apparently no effort was made in the costuming of *Love* to imitate the theatrical device originally used in J.H. Wessel's *Love without Stockings / Kjærlighed uden Strømper*, the parody upon which Andersen's play was directly modelled, of beginning the farce in ordinary domestic clothes and changing gradually to heroic tragedy attire as the mock suspense mounted.[2]

For the lighter genre, then, various combinations of domestic, contemporary costumes usually served the purpose. The scarcity in the Royal Theatre archives of complete costume lists for Andersen's comedies and vaudevilles bears out this assumption. It was rather upon opera and romantic drama that the greatest care and attention was lavished during this period, both in the realm of costuming and of staging. Hence it is not surprising to encounter costume lists intact and executed in great detail for nearly all of Andersen's operas, as well as for such romantic dramas as *Dreams of the King*, *The Mulatto*, and *The Moorish Girl*.

In addition to the costume lists themselves, the Royal Theatre wardrobe inventories and tailor protocols shed light on historical and exotic costuming styles in nineteenth-century plays and operas. Occasionally,

2 Discussed in Krogh, *Danske Teaterbilleder*, pp. 204–6.

these bound journals describe costumes not otherwise included in a play's own costume list. In general, these inventories testify eloquently to the fact that the widespread romantic preoccupation with the depiction of distant, exotic lands and historical epochs on the stage had also reached the foremost theatre in Scandinavia. It is significant that inventories from this period are divided into a large number of very specific ethnographic and historical categories, which are again subdivided to indicate the social status of the character in question. For example, 'Asiatic' costumes included Israelitic, Arabic or Turkish, Persian, Indian, Chinese, Tartan, and Gypsy groups, which were in turn broken down into noble, courtier, warrior, civil servant, and peasant dress. There were similar classifications for 'African' – including Egyptian, Negro, and Moorish – and 'American' costumes. These distinctions can be taken as clear evidence of the increasing romantic interest in picturesque, ethnographic detail. These theoretical distinctions were of course not always so precise in practice; 'Eastern' costumes, for instance, were frequently similar to one another and were used interchangeably.

A marked historical interest is evident in the classification of 'European' costumes. Here, there were two principal nuances to distinguish noble and civilian costumes: 'from the eighteenth century' and 'from older times.' Military uniforms were grouped either as modern, seventeenth- and eighteenth-century, or 'from older times.' In addition to these categories, there were also headings for middle-class, peasant, 'character,' clerical, and servant dress, as well as Greek-Roman-mythological costumes. The general desire, indicated by these classifications, to present at least some suggestion of historical period in the costuming was a factor bearing directly on the production of Andersen's dramatic works, particularly his operatic adaptations of Walter Scott novels.

The Royal Theatre tailor protocols present yet another proof of the fact that it was mainly for the larger operas and pièces à spectacle that the majority of new costumes were created. In presenting *The Festival at Kenilworth*, these protocols indicate that a total of seventy new 'Elizabethan' costume pieces were produced. In the exotic vein, twenty-four new pieces were designed for *The Moorish Girl*, thirteen for *The Mulatto*; in the same year, however, 266 new costume items were manufactured for Oehlenschläger's unsuccessful and highly expensive Arabian fantasy *The Fisherman and his Children*, most of which were immediately reused in *The Moorish Girl*.

The five drawings by Lehmann of scenes from Andersen's Scott operas *The Bride of Lammermoor* and *The Festival at Kenilworth* (Figs. 4–8) are perhaps most reliable in their capacity as costume illustrations, for there are several proofs that they constitute sketches made from the actual productions. The costuming of *Kenilworth* was especially lavish and colourful and represented a serious effort to convey an illusion of the splendour of the historical personages involved. Fig. 6 depicts the meeting of Amy and Leicester towards the close of the first act and their duet, 'You, love, make my heart glad / Each blessed dream revives.' Leicester, according to the *Regieprotokol*, is 'wrapped in a cape, under which a splendid knight's costume with many decorations and the Order of the Garter.' The informative costume list for *Kenilworth* (preserved, through some exception, in the Danish State Archives) affords a more specific description of this 'splendid knight's costume,' a description which furthermore corresponds closely to the figure in Lehmann's drawing. Leicester was attired brilliantly, in high-collared cape, white satin doublet and trunks ornamented with silver, white silk hose, and white shoes with silver rosettes. This 'Elizabethan' costume was supplemented with a silver sword belt and sword, a star on the cape, and several decorations including the Orders of the Garter and the Golden Fleece. Leicester has presumably doffed his white satin beret with white feather in Lehmann's drawing, which is otherwise an accurate representation of the costume used.

Amy's dress in the same picture is also completely accurate, and it typifies the principle that actresses usually refused to appear on stage in anything but the most attractive and fashionable clothes of their own time. Amy wore a dress of red satin with high, slanting collar, gold braid, and full sleeves of white satin, a waistline of gold tassels, a white skirt with gold trim, white stockings, and white flat shoes. It is hardly necessary to remark that this costume was far more in keeping with the highest fashion of the 1830s than with the attire of Elizabethan England. Female costume on the stage was, of course, always heavily influenced by the current mode. In Fig. 2 Cendrillon, who is supposed to be dressed in a mediaeval costume, wears a fashionable Empire dress with the high waist, little puffed sleeves, and heelless slippers of her day.[3] Comparable considerations govern most of the female costumes depicted in H.C.C. Ley's sketch of Andersen's fairy-tale fantasy *More than Pearls and Gold* (Fig. 3).

In Fig. 8, depicting the first scene of the second act in *Kenilworth*, even

3 Cf Laver, *Drama*, p. 198

Queen Elizabeth appears in a fashion similar to Amy's, although her dress is somewhat more elaborate. The Queen's costume consisted of white satin with gold-spangled red trim, a gold tasseled waist, white stockings, and white shoes. The ruff collar was obviously added to suggest the Elizabethan era. The costume also included a royal train trimmed with ermine, not shown in the illustration and apparently donned by the Queen for her exit.

Lucie's bridal costume in the finale of *The Bride of Lammermoor*, which is set around the year 1700, differed surprisingly little from the 'Elizabethan' dresses just described. The heroine's attire, pictured in Fig. 5, consisted of a waist and skirt of white satin, the former richly embroidered with gold, matched with white stockings and white shoes. Lady Ashton's attire in the same sketch – a crimson damask dress with gold trim, a gold-figured silk skirt, a black beret with white feather, white stockings, and white shoes – conforms to similar contemporary lines. The plainer outdoor costume for Lucie's first appearance in *Lammermoor*, somewhat inaccurately depicted in Fig. 4, is also comparable: red woollen hunting dress trimmed with gold buttonholes, a small black hat with a black feather, and black laced boots. Frequently, however, female costumes are not described at all or are mentioned only in very general terms in the costume lists, for the very reason that actresses customarily selected their own fashions. Hence the costumes of the female aristocracy in Andersen's productions were generally dictated by current fashion and the taste of the actress involved. As late as 1865 a letter from H.P. Holst concerning the costuming of *When the Spaniards were here* and preserved in the Royal Theatre archives noted that existing dresses could be converted for the production 'provided the actresses are willing.'

Gentlemen's attire in opera and romantic drama was, as seen in Leicester's costume, frequently elegant, but, unlike the female costumes, male clothing usually indicates a definite, conscious effort to convey at least some impression of historical accuracy. In *Kenilworth* the men wore costumes corresponding to that of Leicester, including a doublet, a jerkin or a cape, the typical Elizabethan ruff collar, wide baggy trunks or breeches, tight-fitting elastic hose or fleshings, a sword, and a feathered hat. In Fig. 8 Leicester, seen kneeling in the picture, exhibits a more courtly version of this basic attire; under a red velvet jerkin with gold trim and sleeves of gold satin, he is dressed in matching red velvet breeches trimmed with gold, and white cotton hose. Added accessories were the customary ruff, a gold sword belt, and natural leather boots handsomely decorated with gold and black velvet. The other male figure beside the throne in this picture is apparently a less accurate representation of Sussex, who wore a black and gold costume similar in style to Leicester's, with lace ruff collar, black velvet jerkin with gold trim and red silk sleeves, matching breeches, gold sword belt, white hose, and neutral leather boots trimmed with gold and black velvet. The arm cape shown in the illustration is evidently the invention of the artist.

The other gentlemen in *Kenilworth* were comparably equipped with 'Elizabethan' attributes. Tony Foster, the castellan, wore gray trunks and matching sleeves which were characteristically 'paned' or striped with red bands. The same applied to Michael Lambourne's costume, which consisted of blue trunks and sleeves paned with white cloth and red bands; a waist belt with pistols and a dagger was added to identify Michael as the adventurer in this opera. Fig. 7 pictures the actor Julius Schwartzen as the nobleman Tressilian in a costume unlike those of the other gentlemen but representing the corresponding period in France, which Schwartzen had worn previously as a French noble in Hérold's opera *Le pré aux clercs*.

In contrast to the male historical costumes of the nobility, which characterized by suggestions of historical period and by finer materials such as silk, satin, or velvet, trimmed with fur, gold, or pearls, the nineteenth-century peasant costume, as it appeared in such Andersen operas as *Kenilworth*, *The Nix*, or *Little Kirsten*, was conventional and stereotyped. Hence Giles Gosling, the inn-keeper in *Kenilworth*, is seen in Fig. 7 wearing a ruff, the standard rustic kofte, or plain 'blue-coat,' which served to identify servants and lower-class characters, matching knee breeches, a red vest, white stockings, and ankle shoes with bows.

Despite the growing interest at this time in 'historical' costuming, exemplified in the 'Elizabethan' attributes of *The Festival at Kenilworth*, the addition of such vivid details in no sense corresponded to accurate historical reproduction. It was not until the close of the nineteenth century that historical costuming on the stage made a close approximation to reality. Nevertheless, the mixed styles of costuming in the productions of Andersen's plays during the first half of the century possessed a certain intrinsic charm, which attracted the audiences of the time. Its character is to be found not in an artificial search for 'historical verisimilitude,' but in the abundant wealth of colours and rich materials, the white silks and satins, red and black velvets, and gold and silver trimmings which glistened in the flattering glow of the dim oil lighting.

In the production of *The Bride of Lammermoor*, costumes were designed to suggest the year 1700, but kilts, plaids, and other Scottish attributes were added to convey the local milieu. Similarly, authentic Scottish ballad and folk music was suggested by Andersen in his preface as a means of denoting local identity.[4] In the opera's climactic scene with the marriage contract, illustrated in Fig. 5, the scoundrel Bucklaw wore a more villainous version of the customary plumed hat, accentuated by false black hair, together with a long coat buttoned up the front and the crossed neck-cloth of the period. A broad leather belt with pistol and sword buckled over the blue coat, high gaiters, and a plaid-lined cloak borrowed from a production of Rossini's *La donna del lago* also in the current repertory served to strengthen the impression of a Scottish laird. The hero Edgar, not seen in either of Lehmann's drawings, wore a similar Scotch costume consisting of a black feathered beret, crossed neck-cloth, dark blue coat like Bucklaw's decorated with gold buttonholes, pistol belt, high gaiters, and a Scottish kilt also borrowed from *La donna del lago* – under which he wore the conventional silk fleshings designed to represent natural skin.

The financial account for the *Lammermoor* production is a convincing example of the care and expense frequently lavished on the costuming of opera and romantic drama in this period. Despite the fact that numerous details in the costumes had been borrowed, and although costume changes were limited solely to Lord and Lady Ashton and Lucie, expenses for costume manufacture amounted in this case to Rdl. 167.3.12. This figure takes on meaning when we realize that it represented five times the expenditure for scenery and seven times the expenditure for rehearsals. In fact, the only cost much larger than costuming was that of 'book and music' – Rdl. 921.5.3. – which included not only the payment of copyists but also the fees paid to composer Ivar Bredal and librettist Andersen as well (Rdl. 604.5.11).[5]

Both *Dreams of the King* and *Little Kirsten* carried the spectator farther back into the past, and the Royal Theatre was obliged to devise an acceptable suggestion of the costuming of the Middle Ages. Although no

4 *Bruden fra Lammermoor*, p. 4

5 'Beregning over hvad det har kostet Theatret at bringe Syngespillet *Bruden fra Lammermoor paa Scenen,' Udgifts-Beregninger for enkelte Stykker af Repertoiret 1831–1841* (Rigsarkivet)

visual material exists to illustrate the costumes used for *Dreams of the King*, the costume lists for this romantic drama afford a detailed impression of their appearance. The female costumes merely reflected contemporary fashion. The male costumes endeavoured, however, to suggest the attire of the mediaeval historical personages at the time of King Christjern II. The pseudo-historical costumes worn by Christjern II, Christian III, Erik Walkendorf, and Faaborg were all basically similar in outline – beret, tunic, sword, hose, and ankle shoes – and reflected the influence of historical painting and relevant engravings. In the course of the one-act drama Christjern appeared in three contrasting costumes, worn over a basic outfit of black tights and ankle shoes to facilitate changes. As the young prince in bourgeois clothing he wore a black hat, tunic, belt, and sword. As the King he assumed a statelier costume comprising a crimson hat trimmed with white fur and a feather, a black tunic with ermine trim, and a red cape with ermine and crowns. Finally, as the royal prisoner in the castle at Sønderborg he (and his double in the dream sequences, played by mimic Andreas Füssel) wore a gray tunic with black trim and green woollen waist. Among the other male characters wearing similar 'mediaeval' costumes, King Christian III was given a particularly elegant disguise for his visit to the prison, consisting of a black beret with a feather, tunic, gray tights, black arm-cape trimmed with sable, sword, and belt.

Especially remarkable is the influence which Samsøe's historical drama *Dyveke* exerted on the costuming of *Dreams of the King*. This familiar, patriotic play from 1796, which had last been performed a decade prior to *Dreams*, treats the same historical period and the same figures as Andersen's romantic drama. The use made of the *Dyveke* settings in the staging of the Andersen play has already been described. In a comparable manner, the costume list reveals that Walkendorf, Christian III, and the Black-friar all wore costumes which utilized the corresponding ones from Samsøe's play. In the revival of *Dreams of the King* in 1857, the *Dyveke* influence became still stronger, perhaps because the Samsøe play had been revived for a series of productions in the 1855–6 season. Both the Black-friar's monk attire and Christjern's second costume as the King were borrowed directly from *Dyveke* in the later production.

There was in general a far more marked tendency in 1857 toward richer and more elaborate costuming. Christjern's royal attire, borrowed from *Dyveke*, was much more extravagant in the later production, consisting of a black velvet beret decorated with pearls and a brass rosette, a black velvet tunic with fur trim and gold-striped, black satin sleeves, an elaborate red velvet cape with arm slits, also trimmed with fur and gold, gray tights, a sword belt with gold buckle, and fine brown boots decorated with fur tops and spurs. The costume of Christian III in the revival was also nobler in material and trim than before. New additions included a velvet doublet with white satin puff-sleeves, matching trunks, white silk hose, a green velvet arm-cape trimmed with dark fur, and fur-trimmed brown boots. Hence although costumes continued to be borrowed from stock pieces such as *Dyveke*, there is nevertheless an indication in the later production of *Dreams of the King* of an intensified quest for a more convincing historical representation of the early sixteenth century. Furthermore, since the settings were the same as those used for the original 1844 production, the scene in Andersen's play depicting King Christjern's *dream* of the poisoning of Dyveke employed the fascinating psychological nuance of using a stage décor and costumes that could be recognized by the audience as the original, traditional elements associated with *Dyveke* on the stage.

Concerning the 'mediaeval' costuming of the earliest productions of Denmark's most popular and most performed opera, *Little Kirsten*, specific information is scarce. A costume list for the premiere in 1846 has not survived, and only the chorus costumes are described for the revival in 1858, at which time the Hartmann and Andersen masterpiece, originally subtitled 'romantic *singspiel* in one act,' was referred to for the first time as a 'romantic opera in two acts.' For the 1858 production there are costume lists for the male and female chorus drawn up by wardrobe supervisor C.C. Thorup as well as a separate list compiled by ballet master August Bournonville, who undertook the chorus and dance direction. These documents indicate clearly that the extras in *Kirsten* were dressed as conventionally idyllic peasants, with a splash of mediaevalism added to indicate the historical period. The eighteen male peasants of the chorus wore tunics, wide belted breeches, coloured stockings, and fur caps. Twenty peasant girls were clad in bright waists and skirts with white kerchiefs, and six bridesmaids wore coloured waists 'in mediaeval style,' white skirts, and green wreaths.

These otherwise rather faceless and operatic peasants were, however, arranged by Bournonville in a diversified ensemble 'that excelled in great precision and energy.'[6] The highpoint of the production was a spectacular

6 Overskou, *Den danske Skueplads*, v, 736

mummer interlude, which was to remain a tradition in later revivals of the opera (see Fig. 51). In this splendid procession the able choreographer combined the peasant chorus with a brilliant assembly of allegorical, preternatural, and historical personages, including King Solomon clad in 'a turban with crown and oriental dress' and carrying 'a sceptre and marvellous book in quarto.' Although our imagination must supply the actual costumes used in this 'production number,' the text of a brief memorandum drawn up by Bournonville evokes an impression of the colourful and exotic effect it must have created:

> Four servants with staves
> Six young girls
> Six couples of knights and ladies, each with small boy.
> The peasants follow, but place themselves on the right.
> *Time* with six small boys places himself centre.
> Spring / Summer / Autumn / Winter
> Night / Adventure (Fortune-teller)
> Will-o'-the-Wisp / Rosmer Merman / Imp / Goblin
> Troll / Wood Troll / King Solomon (Wisdom)
> Thor (Strength) / Valkyries / Warriors
> Sorrow / Peace / Joy
> Avarice / Pride with six dancing couples.
> Time with the small boys follow
> The procession closes with four Pages.

In this emblematic procession of over ninety persons, among whom the audience could also recognize some of Andersen's own fairy-tale characters, the chief function of the conventionalized peasant costumes, apart from their slight mediaeval connotation, was their contribution of varied and pleasing colour combinations to the visual display.

Concerning the actual arrangement of this interlude, Bournonville's chorus memorandum is in the form of a long list of names. Bearing in mind the three open arches in the *Waldemar* backdrop which was used for this scene (Fig. 10), it is perhaps logical to assume that, once Time and his six small boys took their places stage centre, the entrance of the procession alternated between the left and the right arch, shifting as the characters doubly underlined in the list. The procession could then merge and regroup for departure through the central arch.

51 Impression of the mummer interlude in *Little Kirsten*, from a copy of the score
for a production about 1881. Royal Theatre Music Archives

Exotic theatrical costume conveying a sense of the faraway or the fantastic – to which Bournonville's interlude provides an excellent transition – was a factor of utmost importance in the atmosphere of such romantic milieu pieces as Andersen's *The Raven, The Mulatto, The Moorish Girl,* and *The Wedding at Lake Como.* Highly detailed costume lists survive for all four of these productions, testifying to the degree of attention devoted to this aspect of the stage picture. The broad tradition of exotic costuming was, of course, deeply rooted in the older eighteenth-century theatre; indeed, developments during the first half of the nineteenth century frequently evidenced a decline rather than an improvement in unity and harmony of style.[7] In this connection, Andersen's criticism of Fru Heiberg's wretched costume as a Greek princess in Hertz's romantic drama *Swan Feathers / Svanehammen* (1841) comes to mind: 'she was a schoolgirl, and no half fairy from Greece,' he remarked tersely.[8]

Andersen's lively interest in the theatrical possibilities represented by exotic costuming had already received expression in the composition of his first opera libretto, *The Raven,* produced with Hartmann's score in 1832. This delightful operatic fantasy illustrates best the exotic tradition in Andersen's Royal Theatre productions, chiefly because of twelve hand-tinted costume designs discovered in the Royal Theatre library. These sketches, which have lain unnoticed in the theatre's archives for more than a century, were drawn for the revival of *The Raven* in 1865, but the style they represent corresponds largely to that of the original production in 1832. The fact that these drawings (Fig. 52–60) are reliable and were actually followed in practice may be conveniently verified through a comparison with the Royal Theatre's journal of tailor and seamstress payments.

In addition to the *Raven* sketches, a number of other unpublished sources illustrate the process through which the exotic characters of Andersen's imagination were transferred from paper to the stage. It was obvious from the very beginning that the costuming of *The Raven* would involve the Royal Theatre in considerable expense. A letter dated 5 October 1832 from the redoubtable actor and wardrobe supervisor, Doctor J.C. Ryge, to the theatre management and preserved in its archives is so illuminating regarding this aspect of theatre practice that it deserves to be quoted at length:

7 See Nicoll, *Development of the Theatre,* pp. 179–81, for excellent illustrations of eighteenth-century exotic costumes.

8 *Anderseniana,* IX–XIII, 568

To the high Management of the Royal Theatre:

With respect to costuming, the fantastic opera *The Raven* is a very difficult and costly piece to stage at the Royal Theatre. For, despite the fact that the theatre's wardrobe supply contains costumes from [Simone Mayr's opera] *Lanassa*, [Théaulon's fantasy] *La Clochette*, and [F. Kuhlau's opera] *Lulu* which could be used, far more changes would be necessary in *The Raven*, both for the chorus and ballet corps, for which these costumes are far from sufficient. Since time is now *extremely short* ... I must with deepest respect request the high management to excuse me from preparing a most humble and detailed proposal concerning which new wardrobe pieces it will be necessary to procure, a proposal which I could hardly deliver in eight days – but out of confidence in my judgment, experience, and well-known thriftiness [!] to allow me to make the necessary purchases *as needed*, as well as *from next Sunday on* to employ as many extra workers, both tailors and seamstresses, as I may require. That I at a later time both shall and can give a proper, and I trust complete, account of all that I undertake in this connection is a matter of course ...

> With deepest respect,
>
> J. C. RYGE, DR.

P.S. Since the costuming will be Indian, it is highly probable that much of the purchased material can be used again in [Auber's] *Le Dieu et la bayadère*.

Despite the parsimonious Dr Ryge's economical efforts to utilize costumes from previous exotic productions, it became necessary to produce a large number of new exotic, oriental costumes for *The Raven* and, as the wardrobe supervisor foresaw, costume expenses proved to be considerable. The 'complete account' which Ryge mentions in his letter was submitted on 12 February 1833, and it fully confirms the fact that costuming was frequently the largest single production cost at this time. Wardrobe expenses in this case totalled no less than Rdl. 1172.2.7, while staging amounted to Rdl. 235.2.3., the few rehearsals cost only Rdl. 68.2.4 (of which more than 60 per cent was paid to the stagehands), and book and music, including Andersen's and Hartmann's combined fee of Rdl. 567.3.6, came to Rdl. 961.4.9.[9]

The care and expense devoted to the costuming of *The Raven* was, however, repaid by excellent results. A letter written by Andersen four days

9 'Beregning over hvad det har kostet Theatret at bringe Trylle-Operaen *Ravnen paa Scenen,*' *Udgifts-Beregninger* (Rigsarkivet)

after the opening indicates that the author was well satisfied with this aspect of the production:

The costumes are indescribably beautiful; in particular, the four dancing girls were quite enchanting (they wore red silk trousers and white gauze dresses), there were twelve Knights of the Sun in white costumes. Golden helmets with a sun and a gold shield with the sun emblem. They were impressive.[10]

When Andersen's rewritten version of *The Raven* was revived in 1865, costuming was again a key production problem. H.P. Holst, who staged the opera, consulted the author about which costumes to use; in a letter dated 2 January 1865 Andersen wrote: 'Holst wanted to know in what costumes the opera should be played, and I immediately informed him. So I hope that my *Raven* will soon fly into the repertoire.'[11] Presumably on the basis of the (unfortunately lost) reply of Andersen to Holst, a costume proposal and the twelve costume designs reproduced in this study were prepared. In an unpublished letter from Holst to the Royal Theatre dated 16 March 1865 he noted that seventeen of the twenty female costumes in *The Raven* were in stock; the remainder would have to be borrowed if the author was unwilling to substitute pages for women in the text. Although the commedia dell'arte figures originally adopted from Gozzi were given new names and new outward appearances by Andersen for the 1865 revival,[12] most of the other characters in the sketches correspond directly to their counterparts in the 1832 production. For the revival it was necessary to create a total of 135 new costume pieces.

While the letters and other documents just described provide a backstage view of the process by which the exotic costumes for *The Raven* were procured, the actual costume lists and designs illustrate fully the realization of Andersen's characters on the stage. In spite of Ryge's request in the letter cited above, he was apparently not excused from preparing the customary, detailed costume proposal, since such an item bearing his signature, dated 26 October 1832, is to be found in the Royal Theatre's archives. Compared with this document, an undated costume list for Holst's 1865 production is far less detailed and informative, and must be supplemented with facts gathered from the tailor protocol.

10 *Anderseniana*, IX–XIII, 52

11 Topsøe-Jensen, *Breve til Therese og*

Martin Henriques, p. 62

12 *Mit Livs Eventyr*, II, 283–4

Both in the staging and the costuming of *The Raven*, stylistic confusion and inconsistency marred the scenic picture. Gothic and exotic elements were mixed freely, particularly in the 1865 revival where costume items classed as 'European, from older times' and as 'African, Moorish' in the wardrobe guide were combined indiscriminately. There was more than a little truth to the remark made by the sarcastic reviewer for *Folkets Avis* (25 April 1865) about seeing Teuton knights who wandered through settings with Moorish minarets from which Christian churchbells chimed!

Costumes for the 1832 production of the opera seem in many cases to have been more atmospheric and more consistent in style than those for the later revival. Hence the nine halberdiers in the earlier production – the impressive Knights of the Sun so enthusiastically described by Andersen – created a particularly striking impression with their golden helmets and breastplates, tunics and hose of white twilled shirting trimmed with red chintz and golden tassels, sashes of red chintz with golden fringes, small golden sabres on red strings, and oval shields with a golden sun on a field of red. These red and gold costumes, sparkling in the dim glow of the oil lamps lighting the stage, undoubtedly presented a far more picturesque and exotic sight than did the fourteen halberdiers and sixteen warriors in the 1865 production. These later halberdiers (Fig. 52) wore rather conventional attire consisting of coloured berets and tunics, red tights, swords, and turned-down brown boots. The costume worn by the sixteen warriors (Fig. 53) consisted of a belted blouse over tight-fitting fleshings, providing more of a Nordic than an Indian impression.

Similarly, the two types of courtiers – sixteen in all – appearing in the original production seem to have been far more flamboyant and exotic in their attire than the corresponding members of Millo's court in the later version, pictured in Fig. 54. In 1832 the courtiers wore oriental bonnets of chintz or merino, pearl necklaces, shoulder drapery of striped muslin or shawl cloth, coloured or flowered caftans, gaily striped sashes with gold tassels, light, striped hose, and gold laced boots. It is generally symptomatic in contrasting the two productions of *The Raven* that, while in the original version the eight sailors who row Jennaro and the abducted princess Armilla onstage wore exotic, Cingalese costumes borrowed from Galeotti's comic shipwreck ballet *The Cingalese Idol / Afguden paa Ceylon*, the same sailors in 1865 were dressed in tunics, as seen in Fig. 53, borrowed chiefly from Bournonville's decidedly Nordic ballet *Waldemar*.

The stage appearance of Andersen's fantastical figures in *The Raven*

52 Costume sketch for *The Raven*: halberdier. Coloured with green beret,
brown beard, brown alb with purple trim, blue tunic, red tights, and brown
boots. Royal Theatre library

53 Costume sketch for *The Raven*: warriors (left) and sailors (right).
Uncoloured pencil sketch

54 Costume sketch for *The Raven*: courtiers. *above* Page costume with red
beret-like hat, blue tunic with gold trim, grey hose, and brown shoes;
below uncoloured pencil sketch of four courtiers

remained, however, basically similar in both productions of the opera. In the picturesque opening scene in the mountain cave of Norando, the mighty magician is surrounded on three sides by a fantastical chorus of fire, earth, and water spirits. These preternatural beings are in frenzied activity, and their movements contribute visually to the picturesqueness of the scenic display. Three charming, hand-tinted sketches provide a vivid impression of these elemental spirits. The chorus of gnomes, or earth spirits, wore gray tunics and brass bands on head, arms, and legs (Fig. 55). The winged salamanders appeared entirely in red in the costume shown in Fig. 56. The water nymphs were clad in delicate, silvery blue frocks painted with scales (Fig. 57).

Unfortunately no costume designs survive to indicate the appearance of the two most essential groups of preternatural beings in Andersen's Gozzi adaptation, the three mermaids who appear to Jennaro to recite the curse of Norando and the thirteen fearful vampires that Jennaro encounters outside his brother Millo's bedchamber. Ryge's costume list from 1832 provides us, however, with concrete descriptions of both groups. The mermaids could obviously not appear in their traditional topless attire; instead, they wore decorously stylized costumes consisting of a flesh-coloured silk jacket and a light blue skirt, together with long, hanging hair spangled with white pearls. The terrible vampires were dressed in gray headgear and tights and boasted gray bat-wings; there is, however, no evidence that they wore the toothless mask with thick rubber lips which Andersen had envisioned in his stage directions, copied verbatim in the *Regieprotokol*.

The Eastern costumes of the leading characters were particularly effective and picturesque in the earlier production. The male costumes were characterized by richly coloured and ornamented shoulder capes and oriental caftans, decorative tasseled sashes, tights, and turbans decked with pearls and gold. For the heroine Armilla's two costumes the basic elements were a white bobbinet veil, a short Eastern dress, tights, and a bright, fringed sash – the general style is illustrated in the dancing-girl's attire in Fig. 58. For Armilla's first appearance, alighting from a gondola after having been kidnapped by Jennaro, her costume was lavishly adorned and embroidered with silver, while a later costume was trimmed with gold. In the 1865 revival, Armilla's first costume, which included a light blue satin cap trimmed with gold, a red damask apron, a gold satin skirt, and a white silk scarf, was classified as 'African, Moorish,' while

55 Costume sketch for *The Raven*: earth spirit. Coloured with grey tunic and
gold bands on head, arms, and legs

56 Costume sketch for *The Raven*: salamander. Red colouring

57 Costume sketch for *The Raven*: water-nymph. Light blue colouring

her second costume, a long white satin gown, was incongruously European in style.

By far the most lavish examples of exotic attire in *The Raven* were the costumes worn by Millo, the lordly ruler of Frattombrosa for whose sake the lovely Armilla has been abducted. Ryge's costume list contains a wealth of information about the style of Millo's splendid and decorative costuming. For example, his second outfit included an oriental, red velvet headgear trimmed with gold, pearls, and precious stones and decorated with a bird of paradise. Over a light satin caftan trimmed with matching red velvet and a gold border, the king bore a shoulder cape of red shawl-cloth and a necklace of pearls. The costume was rounded off by a red velvet sash with gold fringes, and gold trousers patterned with red velvet and thin gold stripes.

Although the 1865 costume list affords no comparable information about Millo's costume, other than the laconic remark 'black beret with gold,' the corresponding costume drawing conveys a clear impression of this character's appearance. In this coloured sketch (Fig. 59) the round beret is black with gold design, the loose shoulder cape is brown with a gray border, and the tunic is blue with gold trim. The costume is completed by the variegated tasseled sash, loose red trousers, and brown slippers. By comparison, Millo's costume in 1832 appeared far more flamboyant in its use of pearls, gold, and feathers, and more harmoniously coloured in its carrythrough of the scheme of red velvet and gold than the somewhat plainer counterpart utilized in 1865. By the time of the later performance, at the close of Andersen's career as a dramatist, the connection with the older eighteenth-century tradition of the grandly exotic 'Eastern potentate costume,' with its waving plumes, glittering stones, and richly dyed materials, had obviously grown much weaker.

One of the principal changes which Andersen made in his revision of *The Raven* was the substitution of the commedia dell'arte figures originally taken from Gozzi. In the 1832 production, however, these figures appeared in festive costumes bearing some resemblance – at least in colour scheme – to the traditional attire of the Italian masked comedy. Hence Pantalone wore a costume which gave an over-all impression of characteristic black and red, consisting of a black hat and long cape with short sleeves, a red jerkin, reddish knee breeches, red stockings, yellow slippers, and the traditional dagger. Brighella was appropriately dressed in cape, jerkin, and long trousers all in white, decorated with the familiar horizontal

58 Costume sketches for *The Raven*: solo dancers in II. *left* The dancing girl is uncoloured except for red hose. *below* Harald Scharff is shown with directions for blue jerkin, red cap, and brown breeches. *below right* Ferdinand Hoppe has colouring instructions for a red jerkin, grey breeches, and red cap

59 Costume sketch for *The Raven*: Millo, ruler of Frattombrosa

stripes of green velvet braid, and supplemented with a gray hat and gray shoes. Truffaldino appeared in a form of Harlequin costume, with cape, jerkin, and breeches consisting of the time-honoured patchwork in black and white. He wore a patched black, high-crowned hat with black feather, a wide white collar, black sash, and striped stockings. Tartaglia was clad in a version of the Captain costume, with broad ruff collar, a brown silk cape, a brown sash, and long gray gaiters, combined with green plaid knee-breeches, jerkin, and cap. As accessories this bragging soldier bore yellow, cuffed gloves and a military shoulder belt with a so-called 'crispin rapier.' Smeraldina, in contrast, appeared in a conventional exotic costume consisting of a bodice and skirt of green embroidered silk, a yellow sash, long yellow trousers, festive Indian slippers, and a large red and white turban. The costume list gives no indication that any of the commedia dell'arte figures wore masks for the production.

Unfortunately, no illustrations survive of these colourful nineteenth-century editions of the masked comedy types. Because Andersen felt that the commedia figures had been poorly received and misunderstood in the original production of *The Raven*, he decided to substitute other characters for them in the revival. Although the appearances of these replacements are not described in the costume list, the final costume sketch in the series depicts Kløerspaerrude (literally Clubs-Spades-Diamonds), the buffoon role created by Andersen to replace Brighella and Truffaldino. Fig. 60 is a delightful illustration of this gaudy, playing-card jester's costume; the figure in the picture is unmistakably Ludvig Phister, the great Danish comic actor who appeared in the part. The splendid costume design indicates a green hat with red feather, orange hood and collar, and a cream-tinted tunic dotted with orange diamonds and black clubs and spades, under which Clubs-Spades-Diamonds wears a 'body stocking' in which the right sleeve and left leg are red, and the left sleeve and right leg are blue.

This gallery of sketches, taken together with the appropriate documents from the Royal Theatre archives, conveys a rich, vivid impression of the exotic style of costuming that played so essential a part in the romantic theatre's *lebende Bildergallerie*. Andersen's text for *The Raven* was influenced and moulded by two equally significant factors: Hartmann's melodious romantic score and the traditions of the theatre of the exotic. Despite some obvious stylistic inconsistencies in the two productions of *The Raven*, a certain unmistakable charm nevertheless pervades this style, totally independent of the question of geographical or historical 'accuracy.' Particu-

60 Costume sketch for *The Raven*: the jester Clubs-Spades-Diamonds

larly the original 1832 production, with its striped and flowered chintz and shawl-cloth decked with pearls and gold and its vivid array of fantastical figures, seen in the flickering glow of the dim stage lighting, must have made a remarkably festive and theatrical impression on the audiences of the time.

In the 1840 production of Andersen's romantic drama *The Mulatto*, exoticism took the form of picturesque folk scenes of West Indian plantation life. Male costumes here fell into two very broad categories: gentlemen and slaves. (It might be noted, however, that even in 1840 this situation was a historical curiosity in Denmark, which took the lead in 1792 in abolishing the slave trade in its West Indian colonies.) Gentlemen in *The Mulatto* wore a typical nineteenth-century colonial 'planter's costume,' consisting of a coloured or striped coat, white vest and trousers, and broad-brimmed or straw hat; the twenty-six black slaves presented a contrasting picture with the aid of false black hair, black or brown tights, and – presumably – blackface makeup. Ten female slaves are specifically mentioned as wearing masks, confirming the assumption that their male counterparts utilized the far less attractive alternative of lamp black or burnt cork as facial makeup.

The leading ladies in *The Mulatto*, however, Johanne Luise Heiberg as Cecilie and Anna Nielsen as Eleonore, remained remarkably unaffected by the strong regional flavour of their tropical surroundings. Their dresses were more representative of high contemporary fashion than suggestive of colonial Martinique. Fru Heiberg's five costumes in Andersen's drama were in fact strikingly similar to those which she listed in a letter written about 1840 to a colleague at Christiania Theatre, Madame Carl Hagen, who had asked the renowned Danish actress for advice in establishing a fashionable theatrical wardrobe. Fru Heiberg recommended:[13]

1 A duster of dyed jaconet over a dress of white muslin
2 A white bobbinet dress over a red petticoat
3 A dress of red striped gauze with white petticoat
4 A white satin dress and a bobbinet tunic with applied satin sleeves
5 A rose satin duster over a dress of striped gauze.

This all-purpose wardrobe conjures an image of the elegant ladies of the

13 Neiiendam, *Johanne Luise Heiberg*, pp. 24–6

1840s parading, on the stage and off, in their most fashionable gowns, representing a style captured in Denmark in Lehmann's characteristic period drawings.

The costuming of *The Moorish Girl* was, by contrast, a much more haphazard enterprise, combining materials plucked at random from a number of unrelated 'exotic' productions. The demonstrative indifference on the part of the Royal Theatre towards the specific ethnographic environment of *The Moorish Girl* extended to costuming as well, and a large number of the outfits were simply taken directly from Oehlenschläger's Arabian fantasy, *The Fisherman and his Children*, which had been a lavish failure earlier in 1840. These costumes were decidedly oriental in appearance and consisted in the main of an Indian turban, a long dressing-gown-like coat, a sash, a damask caftan or – for the warriors – a breastplate, roomy coloured Turkish breeches, coloured boots or slippers, and a curved scimitar. This attire strongly resembles the eighteenth-century style known as 'Turkish rococo'; Othello, beyond a doubt the theatre's most celebrated Moor, had habitually appeared in this type of conventional Eastern dress, not least in England.[14]

Most of the costumes worn by the Moorish women at the court of King Alhakem were similarly inappropriate. The actress playing Niama 'was nothing more than a huge, well-dressed woman with pants on,' Edvard Collin undiplomatically reported to Andersen.[15] Placed between the two opposing groups, Moors and Spaniards, stood the heroine and title figure, Raphaella. She appeared throughout the play in a stylistically vague and distinctly unflattering attire most resembling a kind of Joan of Arc costume. Over a white flannel dress the Moorish Girl wore a coat of mail and a sword, combined with a black feathered beret and brown boots.

If the Moors in *The Moorish Girl* generally looked like Turks, the Spaniards had a decidedly 'gothic,' Nordic appearance – indeed the term 'spanske' costumes was traditionally applied to the entire realm of 'mediaeval' attire.[16] Even the potentially evocative chorus of drunken lazaros or Spanish beggars in the final act of the play resembled Danish peasants. Pablo, Aurelio, Santiago, and most of the chorus of twenty-four

14 Cf Nicoll, *Development of the Theatre*, pp. 178–80 on this tradition in England. *Othello* itself was not performed at the Royal Theatre until 1904, at which time it proved a failure

15 Topsøe-Jensen, *Brevveksling med Edvard og Henriette Collin*, I, 300–1

16 Cf Krogh, *Teaterbilleder*, pp. 226–7

lazaros wore, over their conventional fleshings, either peasant attire borrowed from C.J. Boye's Nordic history play *Erik* vii or Nordic slave tunics from Oehlenschläger's masterpiece *Hakon Jarl*. Thus, while elsewhere on the Continent and in England at this time available ethnographic sources were freely plundered in order to arrive at more 'correct' costuming, at the Danish Royal Theatre there is little indication that comparable study preceded a production such as *The Moorish Girl*. In this case, despite the monumental works on national costumes, mores, landscapes, and customs that were accessible and were influencing costume designers at many European theatres, the ultimate result depended upon conventional borrowing of stock costumes. Yet, in the Royal Theatre productions of opera and ballet in this period, particularly under the influence of the versatile Bournonville, careful attention to ethnographic detail became a significant factor. It was no coincidence that it was Bournonville who purchased Guilio Ferrario's copiously illustrated, multi-volume work *Il Costume antico e moderno o Storia* ... , published in Milan in 1829, for the Royal Theatre library.[17]

Nor is it surprising that one of the most effectively integrated instances of exotic costuming at this time was Bournonville's production of Andersen and Gläser's *The Wedding at Lake Como*. In a highly complimentary notice the reviewer for *Flyveposten* (31 Jan. 1849) remarked: 'The arrangement of the production bore further witness to the artistically integrating hand of the ballet-master, evident also in the well-planned costuming.' One of the most interesting aspects of the highly detailed, nine-page costume list for this production is its comparatively close attention to Andersen's stage directions, himself a connoisseur of the Italian scene.

At loggerheads with Roderigo and his villainous band in Andersen's text are the hero Renzo and the other Italian peasants, all of whom were clad in the bright peasant tradition established in Bournonville's great Italian ballet successes, notably *Napoli*. In portraying an 'Italian' peasant on the stage, Lombardy and Campania were all one and regional distinctions were quietly ignored. The chief traits of the costume were a black hat, either pointed or broad-brimmed, with a decorative ribbon, a

17 Other significant works on costume at this time included Martinet's *Collection de costumes de théâtre*, depicting costumes of the Parisian theatres from 1796 to 1843, and R. v. Spalart's *Versuch über das Kostüm der vorzüglichsten Völker des Alterthums und des Mittelalters*, issued in numerous instalments from 1797 to 1811.

white shirt, knee-length shorts, a sash, suspenders, and a jacket or tunic in various colour combinations. Renzo's attire was a typical example of this nineteenth-century *Napoli* style: white shirt, green velvet knee-length breeches, and a red silk sash and gaudy handkerchief, to which was added a black pointed hat decorated with a ribbon and a short velvet jacket hung over one shoulder.[18]

Effective costuming was thus essential in bringing to the stage the varied types populating the romantic theatre of H.C. Andersen: Italian bandits and peasants, mediaeval courtiers, Moors and Spaniards, Walter Scott Elizabethans, West Indian slaves, vampires, mermaids, and Frattombrosian rulers. The attire of this character gallery was often influenced by strong, abiding links with the broad conventions of the eighteenth century. In spite of the rising popular interest in the depiction of far-away peoples and places on the stage, many of the older 'exotic' conventions in costuming continued to prevail. Actresses continued the time-honoured practice of wearing, in all situations, the fashionable clothing of the hour. Those attempts that were made in the direction of relative historical or geographical accuracy were romanticized, characterized neither by realism nor by faithful stylistic consistency. Nor are such statements meant to be derogatory. The aim of stage costuming in the productions of Andersen's plays was not to create historical verisimilitude, but rather to add a pleasing and piquant flavour, a taste of the exotic or a dash of history, a splash of colour and a wealth of rich materials to the festive stage picture. And in this purpose the theatre of the nineteenth century frequently succeeded beyond all expectation.

18 The interested reader is referred to the discussion of *Napoli* in Krogh and Kragh-Jacobsen, *Den kongelige danske Ballet*, pp. 242–52, which includes the ballet scenario and pictures illustrating the continuation of the costume tradition in Gennaro's role.

FIVE
Rehearsal and Performance

ALTHOUGH THE NINETEENTH CENTURY is generally regarded as a period when great acting flourished on the stage, a reconstruction of this acting style is not always easy to achieve.[1] Reliable source documents are rare, and many scholars therefore succumb more or less to the temptation of describing a prenaturalistic performance in terms of preconceptions acquired through the naturalistic theatre. But naturalism in the theatre marked a conclusive break with the older, inherited conventions that had survived up until that time, and it can indeed be said that a whole new theatrical 'system' emerged in the 1880s. Throughout most of the nineteenth century, however, the conventions, techniques, and ideals of acting were far different from those of our modern theatre.

Determining, whenever possible, the total number of rehearsals held for a production is of basic importance in any theatre-historical reconstruction. In this respect the Royal Theatre's *Regiejournal*, which dates back to 1781, is a unique and highly valuable source. These volumes contain a precise, chronological record of each day's events, showing the exact number and type of rehearsals held, any irregularities or absences, and the plays performed. By means of these day-to-day journals kept by the stage manager it is thus possible to determine precisely the rehearsal totals for all of Andersen's plays. Such an investigation not only sheds

---

1 This chapter elaborates on an earlier article by the author, 'The Actor in the Nineteenth Century.' Facts about rehearsal totals and procedures have been obtained from four volumes of the Royal Theatre's daily journal: *Regiejournal*, Sept. 1825–Jan. 1837; *Regiejournal*, 2 Jan. 1837–30 April 1848; *Regiejournal*, 1 May 1848–24 May 1859; *Regiejournal*, May 1859–June 1869

added light on the frequently very generalized critical judgments of acting style contained in contemporary newspaper reviews, but also demonstrates clearly that this style had its roots in the basic technique of the eighteenth century.

As might naturally be expected, rehearsal totals varied somewhat according to which type of production was being prepared – opera, vaudeville, comedy, romantic drama, and so on. Somewhat more surprising, however, is the fact that rehearsal practice did not vary to any great degree during the period from Andersen's early plays in the 1830s to his last works in the 1860s. It was not until the production of *When the Spaniards were here* in 1865, directed by the progressive theatre-man F.L. Høedt, that rehearsal totals took a definite swing upward which heralded the future importance the director would come to assume after the emergence of naturalism in the eighties. Throughout the greater part of the century, however, the older practice of few rehearsals continued to prevail, exercising, as we shall see, a marked influence on nearly all aspects of acting style and technique.

The genre which was apparently afforded the least number of formal rehearsals was the vaudeville. For Andersen's vaudevilles an average of only three stage rehearsals and two or three preliminary piano rehearsals was required, ie, about the same number of rehearsals as was customary for all plays during the eighteenth century. Moreover, the length of the vaudeville apparently made little difference in the rehearsal total; thus although the short one-act *Love on St Nicholas Tower* needed three stage and three piano rehearsals, for the double vaudeville *Parting and Meeting* the same number of stage rehearsals and only two piano rehearsals were held. Furthermore, for a play such as *The Invisible Man*, which was first presented by the actors as a benefit summer performance, no more than one piano rehearsal and a single stage rehearsal were considered necessary before the piece was placed in the regular repertory.[2]

2 Bergman, *Regi och Spelstil*, pp. 151–6, finds similar rehearsal totals in Sweden, although the character of his sources is less reliable than the Danish *Regiejournal*. While the Danish rehearsal statistics are comparable to those for Germany, Bergman argues in *Regihistoriska Studier* for considerably higher totals in Paris – a minimum of 6 rehearsals per play at the Comédie Française in the late eighteenth century (p. 63), 15–20 rehearsals for a new programme at the boulevard theatres in the same period (p. 84), and 30–40 rehearsals per play by the 1860s (p. 113). The important question of the nature and purpose of these rehearsals is, however, not answered by mere raw statistics.

Although the more complex genres of opera and romantic drama naturally needed greater preparation, this remained remarkably slight by modern standards. For Andersen's operas an average of five or six stage rehearsals was the norm, in addition to which came a number of piano, quartet, or other music rehearsals that depended on the scope or difficulty of the score. That the latter rehearsals could vary greatly in number can be seen from the fact that while such works as *The Bride of Lammermoor*, *The Raven*, *Little Kirsten*, and *The Nix* required nine to eleven music rehearsals each, *The Wedding at Lake Como*, with its characteristic and successful score, took no fewer than twenty-two music rehearsals to prepare. Moreover, this example is convincing proof that these music rehearsals must undoubtedly have aided in the polishing of chorus movement and blocking as well. Although there were only four actual stage rehearsals for *The Wedding*, Bournonville's mise-en-scène was the object of unanimously enthusiastic praise: 'The stage arrangement in this opera,' wrote the critic for *Fædrelandet* (6 Feb. 1849), 'is executed with taste and finished skill, and offers a sharp contrast to the folly with which the stage has been arranged in recent years in straight plays at the Royal Theatre.'[3] This success was both the result of Bournonville's acknowledged genius and the product of the relatively long series of music rehearsals.

Romantic drama, with its elaborate machinery, lavish costuming, and depiction of local colour, was given slightly more attention than opera. Thus, *The Mulatto* received seven stage rehearsals prior to the opening, *The Moorish Girl* took eight, and the one-act drama *Dreams of the King*, seven. It is perhaps indicative that the totally miscarried failure, *Agnete and the Merman*, was afforded only four stage rehearsals. An ordinary comedy, such as *The Blossom of Happiness*, *The New Maternity Ward*, *Herr Rasmussen*, and *He is not well-born*, took no more than an average of six rehearsals to prepare.

It was, as mentioned, not until Høedt's production of *When the Spaniards were here* in 1865 that the number of stage rehearsals for Andersen's plays increased sharply to ten. (When a double rehearsal on 26 March revealed that Andersen's play 'fell completely apart,' the author arranged for Høedt to take over the direction from H.P. Holst; 'a difficult diplomatic

3 The other reviews were unanimous in praising Bournonville's staging. *Berlingske Tidende* (30 Jan. 1849) found it 'superior,' *Flyveposten* spoke of Bournon- ville's 'artistically integrating hand,' and *Folket* (9 Feb.) extolled his 'customary skill.'

task,' Andersen wrote in his diary, 'but accomplished with Holst's good will.') This was, of course, not the first instance of an increase in rehearsal totals at the Royal Theatre; in 1860 Høedt directed Theodore Barrière's well-made play, *Les faux bonshommes*, for which he held, in the words of one actress, 'countless rehearsals' – ie, a total of nineteen![4] Extensive rehearsals were also devoted to Holst's staging in 1865 of the Andersen and Hartmann opera *The Raven*: a total of eight stage rehearsals, a special rehearsal for Jennaro's transformation to a marble statue in the third act, six music rehearsals, two of which were with full chorus, and five technical rehearsals for the complex staging and lighting. Nevertheless, the results which Holst achieved through this extensive preparation were not particularly gratifying; 'Bournonville could perhaps have staged it differently,' wrote *Folkets Avis* (25 April 1865) with heavy sarcasm, 'but *like this*, no that he could not.'

Usually two or three weeks before the stage and music rehearsals for a play began, it was customary to hold the reading rehearsal (*læseprøve*), which was one of the central elements in the rehearsal practice of that time.[5] At this initial rehearsal, which was conducted in the same way as it had been in the foregoing century, the foundation for the entire production was laid and the individual role interpretations took shape. Afterwards the actors retired to continue work on their parts in private, meeting again several weeks later for the five to seven rehearsals that preceded the opening. The Actors' Regulations of the Royal Theatre from 1856 state explicitly that at this reading rehearsal the actors should already be so well-acquainted with their parts that they might read them aloud with understanding and indication of character.[6] At the beginning of each act, the 'director' of the production indicated the contemplated setting, and at the end of the reading he explained the costumes, props, and the like, at which time the actors could also suggest changes. This read-through by the actors corresponds to the procedure usually followed in Germany at *die Leseprobe*.[7] However, it sometimes also happened that the practice

4 Sødring, *Erindringer*, p. 197

5 There were exceptions, however: for *Little Kirsten*, music rehearsals began nearly three weeks before the actual reading rehearsal on 24 April 1846; eight piano rehearsals were held under the supervision of the composer (Topsøe-Jensen, *Brevveksling med Edvard og*

Henriette Collin, 1, 278)

6 *Reglement ang. Tjenesten ved det Kongelige Theater*, 23 July 1856, p. 11, section 13. These and earlier sets of regulations are collected in the Royal Theatre library and Rigsarkivet.

7 Cf Bergman, *Regihistoriska Studier*, pp. 117–18

of the French reading rehearsal, *la lecture*, was followed at the Royal Theatre. In this case the author himself, with manuscript in hand, a glass of sugared water beside him, and the actors grouped around him in the greenroom, read his own play aloud with as much characterization of the individual roles as possible.[8] It was this alternative which Andersen chose for *When the Spaniards were here*, and in the margin of the *Regiejournal* the stage manager made note of the unusual event: 'The reading was held by the play's author, Professor H.C. Andersen!'[9] However, Julie Sødring, who played Miss Hagenau in *Spaniards*, recalled in her memoirs the unfortunate effect which Andersen's poor reading had on the actors, who were accustomed to reading and interpreting their own parts at this rehearsal 'whereby the character is immediately given in broad outline.'[10]

At the first stage rehearsal several weeks after the read-through, the actors were naturally expected, in view of the average of only six to seven rehearsals for even the most involved romantic dramas, to appear with their parts memorized so they could recite them without hesitation, and this was stated as a specific requirement in the Actors' Regulations.[11] Moreover, it was essential that the actors involved should attend every one of these few rehearsals, since it was often impossible for an offender or his fellow players to make up for an absence. To enforce this rule it had been necessary from the very founding of the Royal Theatre in 1748 to establish a schedule of strict fines for absence, tardiness, or disorderly conduct at rehearsals. The earliest existing *Regiejournal* contains numerous references to absences from rehearsal and resulting fines or excuses; among the more memorable is the remark concerning the actor Adam Gielstrup, who in 1783 missed an entire rehearsal 'because he was gone out to see an execution.'[12] The interesting collection of Actors' Regulations preserved in the Danish State Archives indicates plainly that the practice of fines still remained very necessary in the nineteenth century, as the actors were apparently unbelievably lax in this matter. Sets of regulations dated 1820 and 1832 both follow the older tariff: a fine of one-fiftieth of an actor's monthly wages for absence from the first rehearsal,

8 Cf *ibid.*, p. 105. *Regulativ ang. ... antagne Stykker*, 23 July 1856, p. 3, section 8 gave the author the right to read his play if he chose.

9 *Regiejournal*, May 1859–June 1869, 23 Feb. 1865

10 Sødring, *Erindringer*, p. 205

11 *Reglement ang. Tjenesten*, 1856, p. 12, section 18

12 Krogh, *Det kgl. Teaters ældeste Regiejournal*, p. 37

one-thirtieth for the second, and one-twentieth for the final rehearsal.[13] When by the middle decades of the century the number of rehearsals had increased from the traditional three, it became necessary to establish a somewhat more complex schedule of fines for absence and tardiness. Thus the Royal Theatre Regulations for 1856 stipulate the following fines:

> For absence from a dress rehearsal or any final or sole rehearsal the offender will be fined:
>
> for 5 minutes' absence   1/50th
>   of the monthly salary.
> for 1/4 hour's absence   1/12th
>   of the monthly salary.
> for 1/2 hour's absence   1/6th
>   of the monthly salary.
> for 3/4 hour's absence   1/3rd
>   of the monthly salary (which is full absence).
> Absence from other rehearsals will be fined at one-half of the above rates.[14]

Despite these fines, however, the stage manager's daily journals testify amply to the fairly frequent occurrence of absences or of misconduct during rehearsals of Andersen's plays. For example, in *The Festival at Kenilworth*, Rosenkilde failed entirely to appear for one of the six stage rehearsals, and was fined 1/25th of his salary. For the run-through on the day of the performance, Schneider, Faaborg, and Hansen, who respectively played Tony Foster, Sussex, and the old schoolmaster Holiday, arrived a half hour late, and paid a mulct of 1/50th of their wages. At a later performance of the opera, Erhardine Rantzau incurred the same penalty for 'disorder during the performance.' The dismal failure in 1846 of Andersen's comedy *Herr Rasmussen* can be at least partly ascribed to the actors' attitudes and conduct during rehearsals. Three of the players refused their parts following the reading rehearsal, and one of the produc-

13 *Foreløbig Reglement for Theaterpersonalet,* 1 Sept. 1820 and *Reglement for Theaterpersonalet,* 1 Sept. 1832. On 26 Aug, 1836 the theatre also issued a declaration concerning disorderly conduct at rehearsals because 'the peace and quiet during rehearsals and performances, so necessary and helpful to the discharge of duty, has previously so often been disturbed' (Rigsarkivet).

14 *Reglement ang. Tjenesten,* 1856, p. 16, section 29. These rates were subsequently reduced somewhat by a royal resolution of 15 March 1858 (Rigsarkivet).

tion's six rehearsals was cancelled entirely when Natalia Ryge simply failed to appear, costing the actress 1/25th of her salary.[15] The production of *The Wedding at Lake Como* also suffered under similar difficulties. For a quartet rehearsal of the opera on 18 January 1848, one of the four actors failed entirely to appear and Peter Schram, who played the important role of Abondio, was fined for arriving half-an-hour late.

As these examples indicate, then, nineteenth-century rehearsals were both remarkably imperfect in discipline and few in number by modern standards. Moreover, the *Regiejournal* makes it evident that for revivals of popular plays like *The Mulatto*, *The Invisible Man*, or *The Bride of Lammermoor* in subsequent seasons no additional rehearsals whatsoever were held. It is therefore only logical to assume that this older rehearsal system had a very perceptible impact on performance style and technique.

Under these conditions the problem of role memorizing, a favourite target for critical reprimands throughout the eighteenth century, did not disappear in this period. By way of example, even the star actor N.P. Nielsen was taken severely to task by the critics for his portrayal of Christjern II in *Dreams of the King* because he had not bothered to memorize the part. 'Although none of the others allowed themselves to be guilty of a single noticeable slip,' wrote the reviewer for *Berlingske Tidende* (15 Feb. 1844), 'Mr. Nielsen turned and twisted so many words in his not-so-large role that marked unclearness of diction was the result.'[16]

The limited number of rehearsals had even more far-reaching effects than faulty memorizing, however, and it is therefore hazardous to forget rehearsal practice in evaluating acting style. Although this study is limited specifically to H.C. Andersen's plays, the rehearsal conditions described may be accepted as typical of Royal Theatre productions in general. Exceptions proving the rule are also found, such as a production of *Wilhelm Tell* which received twelve full stage rehearsals in 1842.

One of the major differences between the theatre of the nineteenth century and the modern theatre lies in the question of ensemble acting – a question which is not resolved by a discussion of whether or not actors also rehearsed or were 'coached' outside the theatre, as indeed they were

15 The troubles which plagued the *Herr Rasmussen* production are described in Collin, *H.C. Andersen*, pp. 381 ff, and Bille and Bøgh, *Breve til H.C. Andersen*, pp. 96 ff

16 The only other review describing the acting in this production, in *Ny Portefeuille for 1844*, 1, 7, 167, agrees with the *Berlingske Tidende* criticism.

in many eras of theatrical history. Rather, it seems clear that the rehearsal practice just described demonstrates plainly that so long as no more than six to eight rehearsals were normally required for any full-length play, there could be no possibility of carefully directed ensemble playing of the kind introduced by the naturalists in the 1880s, whose representative in Scandinavia was the gifted director William Bloch. Such ensemble playing, in which the director himself carefully worked with each character and then, to use Bloch's words, 'assembled the various individualities into a musical harmony of conversation in the inspired life of the ensemble,'[17] presumed a system of rehearsal and performance totally different from that which prevailed during Andersen's period of activity as a playwright. Private work to achieve ensemble playing is often mentioned by actors of the older school; for example, Johanne Luise Heiberg describes in her memoirs her work with the romantic idol Michael Wiehe as follows: 'When he had his biggest scenes in the play with me, we worked secretly on these scenes in order to bring an ensemble into the performance.'[18] But the 'ensemble' mentioned here is obviously far different from that which Bloch or Stanislavsky advocated. So long as rehearsal totals did not increase substantially and every actor remained as a consequence sovereign in the preparation of his own role, no amount of 'home rehearsals' by individuals could bring about the precise scenic teamwork of the entire ensemble that characterizes naturalism.

Nevertheless, although ensemble acting did not, and could not, become a reality as long as the older system persisted, the idea and ideal of ensemble was already being discussed in Denmark in the theatrical criticism of the forties and fifties.[19] One of those who spoke out most strongly concerning the lack of ensemble playing at the Danish Royal Theatre was Andersen himself, whose extensive travels brought him into contact with most of the theatres of Europe and made him a knowledgeable connoisseur of theatrical practices. In 1847 in *Das Märchen meines Lebens* he wrote that although the Royal Theatre was a 'good theatre,' comparable to the Burgtheater in Vienna, it lacked the 'military disci-

17 Nathansen, *William Bloch*, p. 46
18 Heiberg, *Et Liv gjenoplevet i Erindringen*, I, 307
19 Notions of ensemble are obviously much older. Around 1770 Diderot made his famous statement in *Paradoxe* *sur le comédien* about 'numberless' rehearsals 'to establish a general unity in the playing.' See *The Paradox of Acting and Masks or Faces?*, intro. by Lee Strasberg (New York 1957), p. 26

pline' necessary for many individuals to form 'an artistic whole.'[20] Eight years later in *The Story of My Life* he heightened his praise to describe the Royal Theatre as 'one of the best in Europe,' and singled out great actors of the age such as N.P. Nielsen, Dr Ryge, Ludvig Phister, and, not least, Johanne Luise Heiberg; his conclusion, however, was the same:

> I feel that the Danish theatre has always lacked discipline, and that is necessary wherever many individuals must form a whole, particularly an artistic whole.[21]

In the same vein, an interesting double article in *Thalia* for 1849 (III, IV) entitled 'A Proposal for a New Method of Stage Direction' and signed A.J. deals at length with the problem identified by Andersen. 'The most important thing about every dramatic production,' wrote the anonymous critic A.J.,

> is *ensemble*, and yet there is nothing which our theatre lacks more than precisely – *ensemble*. We have some excellent actors and actresses who measure up to those of any theatre elsewhere; but we have, on the other hand, such a horde of mediocrities that there is hardly another theatre which can surpass us in this respect. How then can an ensemble be conceivable?

Another critic and dramatist, A.L. Arnesen, in his important review of Andersen's *The Moorish Girl* in *Fædrelandet* (28 Dec. 1840), censured the fact that this production gave the impression of fragments rather than of a co-ordinated whole, and similarly blamed the lack of ensemble on mediocre actors. The solution proposed by Arnesen, however, was that the star actors should be encouraged, by means of *feu* or bonus payments levied according to an actor's rank, to appear in the smaller parts as well. 'I admit,' he argued, 'that I would prefer to see even the most insignificant bit parts played by the best actors and actresses.' Arnesen illustrated his argument by describing the beneficial, almost magical, effect which Johanne Luise Heiberg had had on a production of her husband's *The Critic and the Animal* one evening in which she appeared in an emergency as the servant girl Rose: 'It was not only this one role which acquired an interest it previously never had and later never recovered; but the whole audience became an entirely different audience; and the other actors

20 Andersen, *Mit eget Eventyr uden Digt-ning*, p. 58   21 *Mit Livs Eventyr*, I, 215–16

acquired a spirit, and an *ensemble* and a precision developed that are practically never seen in our theatre.'

It should be obvious, however, that so long as the stage director, because of the rehearsal system, remained without real influence, merely adorning all the roles with virtuosi – whether obtained by means of *feu*, or through more intensive training in an acting school – could hardly be expected to result in more effective ensemble playing. On the contrary, the use of the celebrated Ludvig Phister as the Spanish lazaron Pablo in the fifth act of *The Moorish Girl* resulted in a virtuoso 'number' by the popular actor which had no relation to the serious tone of the tragedy. The satirical periodical *Corsaren* (1 Jan. 1841), maliciously pretending to take Andersen's play as an intentional parody, commented: 'Phister was naturally excellent in this general parody. He sang a song as a Spanish *lazaron* with a Danish peasant accent, and the effect was priceless. The audience roared with laughter, and shouted bravo with all its might!' Andersen wrote ruefully that Phister 'had been so "artistic," so overflowing with humour, that everyone was drawn into the stream of laughter. One had to laugh to the utmost.'[22]

Even in Andersen's last plays in the sixties, the ideal of ensemble playing continued to elude in practice. Clemens Petersen's review of *When the Spaniards were here* voiced advanced views of ensemble playing and criticized that production for wasting the ensemble possibilities inherent in Andersen's thematic device of allowing the young Spaniard, Don Juan de Molina, to be heard but never seen.[23] 'One hears his Spanish song backstage, hears the castanets,' wrote the playwright in this connection. 'His whole personality should, however, stand clear, fine, and noble; without appearing visibly, one should follow him in his love, his flight, and his danger ...'[24] The offstage singing and playing of the Spaniard was intended to be a pervasive, atmospheric element of beauty woven into the life of the scene, in an age before the coming of plastic values and PA systems. Without a director to co-ordinate the acting and the music into a meaningful ensemble, however, the singing of tenor Richard Jastrau became merely a concert performance unrelated to the rest of the play.

In the discussions of ensemble around the middle of the nineteenth century, it occurred to no one among the critics to suggest more rehearsals. Indeed the limited number of rehearsals was an intrinsic part of the earlier

22 *Ibid.*, I, 236
23 *Fædrelandet* (8 April 1865)
24 *Mit Livs Eventyr*, II, 283

theatrical system in which each actor prepared himself independently, and directly resented and mistrusted interference or advice from anyone else. This attitude is well exemplified in a description of Johanne Luise Heiberg of her fiercely independent creation of the role of Fenella in Auber's *La muette de Portici*. Her characterization and interpretation were complete and unchangeable at the very first stage rehearsal. 'When the rehearsal was over,' she relates, 'a number of actors came over to me and gave me good advice. But I said to myself: Talk all you want! I saw the chorus and the stagehands cry, and I'll stick to that.'[25]

Under such circumstances as these, in which the leading actors were convinced that they knew their trade better than anyone else, a director was plainly an unwelcome superfluity, and more than a total of five to seven rehearsals, as Heinrich Laube expressed it in Germany, 'merely tired the actors and led to a mechanization of the acting.'[26]

Although the Royal Theatre's regulations of 1856 expressly established the right of the stage director to inform the actors not only about settings, exits and entrances, and handling of props, but furthermore about their positions on stage, the actors' independence was nevertheless tacitly recognized in the important clause that followed: 'when such cannot be left to their own judgment.'[27] This reservation was deleted somewhat later in a hand-corrected copy preserved in the State Archives, giving the director full authority to decide positions at a special blocking rehearsal. Moreover, this development correlates with the appearance of the important and extensive position plans and movement diagrams for a few large opera productions found in a separate *Regieprotokol* in the State Archives, entitled *Opera og Syngestykke 1857–59*.

The same regulations from 1856 similarly attempted to check the independent attitude of the actors that led them to consider rehearsals merely as a convenient place to memorize their lines, preferring however to 'save' their actual intentions, emotions, and 'tricks' in the part until opening night. Thus August Bournonville, who served in the years 1861–64 as intendant at the Swedish Royal Theatre, complained bitterly of the talented actors in Stockholm who saved their surprises for the opening 'in order to take their colleagues unawares,' and of 'long concealed humour or gushing pathos' that quickly became a stereotype.[28]

25 Heiberg, *Et Liv gjenoplevet i Erindringen*, I, 117

26 Bergman, *Regihistoriska Studier*, p. 215

27 *Reglement ang. Tjenesten*, 1856, p. 13, section 19

28 Bournonville, *Mit Theaterliv*, II, 39

This practice had in theory been forbidden at the Danish national theatre by the earliest regulations, but to little avail. The traditional prohibition contained in a set of regulations from 1813 – 'Rehearsals must be held with audible speech and accompanying actions'[29] – was repeated in precisely the same words in regulations for 1820 (section 11) and 1832 (section 11), followed by the customary clause that the actors must play as far forward as possible and must face towards the audience. It was not until 1856 that the new regulations, influenced by a growing concern with the new concepts of mise-en-scène and integrated ensemble playing, omitted the instructions about frontal playing and expressed instead an increasing awareness of the role of 'intentions' in acting: 'At each subsequent rehearsal the actors are obliged to ... recite their parts and make their pauses decisively, so that everyone can form a clear impression of the intentions of his fellow player.'[30]

But despite evidences of an emerging concern at mid-century with the scenic ideal of ensemble playing, the older rehearsal practice, followed without exception for Andersen's plays, continued to foster a special actor-type, completely sovereign in his work with his part and specialized to the point of virtuosity in a particular type or category.

The division of roles into definite categories or types, each of which had its particular prescribed technique in which an actor then specialized, was, of course, an inheritance from earlier times. This specialization was, moreover, especially sharply defined regarding the two principal genres, tragedy and comedy, and it was difficult for this period to imagine, or accept, an actor performing in both categories. In general, the strength of the idea of specialization was twofold: it existed both as an aesthetic principle and as a practical corollary of the system of independent role preparation.

Violation of this principle in the production of Andersen's first vaudeville, Love on St Nicholas Tower, provoked a veritable storm of reaction. Andersen made the 'mistake' of wanting to cast Anna Wexschall Nielsen, the leading serious actress of the period, in the role of Ellen in his parody of heroic tragedy.[31] The very notion of this classic-romantic tragedienne in the farcical role of the daughter of the tower watchman was a breach of the aesthetic separation of genres of such dimensions that critics were actually morally indignant. Andersen's humourless friend, benefactor,

29 *Regiejournal*, 1807–1814, 389 (Royal Theatre library)

30 *Reglement ang. Tjenesten*, 1856, p. 13, section 20

31 Cf *H.C. Andersens Levnedsbog*, p. 191

correspondent, and sole heir, Edvard Collin, recalled 'the *disgust* with which one regarded this noble actress in this low role.'[32] The emotional language used by Thomas Overskou to describe the 'scandal' which forced Anna Wexschall to resign the part immediately after the opening indicates how seriously the distinction between styles could be taken:

The otherwise so gracious and decorous actress betrayed her nature to such a degree that the audience was shocked at the vulgarity in language, gesture, and bearing with which she played the parody. At first this total transformation of a fine and noble personality provoked considerable applause, but the impression was nevertheless so unpleasant that the actress herself felt its effect, and awoke with surprise to a recognition of the unbecoming in such a low presentation of parody.[33]

Overskou was being less than accurate, however, when he added that the performance of *Love* was hissed and suffered 'harsh treatment.' In fact a marginal note in the *Regiejournal* beside 25 April 1829 reads: 'After the play, performed this evening for the first time, isolated hisses were heard which were however completely drowned out by shouts and applause.' This comment and two of the reviews confirm Andersen's own assertion that 'people had not hissed, people had clapped and shouted: Long live the author!'[34]

Usually the subject of specialization assumed less dramatic proportions. Yet even an actress like Johanne Luise Heiberg, who played the various genres with great versatility, was hesitant to perform the part of Christine in Andersen's brilliant comedy, *The New Maternity Ward*, while still appearing in Henrik Hertz's moving verse drama about a blind princess, *King René's Daughter*. The actress's argument was that it was a violation of decorum to combine simultaneously a lyrical, idealized role with a satirical, ironic portrayal.[35] In this case her caution proved to be unnecessary, and her portrayal of Christine was praised as one of her finest comic presentations. 'It proved,' wrote *Berlingske Tidende* (27 March 1845), 'that

32 Collin, *H.C. Andersen*, p. 134
33 *Den danske Skueplads i dens Historie*, IV, 866. Two reviews in *Kjøbenhavns Posten* (27 April and 22 May 1829) agreed with this view and provoked a tedious polemical exchange with Andersen

lasting for five subsequent numbers (25 and 26 May, 8, 9, 16 June 1829).
34 *Mit Livs Eventyr*, I, 104; *Kjøbenhavns Posten* (27 April 1829), *Dagen* (28 April 1829)
35 Heiberg, *Et Liv gjenoplevet i Erindringen*, I, 370

the stardom of this excellent actress, far from ending with her youth will first truly begin when she starts to take on actual character parts.' Only *Flyveposten* (28 March 1845) was foolish enough to resent the barbed jibes at the press by the actress and the dramatist, and predicted with ill humour – and no accuracy – that Andersen's comedy would never be a box-office success.

In general, however, the practice of specialization in definite role types was an indispensable practical keystone in a system in which the actor had to be equipped to develop his role independently, without any special guidance from a director. Andersen, a perceptive observer of the theatre of his day, was drawing from the reality of contemporary rehearsal practice in his description of the manner in which the actor-hero of his novelette *Lykke-Peer* prepares his role in Ambroise Thomas's opera, *Hamlet*: 'I thought over the character, read something of what has been written about Shakespearean poetry, and then immersed myself on stage in the person and the event; I give my share, and God gives the rest!'[36]

The actor in the nineteenth century was able to recognize types, as well as to categorize emotions under the rubrics that originated in the rhetorical principles of Cicero and Quintilian and were the basis for the various handbooks and manuals of, among others, Riccoboni and Sainte Albine. It is this system which naturalism swept away. Today, an actor's work, carried out in close co-operation with a director, progresses from the inside outward, so to speak. In very broad terms, a character is 'built' of individual responses, habits, and quirks until the 'outside' of the character is also established. In the older system which naturalism replaced, the approach was exactly the opposite: it was the large, sustained *affect*, or over-all emotional impression, rather than the individual idiosyncracy, which was the point of departure in an actor's work. This in turn was part of the general pattern of human outlook at the time. During the nineteenth century, one tended to perceive the 'whole,' the unity of science, or art, or human behaviour. But in modern society, conditioned as it is by such disciplines as non-rational psychology and atomic physics, human perception has ceased to trust the whole, but relies instead on individual impressions or responses or details.

Actors' handbooks modelled on Riccoboni and Sainte Albine gave the actor in the older system a number of stylized rules for expressing a particular emotion, such as pity, jealousy, or fear. Allardyce Nicoll quotes an

36 Andersen, *Lykke-Peer*, p. 52

example of such an Actors' Hand-Book, published by Dicks in the last century; for instance, the emotion of rage demanded:

... rapidity, interruption, rant, harshness, and trepidation. The neck is stretched out, the head forward, often nodding, and shaken in a menacing manner against the object of the passion ... the mouth open, and drawn on each side towards the ears, showing the teeth in a gnashing posture; the feet often stamping; the right arm frequently thrown out and menacing, with the clenched fist shaken, and a general and violent agitation of the whole body.[37]

But it is a mistake to conclude that the conception of 'types' of emotions or characters *a priori* led to monotony or conventional acting. On the contrary, in the hands of a clever and able performer like Johanne Luise Heiberg or Ludvig Phister infinite stylistic variations were possible. For those who *believed* in the concept of type, which in turn supported the system of few rehearsals and virtually no director, it was possible to vary and modulate all the more artfully and stylistically within the traditional form. It was exactly in such skilful and conscious variations of the typical gestures and attitudes that the art of acting consisted.

This principle is illustrated in an interesting document discovered in the course of the present study in the Royal Theatre library, a small copy-book dated 14 June 1837, which contains eleven handwritten pages of instruction outlining the abilities required for becoming a dramatic artist.[38] The thirteen points discussed in this illuminating booklet deal in very broad terms with the problems of developing a dramatic character, and were probably used in the instruction of younger actors at the Royal Theatre. One may derive from this manuscript a number of fresh hints about the question of the actor's style and 'inner technique' in the nine-teenth-century theatre.

The very first ability which is described in the manuscript is 'Fantasy,' which was held to consist first of 'realizing' a role by copying the idealized picture of the type, next of 'individualizing' it by means of exactly the kind of personal modulations and variations referred to above, and finally

37 *History of English Drama*, IV, 49
38 The manuscript is entitled 'Evner, som i større eller mindre Grad forud- æsttes for Enhver der kan gjore Fordring paa at kaldes dramatisk Kunstner' [Abilities which to a greater or lesser degree are prerequisites for anyone who expects to be called a dramatic artist]. Referred to below as 'Abilities of a Dramatic Artist'

of 'sustaining' the over-all impression in all situations. In reality this is the same principle which was expressed, in only slightly different terms, in a review of Andersen's last play, *When the Spaniards were here*; the reviewer for *Berlingske Tidende* (7 April 1865) argued that the single moment on stage should give the impression that 'the actor had considered it as an essential part of a carefully planned whole, whose *Beauty* consists exactly in the fact that variations are subordinated to the over-all concept as necessary facets of it.'

Hertz, in his 'Essay on the Art of Acting' serialized in his *Ugentlige Blade* in 1859, approached the same point in basically comparable terms. The drama, he argued:

is projected by its author from life and reality into the world of thought and imagination. It must be projected back into reality by the actor. The process is reversed. The picture of a human character which has been torn from reality by the author and, being cleansed of accidentals, has been reproduced in his poem must now be returned in this purified state to reality, through a performance which is no less a work of art but in which all the accidentals are elevated to features of significance.

Plasticity in acting, Hertz later continues, 'is clearly identical with the formative process [*Gestaltning*] which is the first and last requirement of all art. A stage portrayal is generally called plastic, however, when it is distinguished by a well-defined shape, a clear repose, and the presentation of the complete figure in a single mould, in all its component variety, not with abstract, isolated, but concrete, interrelated features.'[39]

The basic principle of this acting style was thus to conceive the 'outside' over-all impression first, and then to fit the individual responses to this conception. Naturalistic acting is related to experience – the actor portrays an emotion through, for instance, Stanislavsky's method involving recall of a similar or analogous situation in his own experience. The older acting style, in contrast, was founded on the fundamental classical premise that 'Nature' and human passions can be defined and approached in terms of absolute forms. This performance style presumed an imitation of these absolutes – the actor imitated (presented an active counterpart of) idealized emotions or character impressions from outside himself. By way

---

39 From *Ugentlige Blade*, xxv (30 March 1859), 307f and xxxiv (25 May 1859), 405

of illustration, the story is told by Fru Heiberg of the difficulty she experienced with one of Oehlenschläger's romantic heroines because she was unable to grasp the basic 'tone' of the play from her opening lines. She then persuaded the author to recite the opening lines, and this reading immediately supplied her 'tone,' the main impression or affect upon which she would proceed to develop her entire characterization.[40] The practice of dividing roles into types in which certain actors specialized presupposed, moreover, that the playwright was thoroughly acquainted with the theatrical system for which he wrote. The Royal Theatre regulations from 1856 concerning accepted plays stipulated that the author of an original play had the right to cast the parts himself,[41] and this right was frequently exercised by Andersen. He had a keen sense of practical theatre, and he often visualized specific settings and actors as he wrote. Thus shortly after beginning work on *The Mulatto* in April 1838, he included a complete list of cast and settings for the play in a letter which he wrote to Henriette Hanck.[42] Although for the actual production several changes were made in this plan, it is interesting that the three main characters were played by the actors originally visualized by the dramatist: B.M. Kragh as La Rebelliere, Johanne Luise Heiberg as his ward Cecilie, and Wilhelm Holst as Horatio, the mulatto with whom she falls in love.

Numerous other instances confirm the fact that Andersen often wrote with specific actors in mind. For example, in a letter to his patron, former theatre manager Jonas Collin, dated 30 November 1843 Andersen described the anonymous one-act play, *Dreams of the King*, on which he was working:

History tells of an old soldier who in the prison at Sønderborg was Christjern II's only companion ... he and the King are the main characters, I think they could be well played by Phister and Nielsen; later Christian III appears, who could be played by Holst. The other characters appear only as dream pictures, but are complete figures, namely Madame Sigbrith (Mad. Nielsen), Dyveke (Fru Heiberg), Erik Walkendorf (Stage), the Black-friar (Kragh). See, there you have a complete cast list.[43]

40 Heiberg, *Et Liv gjenoplevet i Erindringen*, I, 278

41 *Regulativ ang ... antagne Stykker*, 1856, p. 2, section 3

42 *Anderseniana*, IX–XIII, 241–2; Andersen wrote a similar letter dated 17 March 1840 supplying a complete cast list for *The Moorish Girl* (*ibid.*, 436).

43 Topsøe-Jensen, *Brevveksling med Jonas Collin d. Ældre*, I, 231

Moreover, this cast list was followed without exception in the actual production of the play.

If an author did make use of his option to cast the parts himself, however, the Theatre Regulations stipulated that he was obliged to cast *all* parts, after which none could be changed within a specified period of time. This required that the playwright be intimately familiar with the concept of traditional types and dominant affects described above. If an actor was cast in a wrong type, or if he was unsuccessful in a role which he otherwise commanded, the author or the theatre manager, not the actor, was frequently blamed by the critics for the fiasco. For example, on the occasion of the failure of *The Moorish Girl*, one reviewer found Edvard Hansen's portrayal of the jealous and traitorous Zavala 'totally unsuccessful' but reasoned: 'The reprimand, however, should perhaps not fall upon him at all, but upon the poet who intended the role for him, and the manager who sent it to him.'[44]

It was not merely that the nineteenth-century dramatist wrote a part with a particular actor 'in mind,' as frequently happens today; much more than this, the role was virtually shaped by the entire system of specialization and types. Seen in this light, it is not difficult to understand why Johanne Luise Heiberg's brusque refusal of the leading role of Raphaella in *The Moorish Girl* – 'I don't play trouser roles,' was her sarcastic retort – led to such strained and bitter relations between Andersen and the powerful House of Heiberg.

Fru Heiberg's unexpected action touched off Andersen's tirade against 'actors or actresses who through talent, through newspaper favouritism, or public favour stand foremost' and 'place themselves frequently above the theatre manager and above the author,' exercising the power of life and death over a play.[45] His correspondence leaves no doubt that he had intended the part of Raphaella for Fru Heiberg, and his diary clearly indicates the influence which her particular talent had on his shaping of the character. An entry for 12 March 1840 reads: 'Visited Fru Heiberg and talked about *The Moorish Girl*; she persuaded me to change the chief character from a quiet, reserved girl to a lively one.' Subsequent entries indicate the course of events that followed: 'Aug. 29: One o'clock read the play for Fru Heiberg, she called it masculine, that it was bombast. My crawling plea to act refused. Answer tomorrow. Furious.' 'Aug. 30:

---

44 *Berlingske Søndagsblad* (27 Dec. 1840).   45 *Mit Livs Eventyr*, I, 216
   See also Collin, *H.C. Andersen*, p. 324.

Fru H. declared she was too weak to act. Furious.'[46] The play itself contains abundant instances of dialogue written specifically for Johanne Luise Heiberg's special abilities. She excelled in evoking the exotic, the mysterious, the erotic, the passionate in a figure – always, however, within the bounds of the neoclassic ideal of *Schöne Wahrheit*. Her dark, foreign appearance, the powerful sensual tension which 'promised a thousand tender things, but held back in smiling purity,'[47] the mixture of fire and ice that was her greatest force, these elements created an unforgettable impression on her audiences and inspired Ibsen's glowing tribute, entitled 'Rhymed Letter to Fru Heiberg,' in 1871:

> ... *She is like a legend that trembles*
> *Behind the veil enfolding it;*
> *She is like a vision that rises*
> *and hovers*
> *Along a secret riddle-path.*[48]

These were the qualities of the actress for whom Andersen intended such romantic, frankly declamatory soliloquies as the following:

> '*Girl, fresh and pure as an almond blossom*
> *Blissfully rejoice that he soon will come!*
> *Agib will return! and so you braid,*
> *While dancing joyfully in field and glade,*
> *In your black hair a purple lily,*
> *A sign to him of fire in your breast!*'
> *And I braided the purple lily*
> *Among my own black tresses,*
> *Awaiting him I do not love!*[49]

Thus when Johanne Luise Heiberg refused the role of Raphaella 'because of illness' and Elise Holst, whose cool, objective, and exalted playing style was the diametrical opposite of Fru Heiberg's attack, was assigned to the part, the outcome was a foregone conclusion. A.L. Arne-

---

46 *Almanakker*, Collinske Samling (Royal Library). Fau Heiberg's sarcastic version of the incident is found in her memoirs, I, 245–8.

47 Neiiendam, *Johanne Luise Heiberg*, p. 2

48 Ibsen, *Samlede Værker*, III, 123–4

49 Andersen, *Samlede Skrifter*, XIII, 53

sen, the only reviewer to recognize the real source of difficulty, tried in *Fædrelandet* (28 Dec. 1840) to define the stylistic ideal inherent in the role and foreign to Elise Holst's type:

As long as beauty, womanhood, quiet feeling, and unforced joy are sufficient for the performance of a role, Mad. Holst is a highly pleasing actress. However, when she must portray *strong emotions and unsubdued passions*, it becomes necessary for her to force both her voice and her gesticulation ... depriving her declamation of all modulation and harmony. In such roles her movement and gesture also become almost *unbeautiful*; at any rate they are not natural.

The critical vocabulary of this review is noteworthy; its criteria of judgment – harmonious declamation, beautiful gesticulation and movement, modulation – are key aspects of the inner technique of the prenaturalistic actor. *Corsaren* (1 Jan 1841) in its typical satirical tone also used Elise Holst's failure as Raphaella as a point of departure for an illuminating parody of the 'romantic' acting style: 'Mad. Holst was masterful in burlesquing the new-fangled furious enthusiasm and exaggeration in tragedies, with an almost inimitable screaming voice which she supplemented with an almost matchlessly apt gesticulation.'[50]

Thus with several of the leading roles in the wrong hands, *The Moorish Girl* was obviously destined for a short and unrewarding run. The play vanished quickly after three performances at the close of the year 1840. Any thoughts the author may have entertained of public revenge on Johanne Luise Heiberg for her refusal to play Raphaella were dampened by Jonas Collin's categorical admonition: 'Speak not a word against Fru Heiberg, it elevates her and crushes you. People will turn their backs on you.'[51] The prudent poet therefore found an outlet for his pique by writing a short, unpublished burlesque in dialogue, entitled *Truth*, which lampooned the performance style of this influential actress. This satirical sketch in doggerel, subtitled 'a plastic declamatory opera without music in one long and one short act, but long enough,' was designed for private reading among friends.[52] Its significance lies in the fact that it derived its

50 Andersen's remark in *Mit Livs Eventyr*, I, 236 that 'the leading role was beautifully and warmly played by Madame Holst' may thus be considered gallant or misinformed.

51 *Almanak*, 11 Nov. 1841, Collinske Samling 10
52 Collinske Samling 21, 4to; reprinted in Høeg, *Om H.C. Andersens "Afreageren"*

satire from the contemporary ideal of picturesque grace and beauty of movement, founded on ballet training and embodied in Johanne Luise Heiberg's portrayal of the title figure in Athalia Schwartz's exotic drama *Ruth* (hence the title of Andersen's satire *Truth*). Andersen's auditors recognized in the parody the familiar declamatory delivery, highly affected and Frenchified pronunciation, and unyielding emphasis on the beautiful form which characterized the performance style of Scandinavia's foremost nineteenth-century actress.

A number of broad observations concerning the inner technique of the nineteenth-century actor and his work with his part can be made on the basis of the copybook manuscript already mentioned, which describes a series of prerequisites for a dramatic artist. Obviously one should not draw too many sweeping conclusions from a pedagogic manuscript such as this, simply because it is not always certain that practice coincided exactly with theory. There were, moreover, a number of various currents running simultaneously within the same style. Nevertheless, it is the stylistic tendency in itself which this copybook's notations serve to illustrate so well.

The significance of the first quality, 'Fantasy,' described in the Royal Theatre manuscript has already been mentioned in connection with role types. 'Taste' was set forth as the next important prerequisite for an actor, a term which in this case is used to mean the necessity of idealizing a character, so that the presentation avoided any disfiguring blemishes or deformities, 'even though these might be found in Nature itself.'[53] The importance of idealizing a role, in conformity with *Schöne Wahrheit*, was an omnipresent influence in this acting style, illustrated in countless scene pictures of the period. Neoclassicism's monumental, exalted dignity in bearing and gesture was merged with the poetic force and often furious passion of romantic acting in order to produce the desired union of 'truth and beauty.' In his novel *The Improvisator*, Andersen provides a vivid portrait of the ideal actress of this period:

Now Dido appears ... her whole being, royal and yet light, lovely grace, charmed everyone ... She stood there, a delicate lovely creature, incomparably beautiful and spiritual, as Raphael might imagine a woman. Her hair, black as ebony, lay upon her beautiful arched forehead; her dark eyes were full of expression. Strong applause was heard, it was Beauty which was being saluted.[54]

53 'Abilities of a Dramatic Artist,' p. 1   54 Andersen, *Improvisatoren*, I, 184

In yet another such portrait, Andersen expressed deep admiration for Adelaide Ristori's Lady Macbeth, which he saw in London in 1857, because the portrayal comprised 'psychologically gripping truth, terrible and yet *within the bounds of the beautiful*. It is impossible before or since that a more true and gripping picture can ever be given of this spiritually and physically ravaged woman.'[55] In his article 'A Visit with Charles Dickens,' he describes in greater detail Ristori's sleepwalker scene, in which outbursts of dialogue were restrained as though they were thoughts escaping as painful sighs:

Never will I forget the strangely dry, deep voice which breathed the words as if they were not speech but thoughts from deep within, revealing themselves in the painful sighs she released – not strong, but so agonizing and shattering that they played on everyone's nerves. It was impossible to forget![56]

Conveying the ideal in a situation and restraining 'agonizing and shattering' romantic passion within the bounds of the beautiful were naturally connected with the practice of sublimation. Thus the scream of the tragic victim must resound in the mind of the spectator, not in his ear. The classic-romantic tragedienne did not shriek at the sight of the torture rack, she merely gave a nervous, girlish shudder. However, the fact that this ideal of restraint could also assume ludicrous proportions is evident from the sarcasm of the review in *Corsaren* (23 Feb. 1844) of Johanne Luise Heiberg's performance as Dyveke in Andersen's *Dreams of the King*:

The King sees her and immediately proposes that she become his mistress. Dyveke immediately says Yes. Progress is unquestionably swift. Of course it costs Dyveke (Fru Heiberg) some effort. In order that the King does not receive her Yes too easily, she wrenches out the words with her familiar nervous anxiety and stretches her head up in an indescribably painful manner so it nearly leaves her shoulders.

55 *Mit Livs Eventyr*, II, 195, my emphasis. A third noteworthy actress portrait by Andersen is that of Rachel as Phèdre: 'This is Truth, this is Nature, but in a different revelation than we in Scandinavia know them' (*ibid.*, I, 278). Cf Høybye, *Andersen et la France*, pp. 26 ff

56 *Samlede Skrifter*, XXVIII, 41; the article first appeared in *Berlingske Tidende*, 24, 28, 31 Jan., 1 and 2 Feb. 1860. Ristori's interpretation of Lady Macbeth probably influenced Johanne Luise Heiberg's portrayal in 1860. The description of Ristori's interpretation, 'My Study of Lady Macbeth,' in Cole and Chinoy, *Actors on Acting*, pp. 396–402, might be compared with Fru Heiberg's memoirs, II, 252–65.

A necessary complement within this style to the requirement of 'Taste,' or idealization of a role, was 'Strength,' the powerful dramatic emotion – *la force* of French tragedy, which Hyppolite Clairon had singled out in her memoirs as the most indispensable prerequisite for an actor.[57] At the Danish Royal Theatre it was the actor Johan Christian Ryge who was the embodiment of Nordic strength, both as a personal quality and as the fulfilment of a specific aesthetic ideal. 'His words,' wrote Bournonville, 'rang like sword blows on copper shields, they pierced to the soul like runes carved in granite boulders. His voice resounded like the shrill tone of the lure through the surf of the North Sea.'[58] This was an acting style which made the severest demands on the physical resources and vocal stamina of the actor, and the manuscript in the Royal Theatre library alludes to the purely physical test of strength which the long declamatory numbers in the big emotional scenes constituted, particularly for the actresses. Conversely, the neoclassic-romantic ideal of strength excluded unconditionally all indecorous declamation or gesture; 'it should be obvious,' warned the author of this manuscript, 'that strength is not evidenced by noise, brawling, or neckbreaking gesticulation.'[59]

Nevertheless, violation of this admonition seems not infrequent in the performance of Andersen's plays, particularly in the fiery and passionate acting of Wilhelm Holst, who played a leading role in several of them. As Horatio in *The Mulatto*, Holst was criticized by P.L. Møller, the reviewer in *Berlingske Søndagsblad* (4 Feb. 1840), for allowing his passionate declamation in emotional scenes to mount to 'an unnatural, monotonous scream.' Holst's enthusiastic poem celebrating the tropical milieu of *The Mulatto* was discussed in connection with staging. The strength of raging passion and heated emotion which Andersen poured into the tropical character of Horatio, and which Holst in his enthusiasm overinterpreted, emerges from a reading of the author's frequent stage directions, which form a kind of mise-en-scène. In the scene in which Horatio is imprisoned in the dank Sugar Mill, stage directions such as the following indicate the powerful, pervasive emotional attitudes intended for this character:

> *exclaims painfully* ...
> *casts himself down on his cot* ...

---

57 Cole and Chinoy, *Actors on Acting*, p. 171

58 Mantzius, *Skuespilkunstens Historie i det 19de Aarhundrede*, p. 56

59 'Abilities of a Dramatic Artist,' p. 2

his entire soul is in agitation ...
he stands for a moment with folded hands,
his exultant gaze turned toward Heaven ...
flings himself down on the bench ...

The Mulatto, remarked Andersen, 'is so burning that one is almost singed by coming too close. I think the flaming sky is pictured in his nature and blood.'[60]

Writing again in *Berlingske Søndagsblad* some months later (27 Dec. 1840), Møller noted what he felt was an improvement in Holst's acting as the far less passionate King of Cordova in *The Moorish Girl*; 'he seems recently to have made progress,' stated the review, 'and particularly to have renounced something of the indecorous in his declamation of passionate dialogue.' Critics are no easy lot to please, however, and in the triple role of Henrik-Ewald-Prince Buris in *Blossom of Happiness*, Holst found himself censured for *lack* of strength and vehemence in his playing; 'despite the unmistakable care he takes to vary his declamation,' wrote *Dansk Album for Litteratur og Kunst* (23 Feb. 1845), sentimentality of approach 'makes it somewhat dull.' In contrast, Fritz Hultmann, made up with a southern appearance as the student Verner in the same play, was warned by the reviewer for *Berlingske Tidende* (17 Feb. 1845) that a warm temperament should not be characterized by 'large, violent and indecorous gesticulation.'

The theoretical background for the principle of strength without boisterous cries and violent movements – 'inexplicable dumb-shows and noise,' as Hamlet called it – is clearly immense. It was not only one of Talma's basic arguments,[61] but can also be traced back to the precepts of Cicero and Quintilian. However, such general theoretical and critical implications fall mainly outside the scope of the present discussion, whose concern is simply to identify the more important practical principles underlying performance style in the nineteenth century.

The attribute termed 'Emotion' in 'Abilities of a Dramatic Artist' was achieved when the actor felt the words which he spoke; this in turn was to be combined with strength and harmonized with the character to produce 'Fire,' an abstraction very similar to that which Talma, for example, called sensibility – 'that faculty of exultation which agitates an actor,

60 *Anderseniana*, IX–XIII, 328   Matthews, *Papers on Acting*, p. 54
61 See Talma's 'Reflections on Acting' in

takes possession of his senses, shakes even his very soul, and enables him to enter into the most tragic situations and the most terrible of the passions as if they were his own.'[62]

The Royal Theatre manuscript also mentions a number of still more generalized acting principles which were most likely included as pedagogic tips for young actors in the Royal Theatre acting school. 'Humour,' the comic spirit or vitality, and 'Boldness,' the self-assurance needed to overcome the nervousness every actor feels when facing an audience, are cited as indispensable qualities which must, however, be subordinated to the all-embracing requirements of 'Taste,' the idealization of the part in compliance with the concept of *Schöne Wahrheit*. Similarly, 'Diligence' and 'Memory' are added as necessary attributes for the aspiring actor. A role was to be memorized perfectly beforehand, so that at rehearsals an actor could 'play' with his part, whereas 'no one endowed by nature with a poor memory should ever take up the dramatic art'[63] – admonitions which should be viewed in the light of prenaturalistic rehearsal practice.

Of more immediate, practical bearing on the performance style of Andersen's plays are the three concluding elements discussed in 'Abilities of a Dramatic Artist': 'Declamation,' 'Mime,' and 'Body Movement.' Especially in the higher drama, particular attention was paid to speech, the shifting pauses, nuances, and stylized crescendos and diminuendos of declamation. The Royal Theatre manuscript from 1837 follows on the whole the distinction which Goethe made between recitation, in which the reciter retains his own individuality and nature, and declamation, which requires that the dramatic artist places himself entirely in the attitude and mood of the character he portrays.[64] The elevated, emotional declamatory style customary in the higher drama of this period was intimately related to the broad, sweeping passions and attitudes of neoclassic-romantic acting. This heightened declamatory technique is, furthermore, the stylistic context for the flowing, contrasting construction of Andersen's dramatic dialogue, samples of which have already been included in the foregoing. One additional illustration of the texture of this dialogue might be Horatio's speech in *The Mulatto* in which he replies to Cecilie's evaluation of his poetic inclinations – a speech which clearly echoes the playwright's own views on art:

62 *Ibid.*, p. 49
63 'Abilities of a Dramatic Artist,' p. 8

64 See Cole and Chinoy, *Actors on Acting*, p. 250

A daily life glides past our common eyes,
A foam-crested picture hovers in the haze.
But poetry, the pearl which deep within it lies,
Can none but the poet, bold sea-diver, raise.

...

To be the people's golden calf is easy.
First they find in him the poet's flame
Who patches scenes from daily life together,
Flat topicality, clear common sense.
Next they see true genius live forever
In him who shadows must in shadows paint,
He who shuns clarity in word and thought.
Obscurity becomes the root of wisdom,
And they comprehend what he cannot.
To be the people's golden calf is easy.[65]

The technique described by Johanne Luise Heiberg of literally adopting a consciously artificial system of Frenchified pronunciation and affected diction in the higher drama is perhaps the most typical manifestation in Scandinavia of this ideal of heightened declamatory style. Even in the drawing-room comedy genre, for which she employed a special 'conversational tone' copied from the salons of polite society, a tone in which 'words ran quickly over the tongue which still retaining sharp, clear, and definite nuances,'[66] formalized, stylized diction still remained the most dominant element. The greater part of the nineteenth century elapsed before this stylistic ideal finally vanished from the stage. As late as 1862 Bournonville wrote to Andersen of his efforts as intendant at the Swedish Royal Theatre in Stockholm to introduce a more 'natural' diction to replace the dominant 'bombastic' declamation: 'it has thus been a great triumph for me to persuade our actors to adopt a more natural diction and to keep their characterizations within the bounds of noble Nature.'[67]

A similar movement in Danish theatre about this time towards a less stylized, declamatory technique lies behind the resounding failure of

65 *Samlede Skrifter*, XII, 19–20
66 Heiberg, *Et Liv gjenoplevet i Erindringen*
   I, 137; see Neiiendam, *Johanne Luise*

Heiberg, p. 18, for details of her artificial speech.
67 Bille and Bøgh, *Breve til H.C. Andersen*,
   p. 63

Agnes Lange in Andersen's last play, *When the Spaniards were here*, in which she played Hermania, the heroine who falls in love with a Spanish officer. Agnes Lange, a successful child actress at her father's Folketheatret who made her Royal Theatre debut in the 1864/5 season, was strongly criticized in *Spaniards* for a subdued, naturalistic delivery which conservative reviewers found 'tedious and unnatural.'[68] 'Miss Lange's diction is so rushed, unclear, and highly unfortunate both in intonation and pronunciation,' commented *Berlingske Tidende* (7 April 1865), 'that this circumstance alone casts a monotony over her portrayal which is by no means inherent in the role ... With an all-levelling individual pathos she demolishes the brilliant portrayal of the dramatist.' Both *Folkets Avis* and *Flyveposten* (8 April 1865) placed the blame for the difficulty on the author's characterization of Hermania; the reviewer for *Dags-Telegrafen* (9 April 1865) however, found 'so much excellence' in the actress's performance, 'particularly in the most pathetic scenes ... that her portrayal should rightly be noted in an approving and commending manner.' There can be little doubt that the background for the heated critical dissention regarding *When the Spaniards were here* was the transition that was taking place from the romantic declamatory style towards a more natural diction.

Just as with declamation, the entire field of mime and body movement was the subject of minute care and attention in the older acting style. Fixed, formalized facial expressions, corresponding to each of the passions and reminiscent of the oratorical precepts of Cicero and Quintilian, were pictured and described in great detail in numerous European theoretical treatises on mime, and were then copied in the living theatre. Charles Lebrun's famous mimic illustrations for 'the passions' – l'admiration, le ravissement, l'amour, le mépris, l'horreur, la crainte, la jalousie, la haine, la joye, la tristesse – had already appeared in 1698 but retained their influence throughout the eighteenth and early nineteenth centuries. Similarly, the descriptions and drawings of a book like J.J. Engel's widely-translated *Idéen zu einer Mimik* (1785), or Johanne Luise Heiberg's own extensive discussion of mime emphasizing activity of the upper countenance – forehead, eyebrows and eyes – in tragedy, and the lower countenance – mouth and cheeks – in comedy are both good examples of the kind of stylized pantomimic ideals which continued to prevail on the

68 See *Dagbladet* (8 April 1865)

European stage during the first part of the nineteenth century.[69] As late as 1866, a German work by Carl Michel dealing with the 'Language of Gesture' appeared, which is a direct descendant of these earlier treatises on mime and which provides both pantomimic exercises to accompany verbal expression and a series of ninety-four photographic illustrations of 'the passions.'[70] Although 'Abilities of a Dramatic Artist' admonishes that such formalized mimic expressions were to be kept within the strict boundaries of the ideal, and were not to be allowed to degenerate into 'grimace,' even a casual glance at the countless existing illustrations of these passions leaves no doubt as to their strong and highly accentuated character.

The introductory remarks on eighteenth-century theatrical conditions referred to the importance which *Le jeu muet* and the technique of reaction assumed in the older system. An effective and artful pantomimic result could be achieved when the characters were grouped in the traditional semicircle on the forestage – a convention which survived long after the dim candle lighting and poor acoustics which originally motivated it had disappeared – and each of them reacted with a different, appropriate passion, in accordance with the prescribed rules for facial expressions and body positions. This strong, heavily emphasized pantomime was, of course, to a great degree the result of a simple technical demand: the need for expressions to be seen in the dim lighting of the Argand oil lamps, which were not replaced by gas lighting at the Royal Theatre until the 1857/8 season. The half-tones and nontheatrical mime so often a part of modern acting technique are, furthermore, possible only in the brilliant illumination of electric lighting.

Hertz treated the whole question of *Le jeu muet* at some length in his 'Essay on the Art of Acting.' 'The ability to play a good listener on stage during a long speech is rare,' this playwright admonished.

Yet if he is fully at home in his part, the actor will find an opportunity to remain silent while at the same time preparing for the lines with which he is to reply. Among the actors to which our theatre can point in recent decades, none has sur-

69 See Heiberg, *Et Liv gjenoplevet i Erindringen*, 'Det Plastiske i Skuespilkunsten,' I, 283–9

70 Carl Michel, *Die Gebärdensprache, dargestellt für Schauspieler sowie für Maler und Bildhauer*. I: Dargestellt als Übungen in Verbindung mit der Wortsprache; II: Erläutert durch 94 mimische Darstellungen (Köln 1886)

passed Fru Heiberg in this regard. She was always the attentive, intelligent listener who often with only a slight, derisive smile, a haughty facial expression, a threatening glance, was able to comment upon or annihilate the lines directed to her. Sympathy, surprise, anger, and every other passion found in her silence their eloquent and most perfect expression.

Effectively balanced tableaux were, in Hertz's view, the product of a judiciously blended use of pantomime:

A scene with a crowd of people, of whom some have a large share, some smaller, and others no share at all in the dialogue, should have the same effect on the audience as a painting in which only the principal figures are placed in the foreground, in full light and drawn with stronger colours. The minor figures, on the other hand, are placed in shadow with fainter outlines and colour application, and hence do not have an effect on the viewer greater than the overall impression allows.[71]

Like pantomime, the technique of gesture and body movement in the older system was firmly bound to the ideals of *Schöne Wahrheit*. The harmonic theatrical figure compositions arranged in bas-relief attitudes can perhaps best be compared to the art of David or the work of the great nineteenth-century Danish sculptor Thorvaldsen. Nor is such a comparison merely figurative. One of the most deep-seated stylistic characteristics of the romantic theatre, as we have seen, was its preoccupation with the stage picture – the conception of the theatre as *eine lebende Bildergallerie*. As such, an intimate relation existed between movement and position on stage, and the art and sculpture of the early nineteenth century. Picturesque attitudes, tableaux, positions, and expressions combined an emotional, almost furious romantic acting style with strict lines and classic dignity: '*la vrai grace, qui est la vraie grace de la nature*' was the accepted goal of the actor.[72] The flowing grace, statuesque carriage, and symmetrical groupings of this style were applied to every aspect of movement and blocking on the stage; they were present:

in a walk, in the apparently most insignificant gestures, in an outstretched hand or arm, in ordinary bendings of the body, in a greeting, in rising and sitting, in a

71 From *Ugentlige Blade*, XXXII (11 May 1859), 381–3

72 de Montabert, *Théorie du geste*, p. 81

sudden run across the stage, in an entrance and in an exit. All of this relies on having power over one's body, and this can only be achieved correctly through the plastic rules of dancing school.[73]

The ideals of statuesque grace were acquired, as Johanne Luise Heiberg suggests, through intensive ballet training. It is on this note that the Royal Theatre manuscript from 1837 concludes, emphasizing however that all of an actor's body movements must be integrated and must stem from the passions of his role, rather than from a mere mannered knowledge of the five ballet positions. It was this commonly invoked critical criterion which, for example, led *Berlingske Tidende* (17 June 1839) to censure the performance of Anton Pätges as Theodor Granner, the importunate suitor in *The Invisible Man*; 'he would probably have won more praise,' wrote the critic, 'if his gestures had been less violent and his positions had been less reminiscent of those seen in ballet.'

In brief, then, the image which emerges of the nineteenth-century actor in the plays of Andersen and his contemporaries is that of a virtuoso, an expert and sovereign craftsman. He was able to create his role independently, with only a few rehearsals and a minimum of advice or interference from a director, on the basis of a whole system of established, formalized emotions, reactions, and expressions. The specialization and recognition of types inherent in this acting style were not only practical measures springing from the rehearsal practices themselves, but were also deeply rooted aesthetic principles as well. However, it is fallacious to assume that this 'classifying' of emotions and reactions led automatically to stereotyped acting. As stated at the outset, it is important to avoid applying naturalistic preconceptions to the prenaturalistic theatre, where it was to a great extent the skilful and conscious variations within a traditional formalized type which comprised the art of a gifted performer.

Nor was the transition, during the last quarter of the century, to a new school of acting greeted as an unconditional manifestation of progress by those familiar with the high standards of the Danish national theatre. Andersen's unenthusiastic reaction to the new acting style represented by the great Ibsen actress Laura Gundersen, during her guest appearance at the Danish Royal Theatre in 1868 as Maria in Bjørnson's *Maria Stuart*

73 Heiberg, *Et Liv gjenoplevet i Erindringen,*
I, 104

in Scotland and Hermione in Shakespeare's *The Winter's Tale*, is worth noting. 'In my opinion,' he recorded in a letter dated 9 September, 'she could be good in her accustomed surroundings in Christiania, also good in our provincial theatres, but nothing to be overjoyed or surprised at on the nation's foremost stage.'[74]

The fundamental goal of the prenaturalistic actor-virtuoso was to convey an over-all impression based on one consistent dominating attitude, rather than to supply a catalogue of detailed quirks and idiosyncrasies. The strong, passionate pathos, heavily accentuated pantomime, and crescendos and diminuendos of declamatory style which contributed to conveying this powerful, single impression were all, however, blended with and tempered by the omnipresent ideal of *Schöne Wahrheit*, the restraining grace of the Beautiful Form.

No attempt, however thorough, to analyze the conventions and ideals of a particular acting style can, of course, ever really hope to recapture entirely the living artistic experience itself. The picture can never be quite complete. The full impression of how an actor truly looked and sounded and moved upon the stage disappears when he is heard no more. Andersen felt this fact strongly concerning the golden age of acting, presided over by such gifted performers as Johanne Luise Heiberg, Anna Nielsen, Johan Christian Ryge, N.P. Nielsen, Wilhelm Holst, and Ludvig Phister, with which he had been associated. 'It is a grand fireworks display that blazes and dies away,' he wrote with nostalgia in *Lykke-Peer*:

A new generation does not know and can not imagine those who from the stage enthralled their grandparents. Youth rejoices perhaps just as loudly and as fervently at the gleam of brass as their elders once did at the gleam of solid gold.

74 Topsøe-Jensen, *Breve til Therese og Martin Henriques*, pp. 99–100

EPILOGUE

The Emergence
of the Director

IF THE PROLOGUE to this study of Hans Christian Andersen and the romantic theatre has been concerned with the theatrical conventions of the eighteenth century and their continuing influence, the epilogue must turn to the evidence indicating the gradual emergence of the director in the modern sense. For the complete system change which ultimately took place with the break-through of naturalism towards the end of the nineteenth century, the modern director as artistic creator and dictator must, of course, be considered a *sine qua non*. The theatre in which Andersen worked, however, was characterized by turmoil and transition leading gradually up to this change; during this period of transition the older forms and recognized conventions blended and merged with new interest in specific, atmospheric detail. Romanticism's particularized scenic *Bildergallierie* and its popular realistic milieu depictions represented a natural stylistic prelude to the emergence of the artistic director-dictator in the closing decades of the century. For the productions of Andersen's plays between 1829 and 1865, however, no single individual created or dictated the entire mise-en-scène. Although the ballet master, whose responsibility included arrangement of mass scenes, processions, and operatic chorus placement, came closest to being an early type of director figure in Scandinavia, the individual production elements – staging and scene design, costuming, rehearsal, and performance – remained essentially decentralized and independent work areas.

However, theoretical discussions and debates in the 1850s, in Denmark and elsewhere, were dominated by the magic concept of stage direction, and the expression of sentiments such as 'Der Regisseur ist der eigentliche artistische Dichter' [The director is the true creative artist] was common enough.[1] Andersen himself was quick to recognize the importance which such new ideas had already assumed outside his own country. His views on the need for a disciplined artistic ensemble were farsighted; he drew attention to the stage direction of Franz v. Dingelstedt's famed productions in Munich in the fifties as an example of 'a separate discipline of which we at home have no knowledge.'[2] His position in this connection is best represented in a noteworthy review of the first night of Charles Kean's production of *The Tempest* in 1857. Kean's management of the Princess's Theatre from 1851 to 1859 marked one of the most notable attempts in the nineteenth century to present physical staging which afforded the greatest degree of archaeological accuracy and pictorial splendour. Historical detail coupled with theatrical effect in every phase of the presentation characterized Kean's celebrated series of Shakespearean productions. Andersen, however, in his article entitled 'A Visit with Charles Dickens,' objected to the over-emphasis upon 'gorgeous and fantastic splendour' in Kean's interpretation. 'After immense expenses had been incurred and countless rehearsals held,' he recorded, 'everyone expectantly awaited the first production of Shakespeare's *The Tempest*; I saw it at the overcrowded performance ... Here everything was afforded that machinery and "stage direction" can provide, and yet after having seen it one felt overwhelmed, exhausted, and empty. Shakespeare was lost in visual pleasure; the exciting poetry was petrified by illustrations; the living word had evaporated. No one tasted the spiritual banquet – it was forgotten for the golden platter on which it was served ... A work of Shakespeare artistically performed between three simple screens is for me a greater enjoyment than here where it disappeared beneath the gorgeous trappings.'[3]

Andersen went on to describe typical Kean 'illustrations' of Shakespeare's text, including a dramatically realistic shipwreck, Juno in a car drawn by splendid peacocks, fantastic landscape pictures, and particularly the wondrous appearances of Ariel. Nor was it without genuine admiration that he recognized the practical prerequisites for Kean's scenic art: electric lighting, 'numerous' rehearsals, highly developed stage

1 *Monatschrift für Theater und Musik*, 1856, p. 27; quoted in Bergman, *Regihistoriska Studier*, p. 151

2 *Mit Livs Eventyr*, II, 140

3 Andersen, *Samlede Skeifter*, XXVIII, 41. See also Marker, 'The First Night of Charles Kean's *The Tempest*.'

machinery – and a patient audience which tolerated the prolonged scene changes in a production that lasted five and a half hours. However, Andersen's basic rejection of Kean's production methods, on the grounds that they overshadowed and went beyond the play itself, was very much conditioned by the heated debate on stage direction which raged just at this time both in the Danish newspapers and in the Royal Theatre administration.[4] His colleague Henrik Hertz clearly shared his mistrust of excessively luxurious stage trappings, while at the same time recognizing the need for realistic staging in certain kinds of drama:

No one will deny that the superfluous, that which extends too far in this direction, involves serious abuses. The attention of the audience, already none too firmly secured, can by such luxuriousness be far too easily distracted from the essentials, from the play, the action, and the dialogue. This does not mean, however, that we should lose sight of the fact that in certain plays, particularly French, which try to reproduce the life of the *salon*, elegance and modernity belong to the essentials of the play. Furniture must correspond fully as well as settings and costumes to the aim of the play, so long as it is chosen with taste and is not crowded.[5]

One of the most relevant contributions to this lively mid-century newspaper polemic, an article entitled 'On Stage Direction' by B.A. (probably August Bournonville), appeared in *Berlingske Tidende* on 30 January 1858. This article, the immediate point of departure for which was the opening of Donizetti's *Lucia di Lammermoor* in December of 1857, dealt chiefly with what stage direction theoretically ought to be. In actual practice it was obviously the older system that still prevailed. Writing to refute discussions of mise-en-scène by Clemens Petersen in *Fædrelandet* (23 Jan. 1858) and by *Flyveposten* (21 Jan 1858), B.A. distinguished between genuine stage direction and mere stage arrangement, rejecting the latter as being 'of subordinate importance.' 'Choosing sets, placing appropriate furniture on stage, and dressing the personnel and supernumeraries' – ie, the co-ordination of physical scenic details which forms one aspect of modern play directing – was, in the eyes of this commentator, a 'very easy and unimportant task' for a director, 'especially since sets and costumes are ... still chosen and decided on by others.' This tacit acceptance of the principles of decentralization in the older system becomes still clearer in a

4 Cf Christensen, *Det Kongelige Theater i Aarene 1852–59*, pp. 245–8   5 *Ugentlige Blade*, VIII (24 Oct. 1858)

subsequent sentence: 'Furthermore, sets and costumes have already improved recently without any help at all from the Theatre's stage director.' The true function of a director, this article argued, was to supply what was termed 'the leading thought.' By this was meant that a director should study and analyze the play closely and then assign the actors their proper positions and movements. Furthermore, he must comprehend each individual role so he 'can influence the performance of individual parts, the dialogue, and the diction, particularly in the case of less experienced actors, and can create an ensemble, not only in the actors' blocking but also in the dialogue, so that continuity is achieved and the performance is rounded into a true artistic whole.'

In a sharply worded rebuttal in *Fædrelandet* (8 Feb. 1858), the influential Ibsen antagonist Clemens Petersen protested that stage arrangement was the single most important function of the director, and criticized 'On Stage Direction' for its exaggerated 'director worship.' He ridiculed the concept of 'the leading thought' by describing a typical performance in which the actors 'mainly hunted for a lead as to what they were supposed to say, with the result that instead of Bournonville's leading thought the audience saw only the actors' leading thoughtlessness.'

This debate undoubtedly contains the theoretical seeds of thought that eventually took root with the evolution of a new theatrical system dominated by the now familiar figure of the omnipotent and omniscient director. At mid-century, however, the practical influence of a director was still limited by the philosophy and practices of the older acting style, including a small number of rehearsals, conventions governing types and affects, and rules for stage positioning. Nor were directorial responsibilities usually vested in one individual: Ibsen's duties at the Bergen National Theatre from 1851 to 1857 included, it will be remembered, the supervision of blocking, gestures, costumes, and sets, but it was Herman Laading who was entrusted with the more important duties of play analysis and actor instruction. Such role instruction was, however, intended mainly for 'less experienced actors,' whereas the accomplished virtuosi remained sovereign in the preparation of their roles. Even Harald Christensen, who as a manager of the Royal Theatre from 1856 to 1859 championed the cause of stage direction, hastened to add that 'the larger the number of great artists working together, the more unnecessary or at least less appropriate such an influence would be.'[6] Thus at mid-century

6 Christensen, *Det Kongelige Theater*, p. 246

the figure of the sovereign director was still a subject for theoretical debate and agitation in Scandinavia rather than an actual fact of life. As absorbing as such theoretical agitation may be, however, its practical impact upon the stage productions of Andersen's plays is not evident until the close of his career as a dramatist. For most of his plays the author's stage directions were simply transferred to the *Regieprotokol*, to form the basis for the physical stage arrangement. Although twenty-three prompt-books for nineteen of Andersen's plays are preserved, none but the last two, for the 1865 productions of *When the Spaniards were here* and *The Raven*, contain other directorial comments than an occasional 'left' or 'right' for an entrance.[7]

Thus, although Bournonville's 'arrangement' of *The Wedding at Lake Como* in 1849 was unanimously praised by the reviewers, no sources survive to suggest the nature or extent of this arrangement. However, the significance of the many chorus rehearsals held for this opera has been discussed. In Bournonville's arrangement and costuming of the chorus for the 1858 revival of *Little Kirsten*, particularly in connection with the mummer procession seen in Fig. 51, one detects a miniature crowd mise-en-scène under the supervision of the ballet master, who was normally responsible for chorus blocking in opera and spectacle pieces. This assumption is also borne out by a *Regieprotokol* entitled *Opera og Synge-stykke 1857–59*, which contains the first evidence of detailed position plans and directions for crowd blocking in a few large opera productions, such as Marschner and Devrient's *Hans Heiling*.[8] However, a description in the same protocol of a revival of *Little Kirsten* includes no such directions.

It is, therefore, upon the promptbooks for the 1865 productions of *When the Spaniards were here* and *The Raven* that we must rely for an impression of the nature of stage 'direction' in Andersen's plays. In the prompt-book for *Spaniards*, containing notes by director Frederik Høedt, there is no suggestion of new or progressive techniques. Scattered pencil markings serve chiefly to indicate an exit, an entrance, a prop, or a sound cue. Occasionally an actor's cross, or a rough floor plan corresponding to the conventional arrangement in Fig. 44, appears. There are no directions,

---

7 All but the promptbook for *The Raven*, which this author discovered in the Royal Theatre library, are preserved in the Royal Library, Det Kgl. Teaters Sufflørarkiv.

8 Det Kgl. Teaters Arkiv, Rigsarkivet, under *Regieprotokoller og Paaklædnings-liste*.

however, indicating motivation or attitude on the part of the actors in this romantic comedy, and what blocking there is usually tends to be a static confirmation of older 'rules.' For example, for a dramatic high-point in the second act at the home of the spinster Miss Hagenau, where the runaway heroine is confronted by her mother, her governess, her fiancé Carl, and Mrs Ballerup, the six-person confrontation was arranged in a traditional semicircle. Hermania was placed on the right side between Carl and Miss Hagenau, so that when she fainted after reading her Spanish soldier's farewell letter she could be helped into an armchair placed conveniently behind her.

The promptbook for H.P. Holst's staging of the revival of *The Raven* contains, in contrast, a comparatively detailed mise-en-scène which sheds some light on the functions of a director at this time. In considering this promptbook one must distinguish between 'direction' of the chorus and of the individual performer. Although it provides explicit instructions for positions and movements in crowd scenes, such chorus arrangement was a characteristic common to the more elaborate opera productions long before this time. Grouping of singing voices is obviously one of the basic prerequisites for any opera performance. However, the detailed individual instructions concerning each personal motivation and reaction which constitute modern direction did not become its primary function before older traditions of rehearsal and performance were swept away by the advent of naturalism.

In Holst's promptbook for *The Raven* extensive directions block the chorus into colourful attitudes and tableaux within the romantic stage picture. In the dramatic opening scene in the mountain cave of Norando, captured in Andersen's charming sketch (Fig. 20), the magician is surrounded on three sides by the fantastical chorus of fire, earth, and water spirits. These preternatural beings are in frenzied activity, and their movements contributed visually to the picturesqueness of the scene. When Deramo rushes in with the news of the kidnapping of Armilla, Norando's daughter, the spirits 'press closer, terrified' on the magician's line 'And she has fled with him–?' On Norando's reply, 'Bleed for revenge! In torment end!' the fire spirits rush to the foreground swinging their torches and the earth spirits brandish their hammers. With the final line, 'Ha, revenge and death!' the chorus spreads to all sides at the sound of 'a terrible thunderclap,' as their master Norando sinks into the floor.

The groupings and movements of the chorus elsewhere in the opera sought in a similar way to reconcile musical demands with the composition of a picturesque stage. With the entrance of Millo's royal, flower-bedecked procession (from the first wing left) at the close of the first act, the large chorus was deployed in a semicircle framing the fraternal reunion, with alto and bass voices holding stage left and tenors and sopranos grouped on the opposite side. A comparable technique was used for the effective bridal procession at the end of the second act. 'The entire stage fills with people of all classes' arranged in a semicircle around the solo dance in the following musical constellation:

BASS	BASS
ALTO	ALTO
TENOR	
SOPRANO	

When the dance was finished the chorus again merged to unite altos and basses upstage and tenors and sopranos downstage.

Among the most interesting aspects of Holst's staging is his treatment of the fantastical elements in *The Raven*. Jennaro's ultimate transformation to a marble statue is, for instance, fully accounted for in Holst's notes. Each of the three partial transformations – to the knees, then to the chest, and finally a complete statue – was accompanied by an underground rumble and 'a blue flame shooting into the air.' For the last step, however, the stage was plunged into pitch darkness: 'the torches are extinguished – hellish noise – a marble statue of Jennaro is shot up [through the main trap] – he himself disappears.'

In addition to crowd directions Holst's promptbook includes numerous instructions about individual movement and expression. Such individual blocking was, however, generally dictated by older positioning practices, particularly the convention of playing 'front and centre.' Placement of individual actors throughout Holst's production is plainly determined by this traditional principle, the utilization of which is easily illustrated by a few examples. For Aniello's opening song in the first act after landing from the galley, he 'goes to the foreground right' for the first stanza, moves to the opposite side for the second stanza, and concludes 'before the prompter' (centre). Similarly the jester Kløerspaerrude's song opening the second act, 'I, Court Supervisor,' is delivered 'walking back and forth in the foreground.' For the love duet later in the same act, Millo 'leads Armilla down before the prompter'; for his subsequent soliloquy Jennaro enters from the first wing left and stops once again 'before the prompter' at the centre of the stage.

Holst's directions for individual expression in *The Raven* are mainly terse pointers indicating basic line readings and emphasizing a formalized, pathetic, and highly declamatory performance style. Typical in this respect is Armilla and Jennaro's first scene together. She is understandably somewhat disturbed at having been abducted; after having landed from the gondola she walks 'haughtily' past him to the opposite end of the stage, while he 'remains at a respectful distance.' At first she continues to ignore him, then replies 'proudly' to his compliments: 'Recognize in me Norando's daughter.' He tries an advance with 'Hear me, princess,' but she answers 'with scorn and contempt'; following his next line she turns her back and again walks away. The ground is now laid for a long, expository explanation on the part of Jennaro to justify his actions, after which Armilla cannot help but be convinced and delivers her exit line 'sorrowfully' and 'apprehensively.'

In general, then, the promptbook for the 1865 revival of *The Raven*, the production which marked the close of Andersen's playwriting career, exemplifies a form of stage direction embodying a logical culmination of romantic theatre techniques, rather than a foreshadowing of anything new. The planned arrangement of mass scenes in a musically practical and scenically effective manner was already a familiar necessity in the eighteenth century and was normally choreographed by the ballet master.[9] Holst's chorus direction in *The Raven* typified the nineteenth-century emphasis upon picturesque tableaux and folk scenes, decorated with bright costumes and atmospheric surroundings. His field-marshal deployment of the chorus in large unit blocks presents, moreover, a striking contrast to the later work of a naturalistic director like William Bloch, whose crowd scenes were to be composed of distinct individuals, each with his own independent personality, movements, and reactions. A classic example of naturalistic chorus direction is Bloch's handling of the fourth act of Ibsen's *An Enemy of the People* in 1883. His directions for the fifty-three crowd members and their actions and reactions fill a separate promptbook of 111 pages, preserved in the Royal Theatre archives.

9 See, for example, Krogh, *Danske Teaterbilleder*, pp. 245–50, for a full account of chorus direction in the production of Naumann's opera *Cora* in 1788.

The individual direction indicated in the promptbooks for *The Raven* and *When the Spaniards were here* reaffirms in writing the style of the pre-naturalistic actor. Positioning of actors in these promptbooks clearly draws upon established conventions governing placement and movement on stage. Instructions regarding the expression of emotion rest squarely on the technique of imitative acting, based on formalized types and affects, and on the ideal of monumental dignity conceived with romantic passion. Yet the very fact that these familiar traditions and conventions were committed to writing in these later promptbooks is no doubt correlated with the awakening interest in the function of stage direction, evidenced at the same time in the revised Royal Theatre regulations of 1856, the agitated newspaper discussions of 1857 and 1858, and the steadily increasing number of rehearsals during the 1860s. Nonetheless, as we have seen, the theatrical style of these last Andersen productions underwent no very radical change on this account.

Andersen himself, although distrustful of the imposition of absolute directorial will which Kean's productions suggested to him, recognized and championed the need for an artistic co-ordinator, and to that end he never tired of recording the absurdities that could arise in the nineteenth-century theatre in the absence of such supervision. One more anecdote will suffice. Visiting a production of Gounod's *Faust* one evening in 1863 in Bordeaux, he thus encountered a Margrethe who 'in pious purity comes home from church with her prayerbook in her hand, takes out her spinning wheel, sits down and sings the ballad about the King of Thule. This Margrethe sat down, but having no further use for the prayerbook she simply flung it, like a rag, into the wings.'[10]

This study has endeavoured to reconstruct the stylistic and theatrical context in which Andersen worked as a dramatist, and to suggest ways in which it helped to shape the art of a nineteenth-century playwright. Its basic premise has been that to know and understand the frame of artistic reference in which Andersen worked is to comprehend better his artistic achievement. To adopt Heinrich Wölfflin's view, alterations from age to age in the mode of imaginative beholding alter the formal possibilities of expression open to the artists of any given period. 'Instead of asking "How do these works affect me, the modern man?" ... the historian must realize what choice of formal possibilities the epoch had at its disposal. An essenti-

10 *Mit Livs Eventyr*, II, 267

ally different interpretation will result.'[11] In this way the artistic intentions of Andersen and his contemporary dramatists were shaped by the singular period of flux and transition in which they wrote, a period marked, as we have seen, by an experimentation that gradually eroded earlier theatrical conventions and traditions. The romantic theatre, representing less a distinct style than a transition between styles, provided no one approach or guiding purpose of its own, but rather a proliferation of different aims and premises.[12] Some of these were new, but others departed from the neoclassical ideals of form, unity, and grace only through shifts of emphasis. Hugo had proclaimed 'freedom' from the 'customs officers of thought.' The Hegelian clash of opposites was a metaphor that aptly described the mixture of realism and fantasy in romantic plays, the blend of classical restraint and fiery passion in the acting of a performer like Fru Heiberg, and the temper of the age in general.

In one of its aspects, which led directly to naturalism, the new movement was characterized by its interest in the specific, its compelling concern with the particular. The romantic theatre deliberately cultivated the local – in folklore, in nationalistic themes, or in atmospheric exoticism. The classical stress on total structure and outline was replaced by a preoccupation with the detail. Strongest of all in Andersen's writing, both dramatic and otherwise, was his enthusiastic response to the cult of 'strangeness' and 'wonder' in the romantic mind, the depiction on the stage of places the audience had never seen and figures that had never been.

And when this brilliantly erratic period of unabashed theatricality finally faded in the intense and probing light of naturalism, the special charm of Hans Christian Andersen's plays, and the context which had fostered them, vanished.

---

11 Wölfflin, *Principles of Art History*, p. vii
12 These remarks are indebted to Bate's matchlessly lucid analyses of romanticism in *Prefaces to Criticism*.

APPENDICES

H.C. Andersen's Dramatic Works

Kongen Drømmer / Dreams of the King	14 Feb. 1844	14
Lykkens Blomst / The Blossom of Happiness	16 Feb. 1845	6
Den nye Barselstue / The New Maternity Ward	26 March 1845	116
Herr Rasmussen	19 March 1846	1
Liden Kirsten / Little Kirsten	12 May 1846	310*
Kunstens Dannevirke / The Bulwark of Art: prologue play for the Royal Theatre centennial	18 Dec. 1848	8
Brylluppet ved Como-Søen / The Wedding at Lake Como	29 Jan. 1849	12
Nøkken / The Nix	12 Feb. 1853	7
Han er ikke født / He is not well-born	27 April 1864	6
Da Spanierne var her / When the Spaniards were here	6 April 1865	7

AT CASINO THEATRE

Meer end Perler og Guld / More than Pearls and Gold	3 Oct. 1849	162
Ole Lukøie / Ole Shuteye	1 March 1850	117†
Hyldemoer / Mother Elder	1 Dec. 1851	60
Paa Langebro / On the Bridge	9 March 1864	19

* Thereby making it the most frequently
performed Danish opera.

† Revived by Folketheatret on 26 Dec.
1897 for 34 performances, and then by
the Royal Theatre on 2 April 1905
for 42 performances.

Bibliography

THE LIST OF BOOKS that follows includes those works which seem to relate in a useful way to the subject of Andersen and nineteenth-century Scandinavian theatre. Regrettably few of them are accessible to the non-reader of the Scandinavian languages. No attempt has been made to list translations into English of Andersen's prose works and tales: a number of bibliographies are available for this purpose, most notably Elias Bredsdorff's *Bibliography of Danish Literature in English Translation* (Copenhagen 1950), which contains a sixty-page listing of Andersen translations. In Andersen's *Samlede Skrifter*, volumes XI–XIV, XVII, and XXXI–XXXII in the first edition and volumes X–XI in the second edition have been the most relevant ones for the present study. No attention has been afforded in this list to the countless Andersen 'biographies' which are, more often than not, copied directly from *Mit Livs Eventyr*.

ALLEVY, M.-A. *La mise-en-scène en France dans la première moitié du 19ième siècle.* Paris 1938

ANDERSEN, H.C. *Billedbog uden Billeder*, ed. A. Sørensen. Copenhagen 1913

– *Bruden fra Lammermoor.* Copenhagen 1832

– *Fodreise fra Holmens Canal til Østpynten af Amager i 1828 og 1829.* Copenhagen 1940

– *Herr Rasmussen*, ed. E. Agerholm. Copenhagen 1913

– *Improvisatoren*, ed. E. Lehmann. 2 vols. Copenhagen 1928

– *Kun en Spillemand.* 2 vols. Copenhagen 1928

– *Lykke-Peer*, ed. B. Grønbech. Copenhagen 1959

– *Mit eget Eventyr uden Digtning*, ed. H. Topsøe-Jensen. Copenhagen 1959
– *Mit Livs Eventyr*, ed. H. Topsøe-Jensen. 2 vols. Copenhagen 1951
– *Samlede Skrifter*. 33 vols. Copenhagen 1853–79
– *Samlede Skrifter*, 2nd ed. 15 vols. Copenhagen 1876–80
ANKER, ØYVIND. *Den danske teatermaleren Troels Lund og Christiania Theater*. Oslo 1962
AUMONT, A. and COLLIN, E. *Det danske Nationaltheater 1748–1889*. 3 vols. Copenhagen 1896
BATE, WALTER JACKSON. *Prefaces to Criticism*. New York 1959
BEIJER, A. 'Om Teaterhistoria,' *Nya Teaterhistoriska Studier* XII (Stockholm 1957), 9–25
BERGMAN, G.M., ed. *Dramaten 175 År: Studier i svensk Scenkonst*. Stockholm 1963
– *Regihistoriska Studier*. Stockholm 1952
– *Regi och Spelstil under Gustaf Lagerbjelkes tid vid Kungl. teatern*. Stockholm 1946
BILLESKOV JANSEN, F.J. *Danmarks Digtekunst*. 3 vols. Copenhagen 1947–58
BILLE, C.ST.A. and BØGH, N. *Breve fra H.C. Andersen*. 2 vols. Copenhagen 1878
– *Breve til H.C. Andersen*. Copenhagen 1877
BLOCH, WILLIAM. *Paa Rejse med H.C. Andersen: Dagbogsoptegnelser*. Copenhagen 1942
BORUP, M. *Johan Ludvig Heiberg*. 3 vols. Copenhagen 1947–9
BOURNONVILLE, AUGUST. *Mit Theaterliv*. 3 vols. Copenhagen 1848–77
BRANDES, GEORG. *Samlede Skrifter*, vol. 2. Copenhagen 1899
BREDSDORFF, ELIAS. *H.C. Andersen og England*. Copenhagen 1954
BRIX, HANS. *Danmarks Digtere*. Copenhagen 1951
– *Det første Skridt: Drengen H.C. Andersens Skuespilarier*. Copenhagen 1943
– *H.C. Andersen og hans Eventyr*. Copenhagen 1907
CHRISTENSEN, H. *Det Kongelige Theater i Aarene 1852–9*. Copenhagen 1890
CLARK, B.H., ed. *European Theories of the Drama*. New York 1957
CLAUSEN, J. and T. KROGH. *Danmark i Fest og Glæde*, vol 4. Copenhagen 1935
COLE, TOBY and H.K. CHINOY. *Actors on Acting*. New York 1954
COLLIN, E. *H.C. Andersen og det Collinske Huus*. Copenhagen 1882
ELLING, CHRISTIAN. *Breve om Italien*. Copenhagen 1945
ENGEL, J.J. *Idéen zu einer Mimik*. Berlin 1845
FENGER, HENNING. *The Heibergs*, trans. with an introduction by F.J. Marker. New York 1970
FITZGERALD, PERCY. *The Kembles*. 2 vols. London [1871]

HAMMERICH, ANGUL. *J.P.E. Hartmann: Biografiske Essays.* Copenhagen 1916

HANSEN, GÜNTHER. *Die Entwicklung das National-Theaters in Odense aus einer deutschen Entreprise, Die Schaubühne,* LIX Emsdetten, Westf. 1963

HANSEN, P. *Den danske Skueplads, illustreret Theaterhistorie.* 3 vols. Copenhagen nd

HARTNOLL, PHYLLIS, ed. *The Oxford Companion to the Theatre.* London 1957

HEIBERG, J.L. *Prosaiske Skrifter.* 11 vols. Copenhagen 1861–2

– *Vaudeviller.* 3 vols. Copenhagen 1895

HEIBERG, JOHANNE LUISE. *Et Liv gjenoplevet i Erindringen,* 3rd ed. 2 vols. Copenhagen 1913

HELWEG, H. *H.C. Andersen ... en psykiatrisk studie,* 2nd ed. Copenhagen 1954

HENRIQUES, ALF. *Shakespeare og Danmark indtil 1840.* Copenhagen 1941

HETSCH, G. *H.C. Andersen og Musikken.* Copenhagen 1930

HOLMSTRÖM, M. *H.C. Andersens Liv och Diktning.* Stockholm 1915

HOVE, RICHARD. *J.P.E. Hartmann.* Copenhagen 1934

HUGHES, GLENN. *A History of the American Theatre 1700–1950.* New York 1951

HØEG, E. *Om H.C. Andersens "Afreageren."* Copenhagen 1940

HØEG, T. *H.C. Andersens Ungdom.* Copenhagen 1934

HØYBYE, P. *H.C. Andersen et la France.* Copenhagen 1960

Ibsen Letters and Speeches, ed. Evert Sprinchorn. New York 1964

IBSEN, HENRIK. *Samlede Værker.* Oslo and Copenhagen 1907

JENSEN, B. 'H.C. Andersens dramatiske Digtning,' *Tilskueren,* XLIV (August 1927), 120–9

JØRGENSEN, AAGE. *H.C. Andersen Litteraturen.* Aarhus 1970

KLINGER, OSKAR. *Die Comedie-Italienne in Paris nach der Sammlung von Gherardi.* Strasbourg 1902

KROGH, TORBEN. *Danske Teaterbilleder fra det 18de Aarhundrede.* Copenhagen 1932

– *Det kgl. Teaters ældeste Regiejournal 1781–87.* Copenhagen 1927

– 'Gamle danske teaterbilleder,' *Ord och Bild,* LXIII (1954), 589–99

– *Heibergs Vaudeviller: Studier over Motiver og Melodier.* Copenhagen 1942

– *Oehlenschlägers Indførelse på den danske Skueplads.* Copenhagen 1954

– *Skuespilleren i det 18de Aarhundrede, belyst gennem danske Kilder.* Copenhagen 1948

– *Studier over de sceniske Opførelser af Holbergs Komedier.* Copenhagen 1929

KROGH, TORBEN and S. KRAGH-JACOBSEN. *Den kongelige danske Ballet.* Copenhagen 1952

LANGELAND-MATHIESEN, A. *Det Kgl. Kjøbenhavnske Skydeselskab og danske Broderskab,* II: *Brødrenes Skydeskiver.* Copenhagen 1934

LARSEN, SVEND. *H.C. Andersen i Tekst og Billeder.* Odense 1925

– 'H.C. Andersens Brevveksling med Henriette Hanck,' *Anderseniana* IX–XIII (Copenhagen 1941–6)

LAVER, JAMES. *Costume through the Ages.* London 1963

– *Drama: Its Costume and Décor.* London 1951

MANTZIUS, KARL. *Skuespilkunstens Historie: Klassicisme og Romantik.* Copenhagen 1916

– *Skuespilkunstens Historie i det 19de Aarhundrede.* Copenhagen 1922

MARKER, F.J. 'The Actor in the Nineteenth Century: Aspects of Rehearsal and Performance in the Prenaturalistic Theatre in Scandinavia,' *Quarterly Journal of Speech,* LI (April 1965), 177–89

– 'The First Night of Charles Kean's *The Tempest* – From the Notebook of Hans Christian Andersen,' *Theatre Notebook,* XXV, 1 (autumn 1970)

– 'H.C. Andersen as a Royal Theatre Actor,' *Anderseniana,* ser. 2, VI (1968), 278–84

– 'H.C. Andersen and the Theatre of the Exotic,' *Anderseniana,* ser. 2, VI (1969), 412–27

– 'Negation in the Blond Kingdom: The Theatre Criticism of Edvard Brandes,' *Educational Theatre Journal,* XX (December 1968), 506–15

MATTHEWS, BRANDER. *Papers on Acting.* New York 1958

MEISLING, S. *Dramatiske Eventyr af Carlo Gozzi.* Copenhagen 1821

MEYER, F.L.W. *Fr. L. Schröder.* 2 vols. Hamburg 1819

MEYER, K.A. *Andersen und seine Werke.* Berlin 1855

MITCHELL, P.M. *A History of Danish Literature.* Copenhagen 1957.

NAGLER, A.M. *A Source Book in Theatrical History.* New York 1962

DE MONTABERT, PAILLOT. *Théorie du geste dans l'art de la peinture renfermant plusieurs préceptes applicables à l'art du théâtre.* Paris 1813

NATHANSEN, H. *William Bloch.* Copenhagen 1928

NEIIENDAM, JAN. 'H.C. Andersen og Hofteatret,' *Anderseniana,* ser. 2, II (1951), 3–11

NEIIENDAM, ROBERT. *Breve fra danske Skuespillere og Skuespillerinder 1748–1864.* 2 vols. Copenhagen 1911–12

– 'Da H.C. Andersens navn første gang blev trykt,' *Anderseniana,* ser. 2, II (1953), 207–15

– *Gennem mange Aar.* Copenhagen 1950

– *Johanne Luise Heiberg.* Copenhagen 1960

– 'Omkring H.C. Andersens dramatik,' *Anderseniana,* ser. 2, II (1954), 327–41

– *To Kvinder i H.C. Andersens Liv.* Copenhagen 1954

NICOLL, ALLARDYCE. *The Development of the Theatre.* London 1937

- *A History of English Drama 1660–1900*, IV. Cambridge 1955

NIELSEN, B.F. *H.C. Andersen Bibliografi: Digterens danske Værker 1822–1875.*
Copenhagen 1942

NIELSEN, LAURITZ. *Katalog over danske og norske Digteres Originalmanuskripter i det Kgl. Bibliotek.* Copenhagen 1941

ODELL, G.C.D. *Shakespeare from Betterton to Irving.* 2 vols. New York 1920

OLRIK, H.G. *H.C. Andersen, Undersøgelser og Kronikker.* Copenhagen 1945

OVERSKOU, THOMAS. *Den danske Skueplads i dens Historie.* 7 vols. Copenhagen
1854–76

- *Den danske Skueplads og Staten.* Copenhagen 1867

- *Haandbog for Yndere og Dyrkere af dansk dramatisk Litteratur og Kunst.* Copenhagen 1879

- *Oplysninger om Theaterforhold i 1849–1858.* Copenhagen 1858

PREISLER, J.D. *Journal over en Reise igiennem Frankerige og Tyskland.* 2 vols.
Copenhagen 1789

PUJOULX, J.B. *Paris à la fin du XVIIIe siècle.* Paris 1801

RAHBEK, K.L. *Breve fra en gammel Skuespiller til hans Søn.* Copenhagen 1782

- *Om Skuespilkunsten.* Copenhagen 1809

Regulativ ang. de til Opførelse paa det kongelige Theater indsendte og antagne Stykker.
Copenhagen 1856

Reglement ang. Tjenesten ved det kongelige Theater. Copenhagen 1832, 1856, et al.

REUMERT, E. *H.C. Andersen og det Melchiorske Hjem.* Copenhagen 1924

RICCOBONI, FRANCESCO. *L'art du théâtre.* Paris 1750

ROSENSTAND-GOISKE, P. *Den dramatiske Journal*, ed. C. Behrens. 2 vols. and
Supplement. Copenhagen 1915–19

RUBOW, POUL. 'H.C. Andersens Parisrejser,' *Danske i Paris gennem Tiderne*, ed.
F. v. Jessen, II (Copenhagen 1938), 170–98

RUBOW, POUL and H. TOPSØE-JENSEN. *H.C. Andersens Romerske Dagbøger.*
Copenhagen 1947

SCHANDORPH, S. *Goldoni og Gozzi.* Copenhagen 1874

SCHMIDT, KARL. *Meddelelser om Skuespil og Theaterforhold i Odense.* Odense
1896

SCHYBERG, F. *Dansk Teaterkritik indtil 1914.* Copenhagen 1937

SCHWANENFLÜGEL, H. *Et Digterliv.* Copenhagen 1905

SOUTHERN, RICHARD. *Changeable Scenery.* London 1951

SØDRING, JULIE. *Erindringer*, 2nd ed. Copenhagen 1951

TENNANT, P.F.D. *Ibsen's Dramatic Technique.* Cambridge 1948

THRANE, CARL. *Weyses Minde.* Copenhagen 1916

TOPSØE-JENSEN, H. *H.C. Andersen og andre Studier*. Odense, 1966*
- *H.C. Andersen og Holberg*. Copenhagen 1956
- *Mit eget Eventyr uden Digtning. En Studie over H.C. Andersen som Selvbiograf*.
  Copenhagen 1940
- *Omkring Levnedsbogen. En Studie over H.C. Andersen som Selvbiograf 1820–1845*.
  Copenhagen 1943
TOPSØE-JENSEN, H., ed. *H.C. Andersens Breve til Therese og Martin Henriques*.
  Copenhagen 1932
- *H.C. Andersens Brevveksling med Edvard og Henriette Collin*. 6 vols. Copenhagen
  1933–7
- *H.C. Andersens Brevveksling med Jonas Collin d. Ældre*. 3 vols. Copenhagen
  1945–8
- *H.C. Andersen og Henriette Wulff. En Brevveksling*. 3 vols. Odense 1959–60
- *H.C. Andersens Levnedsbog 1805–1831*. Copenhagen 1962
WAD, G.L. *Om H.C. Andersens Slægt*. Odense 1905
WHITE, H.A. *Sir Walter Scott's Novels on the Stage*. New Haven 1927
WILKINSON, T. *Memoirs of his own Life*. 4 vols. York 1790
WOEL, CAI M., ed. *Gjenfærdet ved Palnatokes Grav*. Copenhagen 1940
WÖLFFLIN, HEINRICH. *Principles of Art History*. Translated by M. D. Hottinger.
  New York 1932
ZINCK, OTTO. *Fra mit Studenter- og Teater-Liv*. Copenhagen 1906

* *H.C. Andersen og andre Studier* contains a
  bibliography of sixty-two 'Works by or
  about H.C. Andersen' written or
  edited by H. Topsøe-Jensen, the dean
  of all Andersen connoisseurs.

Index

This book

was designed by

WILLIAM RUETER

under the direction of

ALLAN FLEMING

University

of Toronto

Press